AF470817

THE MOST
UPSETTING WOMAN

RICHARD BUCKLE

The Most
Upsetting Woman

AUTOBIOGRAPHY : ONE

COLLINS   ST. JAMES'S PLACE, LONDON 1981

William Collins Sons and Co Ltd
London · Glasgow · Sydney · Auckland
Toronto · Johannesburg

Buckle, Richard
    The most upsetting woman.
    1. Buckle, Richard
    2. Ballet critics – Great Britain – Biography
    I. Title
    792.8'092'4   GV1785.B/

    ISBN 0–00–216326–8

First published in Great Britain 1981
© 1981 Richard Buckle

Photoset in Bembo
Made and Printed in Great Britain by
William Collins Sons & Co Ltd

TO MY DEAREST MAMA
who tried hard to give me
a good start in life
and who,
when I neglected many opportunities,
was stalwart in my defence
against the world

Contents

Illustrations

ILLUSTRATIONS

APOLOGIA

Apologia

'Oh, *don't* write about the family!' exclaimed my mother, one day in the late 1960s when I mentioned my plan for an earlier version of this book; and, 'As an act of friendship, please leave me out of your autobiography and I promise to leave you out of mine,' wrote Lincoln Kirstein, whose friendship and letters had changed the course of my life; and, 'Will you be including any of your journal about Johnny in the same book as your grandmother?' asked David Dougill, fearful that I might desecrate the shrine of that devout woman with a reference to the love which was just beginning to dare to speak its name in our century; and, 'Don't write a book about the Regiment' cautioned Colonel Bill Balfour of Balbirnie, Lieutenant-Colonel Commanding the Scots Guards, who had been informed in October 1939 that the latest candidate for a commission in that corps had perpetrated a novel about Oxford. For that matter, the Duke of Wellington, whom my great-great-grandfather Algernon Greville served as private secretary, laid down that no gentleman would record another gentleman's conversation; and when a first instalment of the famous *Greville Memoirs* by Algernon's brother Charles was posthumously published in 1874 Queen Victoria was 'horrified and indignant' at my uncle's 'indiscretion, indelicacy, ingratitude towards friends, betrayal of confidence and shameful disloyalty towards his sovereign'.

I know the Duke of Wellington was right in a way: there is something underhand about literature, like spying. Yet it was my grandmother herself, the subject of this first volume, who wrote to me in 1940, when she was battling for my benefit with her own memoirs: 'It's very difficult sometimes to know what to leave out – one may leave all the vitality out and spoil the whole thing.' Then it was my Mama, oddly enough, who urged me, when I was still a schoolboy, to preserve the letters I received from Granny, a mother-in-law whose intelligence and gift for self-expression she admired, although she sometimes laughed at her; and Granny's letters were the starting point of this series of books.

For years – from the 1950s onwards – I was obsessed by the idea of constructing one big novel, for I was of Cyril Connolly's opinion that the sole function of the writer is to produce a masterpiece: but I was blocked by the conviction that it was impossible to do anything Proust had not done, except to be concise. Gradually my passion for history and biography, a growing interest in the trivia of daily life which diaries provide, and a new suspicion that readers would be more interested in a factual record than in any fiction based on it inclined me to write a memoir instead of a novel. In 1964 I began the first version of this book – and a few of the following pages were written in that year. I then conceived it as a work in four parts, each taking its theme from the qualities I thought I had inherited from one of my four grandparents. But, although I saw clearly what I had got from Granny Buckle, and although the 'Craven side' of my mother's mother was easily associated with the visual arts – as well as with the world, the flesh and the devil – this scheme was altogether too neat to be valid. Anyway, I was distracted from the book for several years.

In 1971 I went slightly mad. A period of manic excitement, probably caused by change of life, led to the planning of a fantastic, impracticable venture which was followed by near-bankruptcy and total breakdown. At a time when I considered my own character beneath contempt and my whole life wasted, it was the thought of trying to construct something out of my grandmother's papers that started me off once again on a book which would be more about her than about myself. My great friend Astrid Zydower (whom I also considered to be a great sculptor) dabbled in photography. The copies and enlargements she made of faint old snapshots – such as that of Granny in the Wilderness at Eden Gate – fortified me like blessed talismans for the fight which lay ahead. David Dougill, who was then my secretary, typed and helped me shape and reshape several versions of the book: his interest in my material perhaps saved me from throwing in the sponge.

Though my spirits were restored, a new danger loomed; and it took me several years to become aware of it. My fascination for detail, and my greedy hoarding of letters, memoirs or journals, made me quote too extensively from my grandmother's writings, from earlier family papers and from my own war diary. I realized something had gone wrong when I showed work-in-progress to one or two publishers, who looked askance at my fact-crammed chronicles. I began to despair of anyone being interested during my lifetime in the kind of book I wanted to write. The loss of hope, which coincided with my leaving the *Sunday Times* after seventeen years, led to another period of depression even more sinister than the first. It was during this that I began to write the life of Diaghilev.

After a sudden recovery, which struck me at the time as almost miraculous, I was able to finish *Diaghilev*. I then turned back to the abandoned epic. I could not make up my mind whether it should be a book about my grandmother, a book about life in the village of Warcop, or the study of a family in war and peace against an Imperial background. I had given up living in London in 1977 and from then onwards it was my neighbour Jane Harriss who did my typing for me: her liking for what she read about my indomitable grandmother encouraged me, while her sense of discretion, learnt from years of work on the *Times,* enabled her tactfully to suggest, in the matter of personal revelations, when she thought I was going too far.

On 25 November 1978 the exhilaration of New York, which I had been visiting regularly for twenty years, and in particular an encounter with a male stripper, gave me the idea of writing the Adventures of a Middle-aged Englishman in the Magical World of Manhattan. New York always strikes sparks off my imagination – well, so do Paris, Venice, Florence and (now that I no longer live there) London. At John Taras's flat in West 69th Street, when I look through my open bathroom door, across the bedroom and through one of the tall windows framed by exotic plants, I can see over the roofs of Upper Broadway the water tank of the Juilliard School, is part of the Lincoln Center group of buildings, where Balanchine's young dancers take their classes and where Lincoln Kirstein has his office. I was gazing across the roof-tops two days after the Manhattan idea took shape, when I began to consider again what had once been part of my ancient scheme, a book about my 'Craven side', from which I thought came my interest in painting, the theatre, architecture, clothes, fantasy and splendour. In this I would describe my collecting, my experiments in exhibition design and the part I played in founding the Theatre Museum, now a department of the Victoria and Albert Museum. Such a volume could certainly take its place, along with the 'Granny book' and the 'Manhattan book' in my projected work. Then it seemed inevitable that I should fill out the self-portrait with a long-considered reminiscence of my life in ballet, including accounts of my friendship with some of Diaghilev's principal collaborators, whom I knew in their old age; and there ought to be a book about love. My autobiography was shaping itself, and I had soon drawn up a scheme of six volumes, each on a different aspect of my life, but with themes which recurred throughout the series.

I began to work on the Manhattan book, because I was hard up and guessed that it stood a better chance of immediate success on both sides of the Atlantic than the book on Granny; but in November 1979 it struck me as absurd that the six or seven books of the series should not appear in their correct order, so I returned to the volume on my grandmother. On 11 December, after an excursion to Stratford-upon-Avon with my comparatively new great friends, Alexander Schouvaloff, the Curator of our Theatre Museum, and Daria, his wife, with whom I discussed my project, I formed the resolution to make each volume as self-contained as a Mozart *divertimento*, even if my accumulation of themes and their re-statement in the final volume might acquire a Wagnerian complexity. I also decided to lay in the first volume less stress than I had intended on the village of Warcop and to call my 'Granny book' *The Most Upsetting Woman*, taking the phrase from the Plymouth doctor who was moved against his will by Lily Buckle's description of a man she had nursed on his death-bed. The next day, after watching a clever television film about Rupert Brooke, I thought that my father's death in 1918 should be the climax of Granny's story, and that my own youth and experiences during the Second World War ought to take up a mere quarter of the book. I therefore set about condensing the later chapters and paraphrasing the long quotations from my Italian war diaries.

When Daria, a scrupulous but unpredictable critic, undertook to read the latest 'finished' version of my book in typescript, she liked the later chapters so much that she advised cutting down all the earlier part about my grandmother's youth and middle age and about my father, Garry. She was slightly antipathetic to my grandmother's Victorian piety and middle-class point of view, and asked why there was not more about my mother, whom she had met and who struck her as a distinctive personality. It dawned on me at last that to the generality of readers my light-hearted summarizing of diaries or letters would give more pleasure than long quotations from the original documents. My years with the *Observer* and the *Sunday Times,* which taught me to condense and be brief, had borne fruit. In spring 1980 my new agent, David Grossman, thought the passages about my grandmother might be further abbreviated; and in the summer Robin Baird-Smith of Collins, the publisher whom David Grossman interested in my book, urged an even more drastic cutting of Granny's early life to match the compression of my experiences in the Second World War. Thus, 'Our beginnings never know our ends.' We learn the hard way; and 'with windlasses and with assays of bias /By indirections find directions out'. My decimation of my own war experiences so as to give proportionately more space to Lily Buckle had proved so 'effective' in the eyes of my advisers that they wanted a similar operation to be performed on Lily; and my grandmother's papers, which had been my starting point, were to be largely eliminated – at least from Volume One. So the 'Granny book' shrank once more. Meanwhile I was already working on later volumes.

What, it may be asked, had I been or done that justified me in foisting a vast autobiography upon the world? I had no 'message' for mankind, for I was the least theoretical of men, totally unversed in philosophy and logic; and my approach to life's problems was merely pragmatic. I had no 'mission' except to create works of art, give pleasure and beautify the planet. Certainly there were thoughts – or were they too vague to be called thoughts? – rather impulses, or intimations, which since childhood had 'inspired' me: but these were so intangible that if I tried to put them down on paper they might read like the ravings of a village idiot.

I knew, or thought I knew, that in poetry or prose the telling phrase – the unexpected juxtaposition of adjective and noun, which comes to the writer out of the blue – was more potent than pages of description. I therefore guessed that the 'something' I wanted to put across in my book would be more legible between the lines than in the tale itself. Go ahead, Buckle, I signalled, and set down in the plainest possible way the story of how this and that befell you: with luck that 'something' may shine through.

So I take a chance. The diarist hoards experience; the historian looks for a pattern; the genealogist links up mankind. When you are old everything reminds you of something: this *should* make you more poetical. Association and allusion enrich, as the jeweller's cutting tool reveals the second coloured stratum of the *intaglio*. I do not want anything to be wasted: but I know that form must be imposed on chaos. Out of my physical and spiritual adventures, my accumulations of facts, my researches, the works of art I have gorged on, and my treasured landscapes some fragments may be 'shored against my ruins': if only a childish dream of England.

PART I

LILY,
CHRIS AND GARRY

CHAPTER 1

Thoughts of Lily, Wiltshire, 1980

On the way up the lane to fetch the newspapers I found the body of a young rabbit with its eyes pecked out. Like so many things in the daily routine of my Wiltshire valley, this made me think of my grandmother Buckle. 'Rooks are so *vile*,' she had written to me in the early days of the Second World War, 'they peck out the eyes of the young rabbits.' I realized when I first read her letter that she was partly excusing the fact that my grandfather Chris, whose chief happiness was to walk around the fells* and dales of Westmorland with a gun, had started blowing rooks' nests to pieces when he had nothing better to shoot at – except, of course, rabbits. Now, Lily (short for Elizabeth) Buckle loved observing the antics of rabbits, as indeed of all God's creatures; and in 1904, when her husband had been stationed on Salisbury Plain, she had considered it a blessing that from her bed in the Military Secretary's hut, which stood in the park of Tidworth House, occupied by Chris's General, she could watch the rabbits at play before getting up in the morning. In later years, when pain prevented her from sleeping, she used to lie in bed in the Old Cottage at Warcop, thinking of Deepgill, a favourite spot for picnics on the lower slopes of the fells above the village, and of 'the rabbits giving a ball'. That Chris's most regular occupation was killing the pretty creatures – for, unlike grouse, pheasant and partridge, rabbits could be shot all the year round – never struck her as

* 'Fell' is a North-Country word meaning 'mountain', related to the German 'Fels'.

23

inconsistent. Nor, of course, did she think twice about ordering a rabbit pie from the cook, or eating it. This showed her peasant realism.

Yet Granny's view of nature – that is, of the *flora* and *fauna* which adorned and populated the surrounding landscape – was on the whole less a peasant's than that of a pantheistic romantic poet: she found 'sermons in stones and good in everything' – and indeed she tried with some success to be a writer. The stillness of a November morning inspired her, when dashing off another letter to me, to turn even the vile rook into a preacher of God's word. 'The bare lilac bush by my window is all hung with melting hoar frost and its diamond sparkles outshine the crown jewels. There isn't a sound in the village except a rook saying a Collect as he flies slowly across.'

Perhaps Granny's attitudes were no more contradictory than those of any other Victorian wife, mother or grand-mother. Her mixed feelings towards rabbits could be compared to her outlook on men and war. To beget children was everyone's duty, to watch them grow up was an incomparable source of joy, and nothing amused Lily more than the quaint sayings and behaviour of her own descend-ants: but she had an almost morbid expectation of seeing her son and grandsons die in battle – which, in fact, only her son Garry did. Daughters and grand-daughters were rather less important, though they too must 'do their bit'. 'To give your life for your country is so fine,' she wrote to me in 1944, 'you can't grudge it; I never could wish Garry back.' The desirability of dying young and in an heroic manner became even more of a conviction as she herself suffered the disappointments and discomforts of old age. She was sincere in her self-disgust and observed with almost aesthetic qualms the deterioration of her body – and character. So Shelley's line-and-a-half on Keats – 'From the contagion of the world's slow stain/He is secure' – became her favourite quotation. Today's readers, particularly the young, will react with horror to this side of her character. Peace is regarded as the most priceless of desiderata: and even professional soldiers do not exult at the prospect of testing their skills in battle, or long to 'see action' and win honour as, for example, my grandfather did on the outbreak of the Boer War. If there comes a day when war is looked upon once more as a natural occupation of our imperfectible species, when valour is again rated more highly than a better standard of living and when to live till ninety with failing powers ceases to be universally desired, then my grandmother's outlook will appear less perverse.

In Granny's memoir of Garry, which she wrote for my edification, as well as in the autobiography I encouraged her to write as an antidote for boredom during the Second World War, she certainly presented my father in a saintly light. Yet the memoir – along with a horror of everything I had heard about the First World War and a dislike of tennis-playing majors – had the effect of turning me against all things military. As a youth of sixteen I was a pacifist, and at sixty-four I am a pacifist again. In 1939, however, at the age of twenty-three, I did not hesitate to enlist.

As I was not yet two when my father died I cannot remember him and I find it hard to imagine what he was like. If he did in fact turn into the devoted soldier, resigned to martyrdom, whom my grandmother describes, he had certainly passed through the usual phases of lazy boy 'creeping like snail unwillingly to school', and of 'lover, sighing like furnace' in the course of his very few preceding years. My mother Rose, who is still alive and active at eighty-eight, came from a more worldly (in the sense of aristocratic) family than her mother-in-law, whose self-dramatizing excesses embarrassed her, but whose warmth of heart she could still appreciate. She preferred my quiet grandfather, who was such a gentleman, and who, she sensed, could see the funny side of Lily's behaviour even if he was too loyal to comment on it. Rose described my father to me as irresistible, with wonderful eyes and smile, and with an infectious laugh. She also said he was very bad at telling a funny story. She has never been able to prevent herself from being excessively critical, even of those she loved; and her biting comments on my manners and habits of thought when I was young doubtless saved me from some – but not all – of Granny's vulgarities. I have inherited Rose's mocking eye.

My father Garry was very far from being an intellectual. Had he lived he would inevitably have become a general like my grandfather; I should probably have had brothers and sisters; we should have been better off; there would have been a house in the country – possibly Eden Gate at Warcop – and I might have been eager to imitate Garry in preferring shooting and fishing to books and pictures. I sometimes think I am less my father's and mother's son than the offspring of an unholy union between my passionate, earthy, literary grandmother Buckle and my aesthetic, indolent, snobbish and homosexual great-uncle Caryl Craven, who detested Lily and all she stood for.

Our minds are populated by dead friends and relations: in that sense, if in no other, they can be called immortal. Perhaps this referring back to those we have loved and lost is more frequent among people who live alone, as I do. In this hollow in the Wiltshire hills, not far from Salisbury and Wilton, where my grandparents had several temporary homes between 1903 and 1918, how often, coming into a room or looking out of a window, I wonder whether Lily would have liked this or disapproved of that! What would she have said to that vermilion chair against the bookshelves? She had an almost exclusive preference for blue, and thought the use of other primary colours required some explanation. Would she not have been thrilled, looking at that flight of steps I have built outside the dining-room window, which leads up to my little avenue of hawthorn and tamarisk, by the distant glimpse of trees on the crest of Donhead Clift?

Granny could not but have approved the situation of my

cottage among these hills, streams and trees, and she would have sympathized with my steady efforts to make a garden appropriate to the site. Seated on my terrace, she could have enjoyed studying the behaviour not only of rabbits, but of fox and deer, as well as the vile rooks, the pigeons, magpies, jays, blackbirds, thrushes, great tits, blue tits, bullfinches, robins, wrens and an occasional hawk or woodpecker. She would hear both barn owl and screech owl at night in winter.

Lily would be amazed to see me cooking, laying the table and washing up, but distressed beyond measure by the reason for this housework – namely that I have never been married. 'Are there to be no more Norton Buckles?' she wrote despairingly in 1948, shortly before her death, when I was still a bachelor at thirty-two. I think that she faintly suspected, yet could hardly bring herself to believe, the cause of this celibacy. She would be pleased at my mention in last year's Birthday Honours as a 'writer, critic and designer', but mystified when I explained that this was probably occasioned less by the books I have written or the exhibitions I have designed than by my having helped to found the Theatre Museum. 'What on earth is a theatre museum?' she might ask. She had nothing against museums, but associated the theatre (particularly ballet) with impropriety, and I think disliked going to a play because it meant not getting a word in edgeways all evening. Some of the pictures on my cottage walls would puzzle and worry Lily, and I should conceal from her the cost of the gold-leaf on their frames. She would have some difficulty in understanding, when she looked at the framed posters on the walls of the staircase leading to my bedroom, how these were advertisements for exhibitions I had designed. When I was studying at the Regent Street Polytechnic in 1936 she wrote, 'You may pull off some fine design yet': but, 'How,' she might now ask, 'does one design an exhibition – as opposed to a wallpaper?' Diaghilev, Telford, Epstein, Shakespeare, Beaton? At least one of the names would be familiar.

Living as I do in a hollow I can't boast spectacular views; but I have only to walk up the hill which rises to the south and in front of me as I write to enjoy a panorama. If Granny were here the climb would be too much for her, but we should drive circuitously through the lanes up St Bartholomew's Hill to a gap in the hedge and trees which a friend has called

From 'The Opera Box' Drawing by Robin Tanner

the 'Opera Box'. From this we should look down on my cottage, see how the fields and trees slope up from it on every side, then gaze at the downs to the north and north-west. It was a book by J. M. Sargeaunt, a master at Marlborough who took an interest in me, that gave me a clue to the essence of romanticism: he thought it was perfectly expressed in Thomas Campbell's line, ' 'Tis distance lends enchantment to the view.' This idea explained as much to me about my own feelings for landscape as Proust taught me about the ways of society, and about love. A glimpse of blue distance has always acted on me like a drug, sending me into a happy trance. Berenson wrote that the feeling of surrounding space, such as Perugino imparted to the backgrounds of his madonnas, begot in us 'a sense of identification with the universe' which was 'the very essence of the religious emotion – an emotion, by the way, as independent of belief and conduct as love itself'. From the 'Opera Box' I can see to the right the high woods of Beckford's Fonthill, then, to the left, the bosky hill above East Knoyle, where Christopher Wren was born. Beyond rise the Warminster Downs, the south-western extremity of Salisbury Plain, whose colours change with the ripening and cutting of corn. I remember the blustery winter of 1942–3, when I was stationed in a hutted camp in the Deverill valley, and I am comforted by the thought of Bath and Bristol lying on the far side of the smooth-sculpted barrier of hills, which is no barrier to my imagination. I think of Alexander Pope at Stourhead, writing his couplets to be engraved on the base of the nymph in the grotto; and of silver Longleat seen from 'Heaven's Gate' – perhaps by Shakespeare; and of Bolingbroke on his way to confront rhapsodizing Richard – 'How far is it, my lord, to Barkley now?'; and of Lord Bridegwater's children acting Milton's *Comus* at Ludlow Castle; and of Housman on a hilltop near Worcester, brooding on likely lads beyond the horizon of Shropshire, which was a region of romance to him because he hardly knew it.

CHAPTER 2

The Turners at Warcop, 1884

Elizabeth Braithwaite Turner, my father's mother, came on both sides of her family – on all four sides, in fact – from farming stock: but while the Turners farmed in North Devon near the south-western extremity of our island, the Chamleys and Braithwaites were natives of Westmorland in the north-west, near the Lakes and the Scottish border. It is extremely unlikely that any of these Turners or Chamleys had ever travelled outside their counties until the beginning of the nineteenth century, for while the aristocracy ranged freely about the land, farmers didn't. Lily's grandfather Richard married a Frances Colwill, whose brothers died young, so that she probably inherited their money. This was what made it possible for Lily's father Charles (born 1820) to study medicine in London and Paris.

In the village of Warcop, in far-off Westmorland, Lily's mother's mother, Agnes Braithwaite, an only child, inherited from a Coats uncle property in London's Oxford Street, which enabled her husband Matthew Chamley, a Warcop farmer (but who had come 'from over the hills', i.e. Kendal), to add a handsome stuccoed mansion to some older buildings and call the result Warcop House. From then on he passed for a gentleman in underpopulated Westmorland, where authentic gentry were thin on the ground. Matthew and Agnes Chamley paid with the Coats money for their daughter Elizabeth's education at a London academy for young ladies. When her schooling was concluded, on a visit to Devon Elizabeth met the young Dr Turner, who fell in love with her. After overcoming the usual Victorian obstacles, he brought her to Bideford and to bed. They had seven children, besides one who was smothered as a baby by its sleeping nurse. (This episode and her kind father's cold wrath – 'I won't prosecute. Don't let your mistress see you, I give you an hour to be out of the house' – was Lily's earliest memory.)

Soon after Charles Turner died in 1875 his widow and her family moved to a rented house in London; and Lily, who had never been outside Devon before, or more than ten miles from Bideford, was filled with such nostalgia for the cliffs and combes of her native county – described by Rudyard Kipling in *Stalky & Co.* – that she thought she could never be happy till she returned to her old home. Mrs Turner had a plan, however, to rent, and then if she liked it, to buy, a house called Eden Gate, near her brother Tom's Warcop House in Westmorland; and Lily fell in love at first sight with the northern landscape. She never lost her passion for Devon, but from the spring of 1884 onwards Westmorland would share her affections.

> For some reason which I forget [wrote Lily] – probably heavy rain – I could not go out on the evening of our arrival at Warcop; so my vivid recollection of first seeing the new home to which I was to become so devoted is of going out before breakfast next morning and being quite overcome by the beauty of the fells, the river, the old bridge just below the house and the little wood called the Wilderness at the side of the drive, which was thick with dewy primroses and wood anemones. We spread ourselves in the big rooms and revelled in it all with sighs of pleasure and content. Mother enjoyed every minute of the day, had endless discussions with her beloved brother and determined to buy the dear place.

Eden Gate stood near the sixteenth-century bridge over the Eden, at the south-west end of the straggling village. Lily had only to cross the bridge and follow the Bleatarn road to a ridge of high ground opposite her new home in order to look back on the Pennine Hills, which were known locally as 'the fells' as if there were no others. Sometimes this distinctive range appeared grey-blue and distant; sometimes the fells, clear and purple, with patches of shrill green on the lower slopes, seemed to overhang the village, with every detail of rock, scree and tumbledown boundary walls visible in Pre-Raphaelite detail, rendered ominous by the crossing shadows of clouds. Murton Pike was conical, Roman Fell was like the nose of a recumbent emperor, Long Fell had a flatter curve, Middle Fell was a hump, and the base of jagged Helbeck was wooded, with the mysterious Fox Tower rising from its trees. Between the bleak fells and the village, which stood amid chequered fields of corn and pasture, delineated by dry-stone walls and dotted with woods, ran the Roman road north-west from Brough (Verterae) to Carlisle (Luguvalium) and the Scottish border.

Lily's response to the beauty of the world was ecstatic, and she needed no further proof of the existence of God. For what, other than the brain and hand of a supreme artist-craftsman – who, admittedly, put pain, evil and temptation into our lives to test our characters and make us worthier to praise Him in what would otherwise be too enervating and Oriental a paradise – could have devised and wrought the marvellous mechanism of the human body, the wheel of the seasons, the glamour of butterflies, primroses and birdsong, the irregular symmetry of a fern?

The bounty of God made Lily so grateful that she was determined to become a crusader on His behalf. What form her crusade might take it was too early to tell. Along with her unquestioning acceptance of the Church's statutes (although she could already be critical of its ministers) went a loyal belief in the justice of all things British. Had she been born twenty or thirty years later she might have campaigned for the rights of women, for birth control or for social reform. But she was a subject of Queen Victoria, born, moreover, into a middle station of life, without wealth, position or illustrious connections. What good she might be able to achieve in the world could doubtless be made possible only by marriage. Together with her fine dark eyes, clear complexion and trim figure, she had an inner radiance which was bound to prove attractive to men. Well-brought-up women, on the other hand, would always find her too enthusiastic, too demonstrative, too earnest and too eager to take the lead. She had many virtues, but reticence was not among them.

'We spread ourselves in the big rooms.' Who were the 'we' of whom Lily wrote?

I have to take Lily's word for the characters of her mother, her brothers and my two eldest great-aunts: I only knew Aunt Emmie. Writing about them years after their deaths Lily tended to idealize her brothers: her elder sisters were rivals who might perhaps outshine her, and, for all her Christianity, Lily must have been conscious of possessing what is called in theatrical language (a tongue unknown to her) 'star quality', and she liked to shine.

I see Mrs Turner as calm, stately and complacent. Lily wrote that although her mother's grandfather was a farmer, she never had the trace of a North-Country accent. She loved her brother Tom Chamley of Warcop House; and once she had bought Eden Gate, her passion was to improve and enlarge her property. Her stay at the London school (which Lily imagined to have resembled Miss Pinkerton's Academy in *Vanity Fair*) had given her a knowledge of Greek and Roman history and the ability to 'sail into a room': neither accomplishment can have proved very useful in later life. She counted on her sons to make great names and her daughters to make good marriages, and was confident that a dynasty of Turners would arise to positions of ever wider influence, with their empire based on Eden Gate.

Agnes, the eldest daughter, was an invalid with a weak heart, and spent much of her time in that classic Victorian attitude, recumbent on a sofa. It annoyed Lily that Agnes, who was well-read and amusing, would brighten up, forget her delicate health and exert herself to entertain interesting visitors, particularly young men. In old age, when Lily too suffered from her heart and Agnes was dead and gone, she regretted her lack of charity.

Chamley, the eldest son, a soldier and the white hope of the family, was clearly cut out to make a mark in the world. Tall, handsome, athletic and self-assured, he was a bit of a dandy and on the way to becoming a hero. He had done well in the Transvaal under General Wood, who, on becoming Commander-in-Chief, or Sirdar, of the new Egyptian Army, formed to replace the mutinous regiments defeated by the British at Tel-el-Kebir in 1882, had asked him to be one of its twenty-five British officers. Chamley's acceptance brought him a welcome increase of pay, for although still only a Lieutenant in the Shropshire Light Infantry, he was a Major in the Egyptian Army. In the campaign to put down the rebellion of the Mahdi, a Sudanese 'Messiah' who had declared war against the Sudan's Egyptian oppressors, Chamley had lately won distinction, and had been authorized to found the Camel Corps.

Among Chamley's fellow officers, who wore with their white uniforms the red tarboosh bearing the crescent and star of Islam, were Kitchener and Wingate, both of whom became famous. Another, Andrew Haggard, later took to writing books, and in his *Under Crescent and Star* drew such an admiring portrait of Chamley that he appears like the hero of a schoolboy's adventure story, larger than life and impossibly hearty. Haggard described him as 'the *beau idéal* of a soldier . . . all that was bright and powerful . . . very tall, very broad-shouldered . . . a dark face with keen blue eyes . . . downright devil-may-care, goodnatured, hot-tempered and a splendid shot.' He tells stories of the fearless Chamley making incursions behind the enemy lines, nursing the victims of cholera (which he caught), taming a lot of vicious dromedaries and clearing the terrace of Shepheard's Hotel, Cairo, by waving a handful of asps. When Chamley had come home on leave at the end of 1883 Lily, who was anxious to create a good impression on her brother, noticed that he became 'the intimate acquaintance of every camel in the Zoo', and spent his Sunday afternoons there questioning the keepers about camels' habits. Chamley returned to Egypt early in 1884, just before Lily saw Warcop for the first time: but he already knew Warcop, for he had served in the Westmorland Militia, stayed at Warcop House with Uncle Tom and Aunt Janey, shot and fished there; and Eden Gate was intended to be his home.

Nellie, the second daughter, who was so deft at trimming hats, who wept so bitterly at having to go off to India in 1881 married to a man she did not love, and who died there after the birth of her son, had been Lily's favourite sister. Her boy, Kit Birdwood, was brought up by the family at Eden Gate.

Emmie was the most practical and worldly of the girls. If Jesus had dined at Eden Gate, Emmie would have been the Martha who saw to all the arrangements, while Lily would have been the Mary who sat at the Master's feet, drinking in every word. Emmie was sociable and in later life could be relied on to rise to an occasion and speak well in public. She had rather an affected voice, but she also had a sense of humour and was an amused observer of Lily's idealism and self-dramatization. Lily thought that she and Emmie 'never had one idea in common'.

Ted – impetuous, sporting, unintellectual – was fired by a single passion, his devotion to Chamley: he was determined to pass his army exams and serve in Chamley's regiment. Although Emmie was his confidante – for they understood each other over practical matters – Lily was well able to sympathize with Ted's feelings for the wondrous Chamley, which she shared.

Braith was four years younger than Lily. He was the only son whose ambitions went no further than those of his farming ancestors, although he eventually chose to farm in

Australia. In his photograph he looks attractive in an oafish way.

> I can remember doing all the vases at Eden Gate twice a week [wrote Lily], often forty of them. But I cannot recall doing one useful thing in the house or even being expected to, except taking care of little Kit when his nurse was off duty. It was Emmie who was the useful one. Mother did not mind if I read most of the day or played tennis with Ted directly after breakfast. We had a tennis-party every Wednesday. I marked the tennis courts and enjoyed showing Susie Pettiward, when she came to stay, the loveliness of Westmorland.

This Susan had been at school in London with Lily; and her home, Finborough Hall in Suffolk, was the first large country house at which Lily was invited to stay. For nearly three years Lily had been in love with Susan's cousin, Douglas Terry, and she hoped that a glowing account of Eden Gate and the Warcop landscape would reach his ears. It was out of the question for her to write to Douglas, incredible as it must seem to a young person of eighteen today (1980): and the fact that my grandmother Lily, whom I knew, should have suffered under this prohibition brings very close the England of Jane Austen, who was born over two centuries ago.

As the widowed Mr Pettiward of Finborough had only daughters his heir was a Terry nephew. Douglas, a younger brother of this lucky man, was destined for the Church. He was the first young man who listened seriously to Lily's aspirations. They had discussed George Eliot's *Middlemarch* and how to live a good, useful life; they had clasped hands, while 'sitting out' at a dance; and after their first meeting Lily had travelled back by train to London in a blissful dream. That was three years before, however, and no word had been exchanged since: yet Lily's thoughts dwelt obsessively on Douglas. What constancy!

For some reason the men who attracted Lily tended to be clergymen or would-be clergymen. Psychologists may offer varying explanations for this Wagnerian confusion of spirituality and sexual desire. The prototype of Lily's Galahads had been Mr Granville, a good-looking and eloquent Rector of Bideford, whose first sermon on the text 'Lord, what wilt thou have me to do?' changed her life, and who had inspired in her all sorts of devotional and ascetic vows – such as giving up jam on Fridays. 'I can recall awful heart-searching before I was twelve,' wrote Lily, 'as to whether I really went to church to get near God or only to see the Rector's fair head.'

So Lily took her friend Susan walking along the Eden and on the lower slopes of the fells to get a view of the Lake Mountains, among which Wordsworth had died only thirty-four years before, thinking all the time of Douglas Terry.

Red sandstone was the local stone, and of this was built the old bridge with its four bays over the cutwaters, from which one could look down on the swirling Eden without getting in the way of a passing farm cart; so was the little church of St Columba, with its vicarage and school, which, to avoid a zig-zag walk through the village, could be reached by a path across the fields from Eden Gate. The 'church path' had a branch leading across a meadow called 'The Crooks', to Warcop House; this facilitated visits between Mrs Turner and her beloved brother. Certainly Lily would have taken her school-friend up to Deepgill, a picturesque spot at the foot of Long Fell, which had been given by Agnes Chamley to her daughter Elizabeth (Mrs Turner) for her sixteenth birthday, and whose thirty-odd acres eventually came, *via* Lily, to me. On the high pastures above the gill* sheep grazed; in the winding gill itself the men of the family shot rabbits, while the women laid out a picnic among the bracken and hawthorn trees, made a fire and boiled water from the ice-cold stream, on whose slippery stones paddling children struggled to keep their balance. This stream, the

* 'Gill (also Ghyll). A deep rocky cleft, usually wooded and forming the course of a stream.' O.E.D. Scots would say 'glen'; Americans or Canadians 'creek'.

Hayber beck,* provided Warcop's water supply and flowed under several little bridges before joining the Eden in the meadows west of Eden Gate. The village had a post office, two shops, a public house and even, a little way to the east, a station.

Chamley's name was frequently mentioned in the newspapers: he was 'always to the fore in an emergency'. The Mahdi was doing well against the Egyptians, whose only interests in the Sudan were collecting taxes and trading in slaves; and Chamley sympathized with the tribesmen whom it was his duty to fight. In a letter to his mother on 24 April 1884 he wrote: 'They are superior in *every way* to the Egyptians . . . splendid men. With twenty thousand of them I would be in Alexandria in six months and England could not stop me . . .' General Gordon had been sent to Khartoum to evacuate all the Egyptians and British, but on 13 March the Nile had been blocked by the rebels and the telegraph line cut, so that the stage was set for his martyrdom.

On Whit Monday at Warcop the young Turners had planned a picnic with their Chamley cousins, Tim, Sis and Mona, from Warcop House. They were to climb Murton Pike, the little peak which dominated the market town of Appleby. This would entail driving by dog-cart a mile or two along the Roman road in a north-westerly direction, turning right at Coupland Beck, crossing Brackenber Moor (now a golf course), where Chamley had camped with the Westmorland Militia a few years before, and making for the isolated stone hamlets of Hilton and Murton, beyond which there was no road. (Thirty-five years later, when my great-great-aunt Janey Chamley drove my mother and me in her pony-trap for a morning's shopping in Appleby, we always stopped at the inn at Coupland Beck so that I could have a glass of ginger beer.) Then there would be quite a steep climb – the Pike was nearly two thousand feet above sea level – to

* 'Beck' is a North-Country word for 'stream'.

enjoy the view over the Eden valley which was entirely surrounded, except for a gap towards Penrith and Carlisle, by hills. Lily adored picnics all her life. But:

> Soon after breakfast a message came from Uncle Tom – he wished Ted to go across the fields and speak to him. 'Be quick,' we all urged, 'we want to get off before eleven.' Time passed and he did not come. Then Emmie said she would go and hurry them. The lunch was packed and all got ready, but still no one came. At last it was one o'clock and we went into the dining-room. As I gazed forlornly out of the window I suddenly exclaimed, 'Here they are at last! Uncle Tom and Ted and Emmie. What *can* it be?' Mother rose up from the head of the table to meet them. 'My dear Tom! What – ?' but her voice sank down and she turned white. 'Lizzie, my poor dear! Yes, my dear – bad news – poor Chamley. Drowned!' He took her away into the drawing-room and shut the door. Ted rushed wildly upstairs, and we heard from Emmie of the telegram received at Warcop House, and the waiting for its verification from the War Office, and then in a Yorkshire newspaper.

Chamley had been sent up the Nile to buy camels. While swimming in the river and diving for sixpences to amuse the officers of a gun-boat, he had been seized by cramp, and, indomitable swimmer though he was, this had proved fatal. Africa, so aptly called 'the white man's grave', had claimed another victim; and the Turner family had lost its head. The newspapers reported that 'the Khedive and Nubar Pasha [his Prime Minister] had expressed their personal regret to General Wood' on the loss of this young man from Bideford in Devon, who would never raise a family to enjoy the pleasures of Eden Gate.

> Ted had spent whole days on high step-ladders [wrote Lily], putting up Chamley's trophies from South Africa and Egypt in the hall. He had a thousand schemes for fishing with Chamley and shooting rabbits in Deepgill.

And he was working hard at his books, for whatever happened he *must* pass the next army exam and get into Chamley's regiment. Poor Ted. His bedroom had a second door leading into mine, along the wing, and when we went to bed we sometimes had it open a while for freedom in our talk. I see him taking off his boots and suddenly exclaiming, 'Lily! Do you suppose Chamley is singing hymns all day in heaven? He can't be! He'd loathe it! *Where* is he? Oh God! I'd rather be with Chamley if he's in hell, than anywhere without him.'

CHAPTER 3

Courtship and Marriage
of Lily and Chris, 1885–6

Beside Susie Pettiward, Lily's other special friend at Canon Holland's School for Girls in Upper Baker Street had been Isabel Luce, whose family lived in Sussex, but had taken a London house, as the Turners had done, in Regent's Park. Isabel spoke often of her Sussex neighbours, the Buckles of Norton House, Aldingbourne, near Chichester; and when Chris Buckle came up to stay with them to sit for his examinations for the Royal Military Academy, Woolwich, the fact that he had been at Sherborne School in Dorset with Ted Turner caused Mrs Turner to invite him to dinner. It had therefore been in 1880, when Lily was only fifteen, that Chris set eyes on her for the first time: and the impression she made was lasting. Two years later when Lily was at the end of her last school term, there had been 'a sudden outburst of farewell picnics'. Lily went to two of these, but Mrs Turner, leaving for a visit, advised her to accept no more invitations as she was going to the country shortly and the railway tickets cost money. The reason Lily gave for disobeying her mother was that the picnic in Epping Forest was organized by Isabel Luce: but Lily had a romantic devotion to a mistress, who was to make one of the party, and the enchantments of Miss Dingle may have been the real reason for her missing trains and arriving home at 9.30 in the evening. Lily found Agnes, who had not even been warned that she was going on the picnic, in a state of alarm. 'She said I had behaved disgracefully and must go to my room and stay there all next day.' Lily thus missed the 'Break Up' of her school and a flurry of fond farewells. In the afternoon, however, Agnes wanted to go to a tea-party and she told the maid that if any callers came Lily was to be allowed out of captivity to entertain them. Mr Buckle came. When Lily told him how he had set her free from solitary confinement he was 'quite overcome'. ' "*What!* Stayed in your room the whole blessed day! And missed your Break Up! Just because your *sister* told you to! I don't see *myself* staying in like that for *my* elder sister. Hanged if I do!" Then, after a pause, "Look here, will you have to go back to your room after tea, when I go?" "Sure to, but never mind." "Then I shall sit on, and your sister will have to ask me to dinner!" And "sit on" he did.' That was in summer 1882.

The Turners, who were far from being 'in society', lived in Cumberland Terrace almost a village life, the focus of which was Christ Church, Albany Street. The Vicar, Mr Festing, was a friend and had enrolled Lily to take a Bible class for 'shop girls and young beginners on the stage'. 'I cannot have been of much use to them,' wrote Lily, 'for I was more ignorant of a girl's temptations than a modern girl of twelve would be; but I was fond of them – and they were fond of me.' On Ash Wednesday 1885, Emmie and Lily returned from Evensong to find their mother talking by firelight to a tall young man. 'Here is Mr Buckle waiting to see you, Lily,' said Mrs Turner. Lily's response was perhaps more coquettish than rude. 'Oh! I have forgotten who Mr Buckle is.' Christopher Buckle, by now a subaltern in the Royal Artillery, stationed at Woolwich, was over six foot in height, with an erect carriage, a small head and a huge moustache. Lily had obviously *not* forgotten who he was, and he obviously found her more attractive than ever. 'He sat on as before, and mother had to ask him to stay to dinner.'

Mrs Turner knew that Chris was the elder son of 'an old county family', but found him rather dull and thought Lily might easily 'do better'. On a visit to Chris Buckle at Woolwich for a band concert, Lily refused her photograph for his album because he had the portraits of actresses in it.

Nevertheless, she gave him her buttonhole of white violets which, he told her on his next Sunday call at Cumberland Terrace, had brought him luck at cards. Lily announced that men should not play cards for money: but her priggish attitude did not put him off. He atoned by accompanying the Turners to evening service, and was again asked to supper. 'Before Lent was over,' wrote Lily, 'everyone knew there was a love affair in progress.' On Good Friday Lily returned from church – where she prayed that she might make the right decision about Mr Buckle and not fret over Douglas Terry – and from the sick-bed of one of the girls in her Bible class, to find her mother 'worn out' with Chris, who had awaited her arrival all afternoon. Mrs Turner sent the young people into the terrace gardens with Agnes, who soon met another friend to walk with, and Chris and Lily found themselves alone.

We were left to ourselves for quite half an hour, never having had a chance of any private conversation before. The result was that when we came back to an empty drawing-room we found ourselves engaged within five minutes. But, for all the comfort of love and embraces – and they *are* a comfort when one is young and starving for love – we both bargained with each other almost as soon as we drew breath. Chris said, 'Swear you will never stand in the way of the Service!'; and I, much surprised, said that, of course, I never would. And I said, 'I must tell you that I have cared for someone else for three years.' And he replied that he knew that all right and had always known there was another fellow down in Suffolk. I did not ask if 'the Service' included every form of sport, which in his case it certainly did, and *he* did not ask if I had ceased to think of the 'Suffolk fellow', which I had not! But when I had left him to Mother, who was quite nice to him, I considered matters at my bedroom window and prayed we might help each other through life; and I think we have.

While Lily sat waiting for Chris in the terrace gardens on the afternoon of Easter Day she was reading George Eliot's *The Mill on the Floss,* and since she had no understanding of sex or of how women got pregnant she could not make out what had occurred between Hetty and Arthur Donnithorne.

On Easter Monday Lily was astonished to receive another proposal, this time from the Vicar. Mr Festing had to console himself for her refusal by his elevation to the see of St Albans shortly afterwards. All things considered, Lily would have preferred being a clergyman's wife to a soldier's, but she seems to have felt no regret.

Of all the marriages of my recent ancestors it can safely be said that they had one thing in common: one side, the bridegroom's or the bride's, always thought the other not good enough – and sometimes both did. When Lily's father, Dr Turner, married Elizabeth Chamley, the Chamleys were indignant. (They did not know, as I do, that the Turners could trace their yeoman stock at least back to the 1600s.) With Lily's own marriage to Chris neither side was happy. Mrs Turner soon found out that the Buckle 'place' at Norton was not large, the 'park' negligible, and Chris's prospects poor. His grandfather had been a third son, and the big house, Nork, above Epsom, had been sold long ago. The dull proud old Buckles, for their part, felt humiliated. Lily's visit to Norton was depressing beyond words: she had never before been so snubbed. Ugly Mr Buckle complained that he could not find her family in the *Landed Gentry*; remarked that no Buckle had ever married a doctor's daughter before (which was untrue – his own grandfather had); announced that he would halve Chris's allowance instead of doubling it; and decided to make no marriage settlement as Lily looked delicate, and he feared there would be nothing left for Chris's second wife. By the time the old Buckles had married rather late in life, Christopher Richard Buckle had run through most of his money, and his wife Caroline, born Cumberbatch, was impoverished too, as her family's sugar plantations on Barbados were ceasing to pay since the abolition of slavery. A maiden aunt, Mary Buckle, had paid for Chris's education; while the china and silver of another aunt, Mrs Fearnley, married but childless, came to the Buckles of Norton – and eventually to me. Chris had an unsatisfactory younger brother and three dull sisters, who drove into Chichester to shop every afternoon, allowed the attendant at the Lending Library to choose their books for them and lived only for Goodwood Week, when Chris brought home brother officers for the races.

When Chris Buckle went up to stay at Warcop with the Turners, who had by then bought Eden Gate, he took to Westmorland just as fervently as Lily had done the year before. Though no member of his family had lived in Westmorland for a long time, it was a curious coincidence that they had sprung from there. The first Buckle to go south had left his home in the reign of Queen Elizabeth I. It was Lily's engagement to Chris that brought a Buckle back to Westmorland after three hundred years.

The Buckles had once lived on Stainmore, the bleak upland that has to be crossed by the northbound traveller before he descends into the Eden valley. From the high ground he looks down to see Brough Castle, one of the Cliffords' five fortresses, standing out against the paradisal landscape. Cuthbert, the first Buckle to make his name, was the son of a farmer called Christopher, born in 1533. What was the accident of fate, the stroke of luck or the spark of personality that jolted Cuthbert out of his rural rut and sent him trotting southwards towards the ferment of Tudor London – which must have seemed as brave a new world to him as the Americas to Drake? For centuries the horizon of his peasant sires had been bounded by the Westmorland mountains and moors. What was to prevent him from staying on the farm and breeding more Westmorland farmers?

Cuthbert Buckle's early life and his character are as dark to us as those lost years of William Shakespeare's between the christening of his twins at Stratford in 1588 and Robert Greene's attack on him as a successful playwright in 1592. It is, in fact, in 1593, the year after Greene published *A Groatsworth of Wit*, that Buckle steps out of the shadows. He is a vintner; he is married to Elizabeth, daughter of Thomas Marston; he has a son aged three; he is Lord Mayor of London; he has been knighted; he has made a fortune; he lives in the finest house in the city – then suddenly, in the year of his mayoralty, he dies.

It was, of course, an age of change, of adventure. People were going up in the world, and getting around in it. But apart from there being 'something in the air', apart from ambitions aroused by tales of discovery or by the rumour of fortunes to be made, a man needed exceptional determin-ation, talent or charm to rise as Sir Cuthbert Buckle did. Perhaps he picked up a little learning at the school in Brough and was sent to get more at Appleby. Perhaps his beauty was so great that its fame spread through the Eden valley, and he was summoned to the court of Clifford, Earl of Cumberland (an ancestor of Chris on his mother's side and of my mother Rose) and attached to his household at Appleby Castle, and so carried south. Perhaps Thomas Marston was a wine-merchant and Cuthbert went to work for him, then, like Dick Whittington two hundred years earlier, married the boss's daughter.

Sir Cuthbert Buckle's mansion was in Mark Lane, near the Tower; he had property in the parishes of St Dunstan-in-the-East and St Mary-at-Hill; and he was buried in the latter church. In his will he remembered Brough: 'I give to twenty poore maydens borne and dwelling in the parish of Broughe under Staynmore in the county of Westmorland where I was borne to every of them twenty shillings to be paid unto them at the dayes of their marriages . . .'

Cuthbert's son Christopher bought property in Surrey: he too was knighted and he lived at Old Burgh House at Banstead, near Epsom. His son, another Sir Christopher, married Elizabeth Lewis, daughter of a Welsh baronet who had been imprisoned by Cromwell in the Round Tower at Windsor for his 'powerful exertions' in the cause of King Charles. John Evelyn mentions in his diary for 1658 seeing some digging for Roman remains being carried on near the second Sir Christopher's house. About 1690, John Aubrey the antiquarian (and first 'biographer' of Shakespeare) noted, on a visit to Banstead, 'The family of the Buckles is of one hundred years' continuance in this village, though not so much as one monument has been erected in their burial place.' Yet a third Christopher built Nork in 1740 and laid out a park to the east of the Ewell-Reigate road: but the big mansion only remained in the family for a few generations, for it was sold to Lord Egmont in 1846. The most marked tendency of the Buckles was to go to sea and become admirals. Apart from being good sailors, they appear to have had little ambition for going up in the world: they married into few distinguished families and never by any chance got hold of an heiress.

Chris's grandfather Matthew founded the Norton branch of the Buckle family. I have his log-books from the time of his sailing for India as a fourteen-year-old midshipman in 1774. Besides providing evidence of the hard life of seamen before the age of steam they give a hint of his character. When, as a Lieutenant, he sailed on HM Ship *Superbe* from the Cape of Good Hope in December 1779, the death roll was appalling. 'Decr 31st. Died this Month 1 Mid^n 16 Private, besides a Man that jumped over board in a Delirium of a

Fever.' That Christmas Day liquor must have been issued, for on 26 December Matthew Buckle punished three seamen with '12 Lashes for Drunkenness'. Nor was drunken behaviour confined to the lower decks. On 10 October 1781, on board the *Coventry*, 'The Wardroom Mess dined with the Cap^n, soon after the cloth was removed Cap^n Mitchell began talking to Lieu^t Abbot upon Points of Duty, and smartly reprimanded him, telling him he was not fit for a 1st Lieu^t and that he would break him the first opportunity, with many reflections upon the rest of the Officers . . .; upon which I wished him a good afternoon, the rest followed.' The intimidated captain sent a letter asking Matthew if he and the others 'intended to refuse drinking Tea and Suping with him as he did not chuse to receive such a Message by a servant'. Matthew replied that he was 'determined not to eat at his table any more'. After receiving another abject letter, Matthew and the Mess 'thought the appology sufficient and made matters up'.

My grandfather Chris may have inherited from Matthew a disinclination to take any nonsense from his superiors, for it was said that his failure to ingratiate himself with the army commanders, during whose lengthy conferences he used to go to sleep, was a reason for his not being knighted after the First World War. Like Matthew, he was swift to wipe out all memory of an offence, once a wrong had been righted or an apology given. When I was a boy, if I was rude or naughty, his rebuke was as terrifying as a thunderbolt. Afterwards he made a point of being charming and behaving as if nothing had happened. This I found attractive.

Matthew Buckle made some amends for being a younger son by marrying his plain first cousin, the daughter of Admiral Buckle of Nork, the head of the family. His only son, Christopher Richard, the 'old Mr Buckle' of Lily's memoir, also rounded the Cape and made his passage to India as third officer on the merchantman *Catharine* in 1835. He was nineteen at the time; his mother died while he was at sea, his father Matthew seven months after his return.

After her depressing visit to Norton, Lily could write: 'We were both much happier up at Eden Gate, where Chris fell in love with the fells and the river and the whole atmosphere. He never seemed to care for his old home any more – whereas his sisters never cared in the least for any other place.'

But, even at Warcop, all was not perfect. Chris, the most straightforward of men, confessed some youthful irregularities, one of which had resulted in a son who was packed off to Australia; and that night Lily was so upset that she did not go to bed, but paced her room and knelt by the open window overlooking the rose garden, thinking she *could not* marry him after all.

> I knew literally nothing before of sex and its pitfalls and was horror-stricken to learn what an average young officer's life was really like. Walking in the little Wilderness wood, next morning, I said I would rather marry the garden boy – who happened to be passing across the lawn. And Chris said it was just that I didn't understand: all men did the same, and I should find the gardener and my brothers had done everything that he had. He said he should drown himself in the Eden. This overpowered me entirely; and I thought God *must* mean me to marry and take care of him and not mind my own feelings.
>
> Chris was to sail for India on October 1st 1885. It was a stormy Brough Hill Fair day when he left Warcop, and our future looked as dark as the streaming skies.

I suppose that Mrs Turner and Ted regarded Lily's good looks as capital which should be properly invested to bring dividends. Standing on the old bridge one day, Ted told Lily that 'if she was fool enough to marry Buckle she would find herself in the workhouse with half-a-dozen children by the end of the year'. She was so ignorant of the facts of life that she even believed this was possible: but she held firm to her promise to Chris. The time had come for Ted to join his regiment, the Royal Scots, at the Cape of Good Hope.

We saw him off at the little country station with the old 'View Halloo' the brothers always used to give. We never saw him again.

After Ted had sailed nothing seemed likely to happen except the regular Indian mails from Chris, which took six weeks; but something did. Colonel Arthur Wynne came home from Egypt, and as he had been very fond of Chamley Mother asked him up to Eden Gate for a week. He was just forty, but rather worn-looking. A charming man, so kind and good, we all liked him, and it was arranged that he should come again for the Easter weekend. He was so impartial in his manners that on Easter Monday when we took him to Stenkrith for a lunch picnic, Emmie observed to me how nice it would be if Colonel Wynne were to propose to Agnes, who had been talking to him with unusual animation. That evening Emmie and I saw him off on the night train, and as we left the station she suddenly said, 'Lily, I am engaged to Colonel Wynne,' and I was so thunderstruck that I sat down in the hedge. Mother was immensely pleased over this engagement and Arthur Wynne was goodness itself to her up to the end of her life.

They had a great wedding; Eden Gate brimmed over with guests. Sis and Mona Chamley, Janet Irving and myself [all first cousins] were bridesmaids, wearing corn-coloured silk dresses with bouquets of poppies and corn: it was harvest time and I thought poppies went well with the scarlet tunics of the bridegroom's and best man's uniforms. There were triumphal arches and children in white strewing flowers all along the church path, and Emmie had a lovely satin gown and old lace veil: but it was a wild stormy day and the rain drenched down. I was very unhappy as I knelt in the aisle behind the bride. Her long train, which had caught the muddy wheel of the carriage, literally dripped in front of me.

Not long after this I found that when I put my weekly letter for India into the postbox on the hall table it did not always go. Mother's pressure against my engagement had become very insistent and wearing. Finally I wrote a letter – and posted it myself – to tell Chris that I would either marry him now on his subaltern's pay and the hundred a year which was all we had between us from our parents, or break our engagement.

A month later I was giving a lesson in the village school and saw through the window the postman's wife coming across the field path from Eden Gate with an orange envelope in her hand. I rushed out to meet her and she called at the top of her voice, 'It's all right, Miss Lily. He's coming home to marry you!'

While Chris travelled home Lily planned everything on the most economical scale. For her there would be no bridesmaids or triumphal arches. In fact her wedding and the first days of her honeymoon would be as inauspicious of married bliss as her vexed engagement. The wedding would take place from Emmie's and Arthur Wynne's house at Norwood, the South London suburb whither the 'Crystal Palace' had been moved from Hyde Park; and as Chris and Lily would be sailing within three weeks for India, duty dictated that the first days of the honeymoon be spent near the Buckles. Chris arrived back looking 'thin, brown and hollow-eyed'.

On Monday, 13 December Lily woke after a troubled night, and put on a dark-blue travelling dress, a claret-coloured, tight-fitting 'Newmarket' coat with a black velvet collar, and a black velvet toque with a white aigrette in front. 'One last prayer, and as I was coming down the stairs Emmie handed me a telegram from Mother.' Mrs Turner had lost one daughter in India, and a son in Egypt: Ted was in South Africa, and her household at Eden Gate would be reduced to the invalid Agnes, young Braith and Nellie's boy Kit. Her apprehensions were natural, but her eleventh-hour appeal, as it were at the altar steps, was melodramatic. The telegram read: 'Still time to change your mind.'

Lily walked with Emmie and Arthur to St Paul's Church. It was foggy and cold, and only the chancel was lit. In the gloom Lily made out the figure of Chris, kneeling, with his brother seated uneasily beside him. When the curate in a dirty crumpled surplice asked if Christopher Reginald would take Elizabeth Braithwaite to be his wedded wife, the affirmative response came in so loud and clear a voice that it made him jump. Chris stated, as if he were on parade, that he would love her, comfort her and keep her, in sickness and in health, as long as they both should live. In the vestry, an unkempt pew-opener suddenly lit the gas jet over Lily's head to enable her to sign the register, and her bonnet caught fire, so she went off with a scorched aigrette and minus a little curl of front hair, third class, to Arundel. The cold was bitter, the train was slow, the carriage was shared with some workmen. Why the old Buckles were unable or unwilling to put up Chris and Lily at Norton it is hard to imagine, but they did not. The newly-wedded couple found that luncheon at the Norfolk Arms was 'off' and only cold beef was 'on', that their private sitting-room was 'an immense fog-filled ballroom', and that only one of its fires was alight. Next day, the apparition of the Buckle family through sleet and snow was hardly enlivening. On the third day when Chris and Lily returned the visit and were welcomed to Aldingbourne by a peal of bells, Mr Buckle announced that the bellringers must be paid in gold; and this cost Chris as much as the Arundel hotel bill.

Lily told me in later years that, although she was not really passionately attracted to Chris before their wedding, after a few days of married life she was 'head over heels in love': this has always struck me as a classic example of the way physical fulfilment can cast its benison over marriage. She did not refer to this intimate matter in her memoirs, which Chris, of course, would be the first to read. She wrote, however, that during the few days spent at 'dear old Cumberland Terrace', which would soon be given up for good, 'when Chris came rushing back to me for tea, after seeing about uniform and a saddle at Woolwich, it began to feel very nice to be married and independent, and to have an adoring husband to take home to Eden Gate.' The Wynnes too were at Warcop for Christmas. Mrs Turner, making the best of a bad job, 'accepted us quite affectionately and kindly, and gave a dance to show that all was well with both her married daughters'.

CHAPTER 4

Snapshots, 1888–1909

Chris and Lily were to have over sixty 'homes' before they settled down in their old age at Warcop. Their eldest child and only son, conceived in India, was born at Eden Gate in March 1888. He was named Christopher Galbraith, the second name being that of a general who had been kind to Lily in Karachi; and he was always called Garry for short. His childish attempts to say 'Mother' and 'Father' landed Lily and Chris with the foolish names of 'Muddis' and 'Hardie'. I always called my grandfather 'Granhardie'. Woolwich, Aldershot, then Edinburgh. The summers, when not much soldiering was done, were spent at Eden Gate or the Old Cottage, which Mrs Turner had inherited from her mother, and which stood on a triangular 'island' at the other end of the village. Here Doris Eden was born in 1891. A second daughter, Phyllis Norton, always called Tita, was born in Edinburgh in 1893. Lily had more than one miscarriage, probably caused by her lack of moderation in good works, such as nursing the sick, which became an increasing passion. In 1895 the Buckles were stationed on the Isle of Wight, and it was from there that Garry went reluctantly to school at Hamilton House on Lansdown Hill above Bath. A spell at Plymouth preceded a second stay on the Isle of Wight. When Chris went to South Africa in 1898 to fight the Boers Lily was determined to follow him, but it was a year before he thought it possible to send for her. Chris served as Military Secretary to Sir Evelyn Wood from 1903 till 1905, which brought the family to Salisbury and Wilton in Wiltshire.

Garry was at his public school, Marlborough, twenty-five miles away. A third daughter, Judith, was born at Wilton in 1904. Lily nursed her mother through her final illness that summer. Next Chris was posted to Gibraltar. Because of the flowers and the sunsets this was the favourite among Lily's homes; and here she gave birth in 1908 to her last child, Christian. Garry had by this time passed (after an initial failure) into the Royal Military College, Sandhurst; and in 1909 he was commissioned in the Northamptonshire Regiment and posted to India. Christmas 1911, which was spent at Tynemouth in Northumberland, was the last which the whole family enjoyed together. Then Garry applied for a transfer to the West African Frontier Force, which meant an increase of pay at the risk of fever; and Chris was given command of the Harwich garrison.

We have seen how Lily was still afflicted with a lingering passion for Douglas Terry when she became engaged to Chris. Douglas entered the Church belatedly; then in 1893 caught typhoid from a choirboy he was nursing, and died. On the Isle of Wight Lily was violently attracted by a curate, John Holloway, whose voice was like Terry's, and whose sermons stirred her to the core; while Holloway, who was married, fell deeply in love with Lily. Chris was not much perturbed by such aery infidelities, which Lily discussed quite frankly with him. She persuaded Holloway to apply for a curacy elsewhere and, until he could move house, took the train daily, feeling 'very unhappy', to study professional nursing on the other side of the island. Absence did not extinguish Jack Holloway's guilty flame, but he died in 1910. In Gibraltar Lily fell under the spell of its itinerant Bishop, William Collins, whose delicate health and dedicated life made her see him as a martyr as well as a saint. When he died in harness, an obituary she had been asked to write turned into a short biographical sketch, and this was her first published book. Her other books were all of lay sermons disguised as short stories based on real episodes in her life.

Chris was so avid an admirer of female beauty that he was usually attracted by some pretty girl. Lily minded this more than she admitted in her autobiography. His most serious attachment was to Lady Muriel Herbert, the younger daughter of Lord and Lady Pembroke, with whom he rode to hounds in Wiltshire.

From being a bright little boy, whose funny remarks about God and prayer Lily recorded, Garry turned into a rather ugly adolescent, miserable at school, spoilt at home: he was far from intellectual, preferring games to books, and grew up to be not only as keen a shot as his father, but an enthusiastic fisherman, which Chris had never been. A few months at a French crammer's near St Malo turned him into a smart, attractive young man, who 'could not keep girls at arm's length'. He was in love with his cousin (on the Buckle side) Joyce Lambert, whom Lily thought the loveliest girl she had ever seen, but who 'had him on a string' for years. Then Lily encouraged him to become engaged to another cousin, Christine Turner, with whom he had little in common, and whose unhappiness when he severed the connection made him unhappy too. On leave from Africa in 1913 Garry became engaged to Rose Sandford, who was on a visit to her grandmother near Harwich. When he returned to England on sick leave a year later the war with Germany had already broken out. He and Rose were married on 1 September 1914.

Lily's nursing became 'almost a profession' in later years; she specialized in the care of the dying. At Netley Hospital near Southampton, where she worked unofficially but steadily in 1915 and 1916, she was nicknamed 'the Eye-closer'. Her longing to be a heroine in the eyes of another human being, which was less easily satisfied as her children grew up, found fulfilment in the intense communion she was able to establish with young men on the threshold of death: to these she became the triple incarnation of mother, sweetheart and priest. The stories she wrote about Netley

Above: Lily Turner in the Wilderness at Eden Gate, summer 1884. Beyond the wicket gate the 'church path' leads to the church and school. A branch off it to the right, through a field called 'The Crooks', led to Warcop House.

Below: The Eden above Warcop Bridge.

Lily Turner reading a love letter from Chris Buckle in India, Warcop, spring 1886. Drawing by Amy Stobart. The artist, a schoolfriend of Lily's, has written 'Karachi' on the letter.
Lily is seated in her beloved 'bow' at Eden Gate, which may have improved the amenitites of the drawing-room by catching the sun and giving views of the river, but which ruined the look of the house from the outside.

Eden Gate about 1885, when Mrs Turner bought it.

Above: Chris Buckle,
about 1884.

Right: Lily Buckle with Garry,
Edinburgh, 1890.

Rose Buckle at the Old Cottage, Warcop, April 1916. Watercolour by
Dolly Sandford. Rose is sewing baby clothes for the author, who was born
in August. Her Pekinese, Yum-Yum, is seated on a cushion.
Only the south-west corner of the cottage is seen on the right. The house in
the distance, beyond an invisible lane, is Smithy Hill, backed by the trees of
Warcop Hall.

were her best. I can never read them without crying: nor, I learned to my astonishment twenty years after his death, could my grandfather.

Here are a few snapshots from the Buckle family album, taken between the birth of Garry and the outbreak of the First World War.

Warcop, 1888.

It was such a heavy fall of snow the day Garry came into the world, and the big spare room at Eden Gate was full of reflected cold white light. Dr Dalston had driven over from Brough at lunch-time the day before – it was the fifteenth of March 1888 – and the snow drifted so deeply that he could not get back until the next afternoon. In the early dawn Chris was still in his evening clothes when he bent over me and whispered, 'Don't you want to see the son? He's a beauty!' and showed me the crumpled little red face frowning out of a blanket in his arms. But I did not think him a beauty at all: he looked just like his grandfather Buckle when he was annoyed and I had expected – Heaven only knows what a girl expects her first baby to be – a sweetly smiling serene-faced angel trailing obvious clouds of glory and looking at least six weeks old the first minute.

'What do you think of him?' urged Chris, regardless of my exhaustion and disappointed silence, and filled with a perfect satisfaction in the glorious fact that he had a son, a real live Buckle, and certain that however he looked he must be right.

'Funny,' I murmured weakly, and fell asleep.

The snow lasted all the time I was upstairs. I could see Roman Fell from my pillow, whitely majestic as it kept guard over the village at its foot; and the plover could not get food and came down on to the lawn, crying and wheeling round the house.

There was no sign of spring until well on into April when I took Garry for his first walk down the garden and across the old bridge to the path along the river. Everyone at Warcop has to be shown the Eden before they see anything else, and I always loved that path especially. I had taken my love letters there to read over again. I used to read the evening Lesson or Psalm down there in summer, leaning over the little wicket gate at the end of the wood. Looking back, one sees the curve of the wooded banks and the broad smooth reach of water before it begins to tumble and rush along the rocks. So it was the first place to which I carried Garry, and I think the last place he longed to see, for when he grew up it became a favourite spot for fishing, and he said so often when he came wounded back from France, 'I shall be all right if I can get a few days fishing up at Warcop. The river does me more good than anything.'

Warcop, July 1898

Garry was given the holiday task of writing a diary. This painful duty led to the record of an idyllic three weeks, sandwiched between two uncomfortable night journeys.

First of all when I got to Paddington there was nobody to meet me. I had to wait for half-an-hour there before father came. We had to travel all night to get to Westmorland. It was not very nice as we had a drunken man in the carriage. He kept kicking me and putting his head on my father's lap. We got to Penrith at 5 a.m., and as we had two hours to wait we walked to the next station up the river and saw a splendid trout. Mother, Doris and Tita came to meet me at the station. We had strawberries for all the meals.

'Went out fishing . . . shot three rabbits . . . made hay in the orchard . . . picked raspberries for Granny . . . caught a crayfish in the river and some very young trout . . . stalked a leveret and Father shot him . . . Church . . . walked to Sandford Bridge . . . Mother read aloud to us all out of *Swiss Family Robinson* . . . killed a blackbird . . . made two waterfalls in the Eden and went out shooting in Mrs

Preston's park [Warcop Hall] with father . . . after dinner I wound some wool for Mother . . . took the dogs down the beck after water rats . . . I and father between us killed a blackbird and a thrush in the gooseberry nets . . . went to Deepgill with father to cut bracken for ferretting on Saturday . . . shot, played cricket after tea and went up the river . . . I made seven ducks and drakes in one shot . . . saw a water dipper and a water hen . . . target practice and hit bull's-eye three times . . . the river came out in flood and all evening we were watching it . . . a splendid day's ferretting with father and Windsor [Chamley], we killed forty-three rabbits . . . Father, mother and I bicycled up to Helbeck Hall and back, I saw a splendid peacock up there . . . I went for a fourteen-mile bicycle ride to Kirkby Stephen with father . . . went out mushrooming with father, we got about two pounds . . . breakfasted with father at seven o'clock [it was 12 August] and mother and I went part way up to the grouse moor with him . . . ferretting, we got thirty-seven rabbits . . .'

But all this time there was uncertainty about Chris's next posting. On the 19th while he was out grouse-shooting a telegram came: 'Join at Plymouth today'; and Lily had to pack for him, Garry and herself and meet him on his way down from Hilton Moor to catch the night train from Appleby. 'Mother did not have a very good night,' wrote Garry, 'but we had a very good one.'

Lily was pregnant, and had a miscarriage (her second) a few days after their arrival.

Plymouth, 1899

'Will Hammond' was the name Lily gave to the hero of one of her (true) stories, from which extracts follow.

> Will Hammond was a regular young Viking of a boy –
> with double pneumonia. Dr Lock said, 'He's a real good
> fellow, worth saving, keeps a fool of a mother and a
> drunken stepfather and a baby. I'm afraid he'll die anyhow,

but you might just save him.' Let no one ever think that it is easy to go to a new house and intrude on strange people and have the assurance to take over the charge of the sick. It always made my knees play tunes with fright. On this occasion the fat mother wasted no manners on me whatever. 'Yer can look at 'un, an' yer can leave 'un; 'is mother's good enuff for 'un and yer ain't wanted.' When I returned with ice and a soda syphon she had reconsidered things. 'Yer be to bide; the young man's tuked a fancy for 'ee.' A good deal can be done in an hour; when I had got a week's ashes from under the grate, all the dirty rugs turned out, the window wide open, the room fairly clean and Will sponged all over (which he called ''evingly') and he had taken half a tin of Brand's jelly and the milk was on the ice, I felt as happy as a queen. Dr Lock came in after a while and declared the boy was better already; if only the nights did not undo the days he might pull through yet . . . But Will's mates sat up with him and smoked to pass the time . . . I flung open door and window, and stirred the sulky cinder fire, and then turned to the bed and stroked Will's hand a moment as I held him up to get his breath. Talk of love, whoever lacks it has only to try his hand at nursing the poor. I can see Will's blue eyes now as he gasped out, 'I've bin a-praying to God to send you quick, Nurse, iver since five.' He told me about himself . . . and now he supposed he was going to die. As I put his pillow right and asked God to give him a good night I forgot proprieties altogether and bent down and kissed the poor damp forehead. As I walked along to the tram I felt that officers' wives of two-and-thirty were not supposed to kiss young workmen and reflected that Chris might conceivably take that view. But Chris didn't. 'It's time to dress,' he said. 'I'm afraid he'll die. It sounds bad. When I come to the same pass, may you be there to kiss me.' Next morning Will's temperature was down to 102°. 'Why, Will,' said Dr Lock, 'your nurse has saved you.' Will was too polite to contradict. Half-an-hour later the vile needle-point rested at nearly 106°. The breathing got hor-rible. The poor fat mother's face trembled and the tears came trickling down. 'I can't abide to see 'un. Oh deary me, 'ee's makin' faces'; and she rushed stumbling down the stairs. 'Pray the Lord,' he said, 'pray 'im to take me quick.' 'It won't be long now, Will.' 'Lift me 'igher, Nurse.' The brave head was on my shoulder, and the chilly cheek laid against mine . . . How the sunshine glared on the streets as I made my way home; and before I had time to stop him Connor [the soldier-servant] was announcing strange callers in the drawing-room. Feeling myself rather dishevelled, mentally as well as outwardly . . . I went out again to get some air up the hill, and suddenly Dr Lock's dog-cart came along the road. 'Oh, Dr Lock, Will's dead . . .' 'He never had more than one chance in a hundred, you know. For goodness' sake, don't look so broken over it.' I told him a little about the boy's pluck and how he died. He muttered something kind about wishing he had six nurses, and then added emphatically as he drove off, 'All the same you are the most upsetting woman I ever came across.'

He meant that Lily had succeeded in making him want to cry. This, I think, was how she set out to affect people in her short stories, particularly in those describing the soldiers she nursed at Netley Hospital in 1915 and 1916.

Vryburg, South Africa, 1900–1901

The officers Lily entertained in her shack at Vryburg – and she even hired a piano – were suitably appreciative: nevertheless they must have asked themselves what on earth she was doing there at all. (Queen Victoria strongly disapproved of soldiers' wives following their husbands to war.) Lily was particularly attracted to the sick or lonely; young Ralph Venning (later killed 'standing by his guns in Methuen's last fight') was adopted as 'son of the house' and expected to dinner nightly. With a less lovable guest, who drank too much, Lily 'had it out', and he promised to mend his ways. Lily soon found she had earned herself a new name.

There were so many Staff appointments that the officers referred to each other by their initials. The Railway Staff Officer was always spoken of as the R.S.O., the Staff Officer Transport as the S.O.T., and so on. One evening when Lily had several officers to dinner she remarked that she should start some grand initials of her own – M.C.W. for Mere Captain's Wife. At this a young subaltern blurted out, 'Oh, but you've had initials ever since you've been here,' then became embarrassed and began to murmur that it was all rot, and of course she wasn't really old. Lily protested that she was thirty-four and insisted on knowing what her title was – even if it was A.L. for Aged Lunatic. The subaltern said it was frightful cheek, but they all called her 'M.O.A. – Mother of All'. She thought this was 'the dearest name any woman could wish for'.

Life was not easy: the Boers kept cutting communications. They prevented the Christmas mail from getting through; they intercepted columns sent out by Chris; they stole his cattle. Even at night the heat was intense, and because of the dust Lily had to wash her hair every other day. The new century, however, began with a thunderstorm, which cleared the air. The Buckles were on a two-day trip to Mafeking – where Chris had business and Lily bought brooches made of Mauser shell and 'a queer Kaffir stick for Uncle Tom' – when they heard of the Queen's illness. Back at Vryburg, before breakfast on 24 January, Lily heard the Queen was dead. At morning prayers Chris, Lily, Gunner Richardson and Basuto Joanna prayed for the new King.

On 4 February the rains came at last:

> Torrents and deluges which turned our garden path into a roaring river in a few hours. They have made life here quite a different thing, and I was able to go for a long cool ride with Chris, out round his Government farm. There we found over a hundred rebel cattle calmly grazing and drove them all in before us. I wondered if Doris and Tita

would recognize me if they saw me heading back oxen and cantering after stray bulls and cows.

Warcop, Summer 1909

Mrs Turner, Ted and Agnes were by this time dead. Shortly after Ted's arrival in South Africa he had sent home for a pack of hounds, just as Chamley had done. He was seconded to the service of the Chartered Company, became a friend of Cecil Rhodes, and invested every penny he had in the original shares of the company's land. He married Roberta Graham of The Mains, Wynberg, who came of an ancient Scottish house which produced a number of distinguished public servants for Cape Colony. They had no children. In 1892 Ted was offered the appointment of first Resident Magistrate of Salisbury, Rhodesia, but before taking it up he went as representative of the Chartered Company to plot the boundary with Portuguese East Africa. Near the confluence of the Lundi and Sabi rivers he died of malaria. In 1904 Mrs Turner died at the Old Cottage, nursed by Lily. Agnes only survived her briefly. (Kit Birdwood was killed at Gallipoli, in 1915.)

Eden Gate was standing empty and unlet. Lily decided that the family must have the pleasure of spending the summer there, and she travelled to Westmorland alone to get the house ready for them. The place seemed full of ghosts. Only Emmie and Lily – and Braith in far-off Australia – remained.

> I drove up to the house in the evening in heavy rain, and as the hired carriage pulled up at the door my heart quite twisted with the pain of it all. We had been such a cheery party there in the old days, and mother was always waiting with such a welcome. There was no one now, only old Pax the retriever, and the gardener and cook. I wandered through the deserted rooms one after another; the familiar carpets stood up in rolls; the pictures, chairs

books were dusty and awry. Next day, Sunday, still it rained, but I started down across the dripping garden to go to early service, and opened the little wicket gate to find no church path – not a sign of it. The tenants had never used it, I suppose: anyhow it had grown entirely into part of the big drenching hayfield – and it was far too late to turn back and go all round by the road.

But Lily later saw a Providence in this desolation.

If Eden Gate had not been so unbearable as it was I might not have hurried to get in women to clean and freshen all the shut-up rooms at once, and men to re-cut and dig the church path. As it was, I set to and we all worked hard and in a week the place began to look sweet and useable and cared for again. Then, one afternoon, I walked across the fields to fetch the second post, opened the paper and saw that Mary Collins [the Bishop of Gibraltar's wife] had died in town. Oh, poor Bishop! Within an hour I was back at the post office with a letter. If he wanted to get away from everything and everyone I could give him a set of rooms all to himself where he could slip down to the river or up among the fells, and he need not even see me at meals unless he liked. The children were due, and Chris was landing from Gibraltar when the Bishop wrote that, 'since he could not be in Paradise with his dear one he would sooner be at Eden Gate than anywhere'. I think it must have been the name that drew him.

The girls filled the house with flowers, and the big chintz armchair in the window of his bedroom did really face a most heavenly view: rose garden beneath, wood beyond, and then the swelling purple curves of Roman Fell and Helbeck. The writing-table in the library was better still, with the lawns outside the window sloping down in terraces to the Eden, whose murmur over the rocks and stones by the old bridge could be heard all day long.

When Bishop Collins arrived he was 'so ill, so spent and weary' that he seemed to Lily on the point of death himself. 'Yet he noticed each turn and changing view . . . Every night he slipped away early to dress, and I always found him along the wing in Judith's room when the gong went. One evening I overheard a fragment of their conversation. Judith was being rather patronizing. "Well, good night, Bishop darling," (sounds of earnest and numerous kisses), "I know you'd like to come and talk to me in the morning as well as the evening, but you can't, you know, darling, we're so undecent when we're dressing."' Lily ventured to tell the Bishop that she thought his own life was nearly over. 'He looked at me with candid amazement and oh! such joyful amazement too, like a child. "You mean to say you think I am going to die quite soon?" "Why, my dear Bishop, of course you are, it's written on your face. Even the most ignorant can see it." "How soon?" "I suppose it might be a year if you took any sort of care of yourself."'

Chris's sympathy for the Bishop was expressed in few words, but he liked him and did not grudge him Lily's devotion. The extinction of the entire Church Militant here on earth would not have interrupted his grouse-shooting. Between Lily's two beloveds there was an exact division of labour. Then, when Garry arrived from India she would for the only time in her life have the three men she loved best under one roof – and the roof of Eden Gate at Warcop, too! For once she could not say with Browning – as I often heard her say in old age – 'Never the time and the place/And the loved one all together.'

Garry, weak with fever, had to have an awkward interview with Chris over the payment of racing debts. The Bishop sat up late talking to him, and told Lily, 'He is very unusual. He will never be small, he *might* sin deeply, but I *think* he will be a great man. He has such a big heart.'

Shortly afterwards, Eden Gate was sold to Gerard Thompson of Stobars near Kirkby Stephen. From then on, the Old Cottage would be Garry's only home – or rather, his *point de repaire*. Twenty-five years later I should be dreaming of buying back Eden Gate myself, but the only nights I ever slept under its roof were as a guest when my grandfather was dying at the Old Cottage.

CHAPTER 5

Garry and Rose, 1913–18

It was during a tennis-party at Mistley Place in August 1913, that Rose Sandford heard 'a marvellous laugh'. It was Garry Buckle's. At their third meeting four days later he rowed her on the lake and proposed to her. He said, 'I've got no *money*'; and Rose told him she hadn't got a penny either. She was one of the four daughters of Constance Sandford (*née* Craven) whose husband Francis had died ten years before. Rose's twin Violet was extremely pretty, and Rose was used to being pointed out as the plain one of the family on account of her big nose, which made her shy in society for the rest of her life. Still, she was the first sister to get a husband. Lily was surprised that Rose was no striking beauty, although she had a pretty complexion and a mass of fair brown hair; and she was concerned about the nature of the engagement. Disliking anything that was not open and above board, she was upset to find that Rose intended to conceal her plans from her family. Rose had suffered enough in her youth to learn when to be patient, observe how the land lay, await an opportunity and say nothing. She knew what snobs her mother and her unmarried uncle Caryl Craven were. Grandma Sandford, with whom she was staying in Essex, was formidable too. A Buckle who could be found in the *Landed Gentry* might just pass muster, but a Buckle without any land at all would probably not: yet the time must surely come when her mother would be relieved to get *one* daughter off her hands. To *say nothing* was something that Lily had never learnt.

The outbreak of war, a year later, put an end to these hesitations. Garry and Rose had their honeymoon at Warcop. To Rose the fells seemed, on first sight, incredibly bleak; and the 'raw Warcop women' stared dourly at this dressed-up lady from the south with a Pekinese under her arm. However, she soon took to Westmorland as enthusiastically as her in-laws had done in the 1880s. No one had ever taught her the rudiments of housekeeping, and she found to her embarrassment that she 'did not even know how to order pepper'.

The married life of Garry and Rose began a few weeks after the outbreak of war and ended four months before the Armistice. Because he was suffering from the aftermath of fever, Garry missed the early mobile phase of the war; and the squalid form of campaigning known as 'trench warfare' was his lot. On his way back to France in the winter of 1915 he met his parents at the Artillery Hotel, that gloomy building surrounding two courtyards in Victoria Street, which was to be the scene of several farewells, and told them Rose had hope of a baby. 'His face was so proud and yet sad – but we were overjoyed,' wrote Lily. He was awarded the Military Cross in the 1916 New Year's Honours, and when the long, bloody battle of the Somme began that summer he was in command of his battalion.

When Garry came to Warcop for leave in June 1916 Lily wrote:

> I was nursing poor Rose, who had been very ill with nephritis. She was not able to leave her bed, so I met Garry at the station on a dark, lowering early morning, and he was full of bad news: Lord Kitchener's death from a mine at sea and the first telegrams about the Battle of Jutland, which were so ill-worded that for two days we thought our navy had suffered a defeat. After a tub and a shave and a blessed change of clothes, Garry satisfied himself that Rose was really better, and we went down the village to find Jock, his beloved old greyhound, who lived with Tommy

Hall the postman in order to get enough exercise when his master was away. As we went along by the beck, Hall and Jock appeared round the corner of Shoregill and Garry whistled – a long special whistle with which he always called his dogs. Jock threw up his head as if he had been shot and in one wild rush was on his hind legs with both paws on Garry's shoulders barking with such wild torrents of barks that all the village rushed to their doors to see what it could be. 'Steady, old man! Down, Jock, down!' said Garry, but the great hound was almost mad with joy. I never saw any beast so beyond itself.

I felt very sorry for Rose during that leave; she had to lie upstairs, weak and in great discomfort, and Garry had to fish by himself. He knew well enough that he must get all the good out of his leave that was possible, or he could never command the regiment. I used to slip down to the river to watch him for a few minutes, or to walk back with him, but Rose had no nurse but me and could not be left long. In a very few days he had to go back to France, and this time it was pure agony to him. The baby was expected in six weeks; Rose was in a very weak state; and the fighting in France was at its hardest.

I can see the lamp-lit supper table in the little dining-room, and Garry trying in vain to eat. I can hear him rush upstairs to Rose, and hear her sobs, and I can see myself waiting for him in the passage. All very well to talk of bravery and courage, but in this war the men – and especially the infantry – lived in hell month after month, then, after ten days at home, had to face hell again. The wonder was not that some went mad but that any kept sane. I know I was horribly afraid for Garry's nerve that night, and when he held me tight in a long almost shuddering kiss I cut it short and said in a loud voice, 'Go on, Garry. *You* will lead them to victory now you are Colonel. Don't keep the car waiting,' and he was gone in an instant. Dr Sprott, who gave him a lift to catch the night train at Penrith, said to me next day, 'I have often felt sorry for a man, but I never felt as sorry in my life before as I did for Colonel Buckle last night.'

Lily had a habit of chewing peppermints as she sat with Rose, which got on the latter's nerves: nevertheless, Rose was better before the baby arrived, and could walk down the lane to church every evening at five. Tita, Judith and Christian came for their holidays. On Sunday, 6 August 1916, Dr Sprott was summoned from Appleby. It was a fine day, and I was born about two in the afternoon.

I was reluctant to accept baptism at Warcop Church, screaming and pulling the beard of Parson Shaw. My god-parents were my great-aunt Dolly Sandford and two fellow-officers of my father's who never set eyes on me as they were both killed in the war. In September Garry had a recurrence of fever, came home on sick leave and saw his son for the first time.

That winter Garry persuaded Lily to give up her work at Netley Hospital which, after two years, was wearing her out. Lily took a house in the corner of Kingsbury Square at Wilton, with a garden giving on the Pembrokes' park; and Judith and Christian went daily to the Godolphin School in Salisbury, as Doris and Tita had done twelve years before.

Garry was awarded the Distinguished Service Order in May 1917. Chris was commanding the artillery of the Second Army, and on 21 July when the 23rd Infantry Brigade went into battle from trenches near the Menin Road and Garry, with a head wound, led his men forward, the barrage which preceded their advance was laid on by Chris. Lily recorded: 'They had often said how fine it would be if only they could fight together, but I had a letter from Chris, written next day, in which he confessed that after all he had felt worried and had not really liked it a bit.' All the same, another general told Lily that, 'The only man *enjoying* this war is Chris Buckle.'

On leave with his head wound that August Garry fished at Warcop, where the Eden was 'so low you could see every trout in the river', but met Lily at the Artillery Hotel in London, on his way back to France in September.

I used to be afraid to look at Garry lest he should see in my face how I was trying to stamp every line into my memory. That night I couldn't sleep, and I could see his electric light shining under the crack of the door, so at last I got up and crept softly in. He was asleep, lying on his back with a drill book open in his hand. He looked so pale and so beautiful, like a young knight's figure on a tomb. As I stood looking at him, he opened his eyes and smiled directly, and said, 'Bad Muddis, go to sleep'; so I turned out his light and left him.

Next day Lily and Garry attended Matins in Westminster Abbey. After lunch they sat in the Green Park. It was 'hot and airless' and they felt 'tongue-tied and heavy'.

Then we went to see old Mrs Sandford in Hertford Street, but Garry sat almost entirely silent. In the evening we spoke of second sight, and Garry said how queer it was that he could tell, before an attack, which men would fall, and that one evening in the trenches they had been talking about it and he said he would nudge his adjutant's arm for each man who had that look of coming death in his face as they passed up the trench, and he did, and none of those men came through. I knew exactly the look he meant, it is an unmistakable expression – and it was in his own photograph which he had taken that autumn.

After six weeks in France Garry was wounded in the foot. General Heneker told him it was useless for him to attempt another winter in the trenches: he must go home and get fit, and they would have him back in the spring as a Brigadier and save his life yet. Garry took over a Highland Training Battalion at Kirkcaldy in Fife. A furnished house was found; and Rose, Nanny and I were installed. Rose said the town smelt of linoleum – there was a factory nearby. I was beginning to talk. Garry found the Highland recruits were like children who had never been away from home before. One of them, a widow's only son, was so homesick that Garry made him his servant, and he helped look after me.

The Bolshevik revolution in Russia, which led to an armistice between the Soviet republic and the Central Powers, was followed by the Italian rout at Caporetto; and Chris went to command the British artillery with six divisions which were sent to Italy. Now that the United States were engaged the Entente could expect unlimited reinforcements. It was clear to Ludendorff that the war had to be won or lost in 1918. The story of 1918, therefore, is of several devastating German attacks between 21 March and 15 July, of confusion caused by the German armies gaining too much too quickly, of the seizure of initiative by Foch, and of the consequent wave of Allied victories.

Lily had moved from Wilton to Bemerton, the village in the water-meadows between Wilton and Salisbury, where George Herbert had been parson and written his poems. Bemerton House, which can be seen from the train to this day, was square, white and plain like an 1830 vicarage, with a tennis-lawn and a fir tree; and it was to be Lily's last war-time home. During Chris's leave in February 1918, Garry came down from Scotland for two nights to see him.

> It was a black visit [wrote Lily]. The war was at its worst; the best men doubted if the army could hold out; and all the pick of our men seemed to be gone. Watching Chris and Garry walk down the drive together, their figures the same height and looking such a pair of friends, I thought, 'Will they ever go for a walk together again?' and they never did. That evening the children had dinner with us, Tita, Judith and Christian only ten, and Garry looked up the table and said, 'And what do *you* mean to do with your lives?' Judith said she should be an explorer and bring home creatures for the Zoo: she had a scheme for having the deck of a ship glazed and kept hot for bringing home humming-birds. Christian said she meant to take care of people. He was so interested in all they said and looked at them so earnestly as they chattered. It was extraordinarily bitter dark weather. I could not talk at all. The only moment Garry looked brighter was when he

spoke of little Richard, now just a year and eight months old. He told me how the boy loved to hear the band and looked out for him from his pram on the parade ground. Garry had gone up to the nursery one evening and the door was ajar, and he could see Richard standing up in his cot; but the moment he came in the child had lain down quick as a flash and pretended to be asleep. When Garry said, 'Now, youngster, this won't do, you know,' and tucked him up, Richard burst out laughing in his face. I never heard any man speak of his baby with such a tone of yearning affection as Garry did.

At the beginning of April Garry telegraphed to General Heneker that his foot was all right and that he was ready to fill any vacancy. He was obviously needed. On the seventh he wrote from Kirkcaldy to Lily:

> I got a wire this afternoon telling me to proceed to France on Wednesday, leaving Charing Cross at 11.10 a.m. Not much notice, is it! It will take us all our time to get packed up and the house ready for leaving. We shall go down by the night train on Tuesday and straight across to Charing Cross and could breakfast with you there at about ten, if that suits you: but it seems scarcely worth while for you to come up just for an hour ... We were in the middle of making our arrangements for going to Warcop for ten days' leave on Friday when the wire came ...

Garry took Rose, Nanny and myself across London from King's Cross to Waterloo and put us on the train to Salisbury. 'I love you more every time,' he said to Rose. It was his last sight of us. His mother was waiting with Doris at Charing Cross. She had arrived at 8.30 and was walking up and down outside the station entrance, 'fearing to miss a minute of him'. Doris was a nurse at St Thomas's Hospital, and had been on night duty, so was able to get off for an hour. Lily wrote:

> Suddenly I saw a taxi driver smile and salute as his fare over-paid him, and I said, 'That's Garry with his back to us.' We had had so many partings at Charing Cross since

the war began, but this was quite different. He was almost speechless and I said, 'Oh, how you must want your breakfast after travelling all night!' but he only shook his head and then muttered that Dicky had cried a lot and he was afraid the little chap had caught a chill; and then, quite suddenly, after a minute or two, he said rather loudly – so that a man passing turned to look at him – 'I don't like leaving my son with a pain in his tummy,' and the tears ran down his face. We pushed our way into the crowded dining-room and tried to order him a good breakfast, but the waiter said, 'Only one course allowed.' Garry turned the haddock about with his fork and drank his tea, but I think his love was in his throat, as he said when he was a small boy, and he could not eat. He had forgotten his trench pillow, and Doris was so good – she dashed off to buy him one while we tried to talk. I told him that [my cousin] Letty Irving had just been married to Gerard Thompson, who had bought Eden Gate years before, but never lived in it. Garry said, 'My dream will never come true now. I always wanted to live at Eden Gate again more than anything in the world.' And I said, 'But you never could have afforded it, you know.' 'Oh well, if they made me a general and you and father lived there too. I often planned it for after the war.' Then he paused a moment and said, 'But I don't think there *will* be any "after the war"'; and then I knew that he felt as I did.

The platform was crowded, and Doris came rushing along with the trench pillow. There was everything still to be said and we could not say a word of it, and the seats were filling up. He got into a corner of the crowded Pullman and put his hand out of the window. I put mine on his. He looked as handsome as ever because his features were so finely drawn, but more worn and sad than I had ever known him. As the train began to move I ran along with it. 'You will pull things right if any man can,' I said in farewell; but he never smiled, only said, 'Muddis, Muddis, the train is moving.'

Ludendorff's second offensive, this time against the British in

Flanders, had been launched on 9 April. So effective was the German advance towards Hazebrouck, the railway junction of the north, that preparations were even made by Haig's headquarters for the evacuation and demolition of Calais and for flooding the country west of Dunkirk. It was then that Haig issued his celebrated Order of the Day: '. . . Victory will belong to the side that holds out longest . . . There is no other course open but to fight it out! Every position must be held to the last man: there must be no retirement. With our backs to the wall and believing in the justice of our cause, each one of us must fight on to the end.'

Garry was sent first to command a battalion of the East Kents, and fought with them in the battle of Villers-Bretonneux; then, since my godfather Colonel Latham, who had succeeded him in command of the Second Northamptons, was killed, he returned to command his old battalion. On 7 May he wrote to Lily: 'I am back with the 58th, in a land of oxen and nightingales'; and a week later: 'Don't worry because I don't write often. I am always thinking of you and thanking God for such a splendid mother.'

In May Ludendorff turned his attention from Flanders, where he had found the British too strong for him, towards the much-contested Chemin des Dames near Soissons. Pétain had expected an attack here in March, and the fact that none came made him think that the Germans considered it impregnable, owing to the many machine-gun posts which covered the steep approach from the river Ailette. It was, in consequence, very lightly held by five depleted British divisions borrowed from Haig 'to rest' there. Among these were the Fifth Army Division, which included the 2nd Battalion Northamptons, commanded by Garry. Ludendorff's bold plan was that his troops should cross the Ailette, climb the three-hundred-foot slope to Chemin des Dames and, if successful in capturing the main positions, push on across the sixty-yard-wide Aisne beyond. The Germans' carefully planned attack was totally unexpected. 'As late as 25

May French army headquarters were so completely deceived as to state there was no evidence that the Germans had made any preparations which would enable them to attack at short notice.' A warning by the 'inexperienced American Intelligence' had been ignored by Foch. On Saturday 26 May Garry wrote to Chris: 'This is a glorious country, all the woods are full of lilies of the valley, and I have seen all sorts of rare birds. There are two lesser bustards just behind our sector . . .'

> On the 26th [wrote Cruttwell,* whom I have quoted or paraphrased above] the curtain of mystery was dramatically raised so as to allow the French to foresee the fate which it was now too late to prevent. A German under-officer and private were captured in a patrol scuffle. The latter gave a full account of the German plan. Nothing could be done except to warn the trench divisions of the unsuspected bolt which would fall on them within twelve hours, and to send preliminary orders for eight divisions to start at full speed from the northern reserve.

On Sunday, wrote Lily, 'all was peaceful and quiet on the Aisne; village church bells were ringing, the sun shone warmly all day long, and the ground about the trenches was full of flowers. It was not until 3.45 in the afternoon that the brigade-major at 23rd Infantry Brigade headquarters received a little pink telephone form. He was stretched in the sun outside the dug-out when the signaller came up and gave it to him. "The enemy will attack on a wide front at 1 a.m. tomorrow, 27th".'

Lily's information about the next few hours came from Garry's Adjutant, whom she went to see in hospital, and from his Sergeant-major, interviewed by Chris. Captain Blake said:

> The Brigadier came down the steps of the dug-out and asked to see the Colonel, who was up in the front trenches

* C. R. M. F. Cruttwell, *A History of the Great War*.

doing his rounds. He then told me that there was to be a big attack at 1 a.m.: he said the Colonel knew exactly what to do. When the Colonel came in he was rung up from Brigade Headquarters, and I know they must have told him to thin out the men and officers in the front trenches because I heard him answer that the line was too thin already; but he would send back his Second-in-Command. Then the Major got up and the Colonel shook hands with him and he said goodbye and went out.

Blake went to sleep after this. Whether Garry slept too we cannot know, but at 1.35 a.m. on the 27th he sent a telephone message, the text of which in his writing was found hanging on a rusty nail six months later. 'All platoon commanders will remain with their platoons and ensure that the trenches are manned immediately the bombardment lifts . . . No short bombardment can possibly cut our wire and if sentries are alert it cannot be cut by hand. If they try it shoot the devils. C. G. Buckle.' But the wire was cut, and the front trenches were overrun and outflanked by the enemy. About 4 a.m. an officer of the Worcesters rushed down into Garry's dug-out to say that they were surrounded by Germans. Garry ran up the steps, followed by his staff. Although it was daylight the mist was very thick: they could see the enemy thirty yards away coming towards them and realized they were cut off from the front line.

A moment of decision — *the* moment of decision for which he had been born, bred and trained, and which he had probably long foreseen with dread or with resignation, was upon Garry. He did not have to die. It was almost pointless. His battalion in the forward trenches had been overrun: they were all either dead, wounded or prisoners. The Germans were coming on towards him. He would send his Adjutant and his Sergeant-major hurrying back, and the 'sensible' thing would be to go with them. Garry had little time to consider — but lifetimes of thought can be condensed into thirty seconds. Perhaps he thought of what his soldier father would have done in the circumstances or what his Bible-reading mother would consider right; that his death would leave Rose, whom he loved more than anything in the world, unprovided for; that he would never see me grow up. Obviously he had at the back of his mind Haig's order, issued just over a month before, that every position must be held to the last man. When his staff of two had made off for Brigade Headquarters, as was necessary – and it was they who told Chris and Lily the tale – *he* would be the last man. Should a colonel outlive his battalion? He had the chance to kill at least one more German before he died. He did exactly what his father would have done, interpreted Haig's words literally and obeyed orders.

My father went down the steps of his dug-out to fetch his revolver. Before the Adjutant and the Sergeant-major retired through the mist they saw him running towards the advancing Germans. Two of these were later found buried beside him.

Some time after four o'clock that morning, in her bedroom at Bemerton House, near Salisbury, Lily woke with a violent shock and found herself standing in the middle of the room. She knew that Garry was mortally wounded; and she prayed that his suffering might soon be over. As the sun rose over the trees and downs of Wiltshire she felt a sudden calm and thought the end must have come. Before seven Tita passed down the landing, and Lily called her in to tell her Garry was dead. Often, when I read Lily's account of this incident in later years, her conviction of Garry's death struck me as too good to be true; and in 1980 I wrote to ask my Aunt Tita if she recalled the episode.

She replied, 'Yes, I perfectly remember Granny calling me into her bedroom (on my way to the bathroom), and telling me that she knew your father had been killed. She told me that she woke (I think about 5 a.m.) and was sure he was in agony and she got his photograph and held it to her breast for an hour or more; and then she was sure that all was over and that he was at peace. *I didn't believe he had been killed for a long time – but of course she was right.*'

Lily went to pray in George Herbert's little church, tried to weed the garden, and wrote to Chris. Later she walked over the fields to Netherhampton House to ask Sir Henry Newbolt, who came down from the Admiralty on the afternoon train, whether there had been news of fresh fighting on the Aisne. The author of 'Drake's Drum' confirmed that there had been a sudden big attack there and that the British had been obliged to retreat. Next day *The Times* reported this. A few days later came the official telegram saying that Garry was missing. Lily went up to Warcop. Rose had her aunt Dolly Sandford with her; and they 'took the line that Garry was a prisoner, and therefore safer than before'. Lily did not tell them of her experience on the morning of 27 May: this would be revealed later, when another War Office telegram arrived. Lily wrote:

> I walked up to Deepgill by myself, and read the funeral service kneeling by the big stone which Garry had rolled down to be my seat. It was a wonderful morning, warm and clear, and full of the scent of gorse and broom which made the hillside almost golden; and when I rose up from my knees a blue butterfly settled on the stone, sunning its wings.

Rose thought that Chris felt Garry's death every bit as deeply as Lily: but he was not a man to indulge himself in expressions of grief. Lily wrote: 'I thought when Chris came on leave to Bemerton, a few weeks later, that we might talk together and he would tell me more, but he did not want to speak of Garry at all. He hired horses to ride with Lady Muriel Herbert in Grovely Wood. Later on, Dicky, running about and full of baby talk, was my best comforter. He ran up the drive at Bemerton shouting out "Granhardie!"; and when I said, "He's not here, Dicky," he exclaimed, "Oh, *don't* say *he's* gone to a beastly dug-out in the sky!"'

PART II

THE
YOUTH OF DICK

CHAPTER 6

From Warcop to Overstrand, 1920–9

By the time of her death, thirty years after Garry's, Lily would have twenty-one descendants: but I was the only son's only son, her only Buckle. From her armchair, covered in a particularly unsubtle colour which my mother derisively called 'Buckle blue', and from her narrow bed which was like an iron hospital bed, the dynamo of Lily's energy electrified her loved ones throughout the world. The children must be educated; the poor must be taken care of; books must be written to save a few cherished characters from oblivion; an enormous correspondence must be engaged in; Chris must be fed and kept happy; God must, of course, be worshipped; but above all Dick must be encouraged to work, to grow in wisdom and character, to serve God and King and to play his part in the history of England.

Lily's possessive love of me, to which I responded the more warmly because I saw less of her than I saw of my mother, was not so jealous that she could not sympathize with Rose's situation. Rose had lost the adored, loving and irreplaceable Garry. She was left with her widow's pension and very little else to bring up single-handed a boy who might well prove difficult, and whose sturdy Buckle blood was tainted by the bluer but suspect blood of the Cravens. My grandmother foresaw the difficulties, which Rose's upbringing by Connie Sandford had hardly prepared her to overcome. 'Poor little Mummy!' I used to hear Lily exclaim, sighing to herself.

I'm forever blowing bubbles,
Pretty bubbles in the air;
They fly so high,
Nearly reach the sky,
Then in a dream they fade and die.

This silly popular song, the first I can remember, used to be played and sung by my mother at the piano, and is one of the earliest recollections of my childhood at Warcop. Rose's long, light-brown hair was gathered into an enormous *chignon* or 'bun' at the back. She may have been desolate for the loss of my father, but I remember her in those days as light-hearted and gay, giggling with her friend Jemima – the name (her idea of the feminine of Jim) she gave to Alice (Mrs Jim Wild) of Warcop Hall. Several of Garry's cousins proposed to Rose in rapid succession. Of course she would have been better off if she had married again: but she was fastidious. Dirty finger-nails, an awful umbrella, the way a man sucked his pipe or the fact that he bought and offered chocolates on a visit to the theatre would put her off. She was rather a tease. Nanny – Scottish, small, pretty and plump – was perhaps more motherly. When I was born Isobel Ross had been on a visit to her sister, who was married to the gardener at Eden Gate. Lily heard that she had nursed a little boy before, and walked round to interview her. She came to look after me within a few days of my birth and remained for life. When I ceased to need a Nanny she continued as cook-housekeeper, and for fifty years was our only servant. I had an obsession that my mother or Nanny or both would disappear and leave me alone in the world. If I had been naughty I would reassure myself, before going to bed, that Nanny had not packed her luggage in preparation for flight: if her silver hair-brushes were still on her dressing-table I felt safe. My bedroom door was left open so that I could call out to my mother and hear her answer from the rooms below, until I fell asleep. One night I called and called, and there was no answer. In tears and terror I rushed downstairs, only to find

Rose and Jemima laughing at me in the dining-room. These anxieties presaged the torments of imaginative jealousy I would suffer in the course of my love affairs.

In 1921, Great-grandma Sandford, born Greville, was to be ninety years old. She was a grand-daughter of the Lady Charlotte Greville (daughter of the Prime Minister Duke of Portland) who was a close friend of the great Duke of Wellington; and she was niece of Charles, the famous diarist, and daughter of Algernon Greville. Even in her youth Great-grandma was evidently plain and dumpy, for when she found a husband in 1858 her uncle Charles wrote to Henry Reeve, a celebrated contributor to the *Times*:

> Augusta Greville is going to be married to a Mr Peacock [*sic*], a man thirty years of age [he was 38], very eligible in all ways, and with £10,000 if not £15,000 a year, house in country and in town: was there ever such luck, for a girl without any pretensions or attractions to make such a match? The Duchess of Richmond seems to have done it all . . . The only objection I have heard to him [Peacocke] is that he has a glass eye, but if his whole body was made of crystal I should think it a capital match for her.

The Duchess of Richmond was Great-grandma's elder sister. George Peacocke was an MP and a crony of Disraeli's and Lord Salisbury's. It was because he represented Malden in Essex that he and his wife usually took a house in Suffolk or Essex for the summer months, a habit which Great-grandma continued after his death. This was how Rose, staying with her grandmother, came to meet Garry. In 1866 Peacocke changed his name to Sandford, because he was the last surviving descendant of the Irish branch of the Sandfords of Sandford in Shropshire. He died in 1879. The Peacocke-Sandfords had four daughters and two sons: Aunt May, religious; Francis, my grandfather; Cecil, died young; Aunt Alice, intellectual; Aunt Blanche, amusing and married; and Aunt Dolly, artistic. Dolly and Rose's special friend, in whom she confided when she was secretly engaged to Garry; and she became mine. She was also my godmother.

Francis sounds gayer and more worldly than the rest of his family: he was funny and charming, a good amateur actor and in the Grenadier Guards. He served in the Egyptian campaign. He married the high-spirited Constance Craven. They lived beyond their means, and whether because of his wife's extravagance or not, Francis took to drink and died of it in 1904. So Connie Sandford, always known to me as 'Granmumkie', was left very hard up with four daughters, of whom the two younger, Rose and Violet, were twins. She would much have preferred sons. Connie resented her well-off mother-in-law's meanness with money: but I suppose old Mrs Sandford told herself that anything she gave Connie would be frittered away.

Rose remembered her father with affection, but she also remembered him, when he had DT's, trying to throw a chest-of-drawers over the banisters in Rutland Gate. When the family retired to Hampshire, where Francis died, she recalled bowler-hatted bailiffs in the house and herself being refused credit in the village shops because of her mother's unpaid bills. The growing girls felt the pinch of poverty in their feet, for their shoes were always too small for them; and Rose's little toes were deformed like a Chinese aristocrat's. She had had a miserable childhood and longed for education, but a series of foolish second-rate governesses taught her nothing. Caryl Craven, Connie's unmarried younger brother, used to help out by buying clothes for Eva and Cynthia, the elder girls, who spent much of the time at Crichel in Dorset with their mother's first cousin, Lady Alington. Great-grandma Sandford befriended the younger girls; and they stayed with her every summer.

It was shortly before my own fifth birthday that Rose, Nanny and I travelled down from Warcop to London to be present on Great-grandma's ninetieth. I remember the journey. It was a scorching summer day and our third-class carriage was crowded. The train had no corridor. My mother was suffering from hay-fever and I had diarrhoea. Nanny was obliged to rush me out at stations, but sometimes I could not wait. When we arrived in the late afternoon at 33 Hertford Street (where the Hilton Hotel now stands), Grandma's birthday party was in progress in the upstairs drawing-room, in which Garry had sat silent nearly four years before. Besides my three Sandford aunts and four great-aunts there were a number of old ladies dressed in identical black. When told to go and kiss my great-grandmother I did not know which she was. Since Grandma had not altogether approved of Rose marrying Garry and certainly not of his getting killed and leaving Rose penniless, my mother was hoping I would make a good impression. This I apparently did. The story goes (for this part is hearsay) that I said, 'Oh, Grandma, I didn't know you would be so *very* old!' I got a footstool for her feet and wrapped a rug round her knees and treated her like one of my dolls. This amused her and she exclaimed, 'Dear little feller, dear little feller,' as I fussed around. (Grandma used to say 'yaller' and 'spittacles' and 'cup o' tay'. Dolly, her last surviving daughter, would use such Regency expressions as 'Ain't she a pooty gel?' right into the 1950s.)

Then, after all the heat and fatigue, I remember sitting up in a big cool bed in a dark-green room, fanned by a breeze which came in with the evening sun from Hyde Park, receiving the homage of selected aunts. This is my only recollection of 'the Nursery' at Hertford Street, which, I am told, Nanny and I sometimes occupied, as had Rose and Garry, during the war. It must have been the first London bedroom I ever slept in.

Next morning I was photographed with Grandma in Hamilton Gardens. These gardens at the south-east corner of Hyde Park were still exclusive and only the neighbouring householders had keys to them. Today Byron still sits brooding where he did, on his red marble base, but the railings have been removed and shrubs uprooted; and the eroded Gardens now appear as a mere island off the coast of Hyde Park, separated by a channel of traffic. To the end of her life my great-aunt Dolly – who like my grandfather and all her sisters had been born in Hertford Street – used to exclaim on the mention of some family, 'Oh, we played with them in the Gardins.' This was tantamount to a guarantee of respectability, like another well-worn phrase, 'They're cousins of ours.' I was told in later years that Grandma used to walk twice every Sunday, usually with Aunt May, to St Paul's, Knightsbridge, where she had been married in 1858: this entailed crossing the Gardens twice, and unlocking and relocking two gates. Dolly, who did not go much to church – and, for that matter, did not like her eldest sister May – would probably be painting in the sitting-room in Hertford Street which she shared with Alice ('almost a suffragette'), or developing photographs in a bathroom. She rolled her own cigarettes, and smoked one a day, after luncheon.

Grandma's father, Algernon Greville, had fought in the Grenadiers at Waterloo when he was only sixteen; after that, as Private Secretary to the Duke of Wellington, he had worked at Apsley House, to the south of the Gardens. It was from a window in the latter mansion that my mother (aged five) had watched Queen Victoria's Diamond Jubilee procession in 1897: she retained ever after a memory of the little old lady amid a magnificence of maharajahs. Grandma was descended from King Henry VII, from the poet Surrey, who invented blank verse, from Queen Elizabeth's Secretary Cecil and from her favourite Essex, from Shakespeare's patron Southampton, and, on her mother's side, from King Charles II and Nell Gwynn. When I grew up I should regard her as a precious link with history and be glad that two photographs had been taken of us together by my mother Rose.

Eden Gate, where Garry had been born and which belonged to Gerard Thompson, the husband of Lily's cousin

Lettie, stood empty. Lettie's sister Janet began to rent the Old Cottage where Lily's mother had died and where I was born. For a time my mother and I lived at Smithy Hill, where she and my father had spent their honeymoon: this belonged to my great-great-aunt Janey, who had continued to live at Warcop House after the death of her husband Tom Chamley. Warcop Hall, whose park was opposite Warcop House, had nothing to do with my relations, and the Prestons and Wilds who lived in it were usually at war with the Chamleys – though Mrs Jim Wild, as mentioned, was my mother's most intimate friend in the neighbourhood. By the time Great-grandma Sandford died, soon after the birthday party I attended, we were living at The Fox, a former pub. It was only a cottage – two rooms up, two down, with a longish room built out at the back over a barn, which was the drawing-room. The four south-facing rooms – dining-room, kitchen, my mother's bedroom and Nanny's and mine – had one window each and looked out on the beck, which came down from Deepgill, on the bridge over it, on the maypole round which gipsy caravans sometimes assembled, and on the red sandstone obelisk of the new war memorial which was engraved with my father's name among others, and by kissing which at the opening ceremony Lily horrified my mother. (Lily's theatrical demonstration, however, made a lasting impression on one small boy who was present, the village tailor's son, who later became Postmaster-General in Harold Wilson's government and a peer.) Like nearly all the Warcop houses, The Fox was built of sandstone, white-washed, with black quoins. Beatrix Potter's water-colours have immortalized this local style.

But it was Dolly Sandford who recorded our village in water-colour when she came to stay with her favourite niece; Rose did a little sketching too; and I began to imitate them. I had painted almost before I could spell, but not landscape: my first remembered water-colour was of Queen Mary. Dolly was 'four-foot-nothing' and 'a character'. She was supposed to feel faint if she lifted her arms above her head, so could not travel without a lady's maid to do her hair. I think the Sandford great-aunts had one lady's maid between two: but since these confidential domestics had presumably to be allowed a fortnight's holiday a year Dolly would sometimes have to rely on my mother. Dolly had been engaged – it must have been half a century before – to marry her second cousin Granville Egerton (a grandson of the Harriet Greville who had married the first Earl of Ellesmere). It was said that her trousseau had been ready and her wedding dress hanging in the cupboard when he jilted her. Whether it was true that 'she never got over this', and whether her way of always being busy with the trivialities of daily life had begun as a plucky method of not dwelling on her disappointment, I cannot tell. As both my godfathers had been killed Dolly was my only god-parent, and no man ever had a better one, although she never mentioned religion to me. Her real names were Caroline Amabel. I don't know where the Amabel came from, but both *her* god-mothers had been called Caroline, and both of them, the Duchess Dowager of Richmond and Lady Downshire, were daughters of heroes in the Napoleonic wars – Lord Anglesey (the Uxbridge who lost his leg at Waterloo) and Field-Marshal Lord Combermere. My father's god-mother, Susan Pettiward, was a great-grand-niece of Nelson. My mother's godfather, Prince Edward of Saxe-Weimar, married to a Gordon-Lennox, was grandson of the Grand Duke of Weimar whom Goethe served.

Dolly regulated her days, which were beset with paraphernalia. After breakfast, which always consisted of a poached egg with the white slowly and meticulously removed, and a Cox's Orange Pippin, she would bring her special cushions and two bags into the drawing-room. One bag contained two spectacle cases, a writing-pad, ink, fountain pen, letters to be answered and the small account books into which every minute expenditure was entered; the other held sketch-books, pencils, the necessaries for rolling cigarettes, playing cards for patience and some more oracular cards used in a process of fortune-telling called 'Consult Napoleon!' For sketching out-of-doors, folding easels, a white linen green-lined parasol, an apron, black japanned paint-boxes and a water-bottle had to be strapped on to her bicycle; and the fine straw hat with its black velvet ribbon was secured by a silk scarf, tied under the chin.

Had she been born fifty years later Dolly would probably have been a serious artist. She was talented and she worked almost daily. As it was out of the question for her to go to the Slade, she carried on for decades a correspondence course with a professional painter, who returned her water-colours with criticism. When the Hertford Street household broke up on Great-grandma's death, Aunt May went to live with three maids at Finchley in the parish of a pious lady who ruled her life; and Alice and Dolly shared a rented house. Then Alice died and Dolly took a lease of 32 Tedworth Square, Chelsea, to be near the Thames which Whistler and Steer had painted and which she saw through their eyes. From that time Dolly bicycled daily to the Chelsea School of Art, where Sickert once threw her india-rubber out of the window. It was not till she was knocked off her bicycle in the late 1920s that she bought a car, a large open Armstrong-Siddeley, and learned to drive it herself.

Dolly had a number of individual expressions. If Rose had done something ingenious or said something particularly apposite Dolly would express her approval with the odd phrase, 'Oh you [*accelerando*] kippie-little-fellie!' But if you had a brainwave which led to nothing it was called, 'one of those *frightfully* good ideas'. Should some social disaster threaten she would put on a flustered voice to quote an ancient family joke: 'Nothing to be done! Nothing to be done! Can't possibly do anything!' A boastful remark would be squashed with, '*That* was grand, *wasn't* it, dear?' The recently ennobled were known as 'mushrooms'. A woman who came to call and stayed too long would be said to have 'brought her sitting britches'. Last thing at night, before gathering up her belongings and going to bed, Dolly would automatically exclaim 'Pat the cushions, pat the cushions.' She had a special voice – which might be described as 'wide-eyed' – for making magical pronouncements. There were ditties she sang to herself, the origins of which were lost in the mists of Victorian antiquity, and little spells she intoned as she went about her daily business, preoccupied as a pigeon. 'Cuckoo! Cherry-tree! Catch a bird and give him to me.' That was fairly straightforward, but I never discovered the source of 'Pica – pica – pica – [*accelerando*] dilly – dilly – dilly!'

'Cuckoo', in fact, was one of her earliest names for me. There was some joke about my being a cuckoo in the nest, a foundling or illegitimate. Hence other names, 'The Bastard' and 'Fitzpyx'. (The derivation of Pyx was: Richard, Dicky, Dixy, Pixy, Pyx.) When I was in a bad temper I was called 'The Black Prince'. Dolly had once been to Egypt, where she was hauled up the Great Pyramid. She and I dressed up as Arabs and went round Warcop exacting 'baksheesh' from the surprised inhabitants.

Another dressing-up that took place was for the annual Rush-bearing. Warcop and Musgrave were almost the only two villages to continue this ancient ceremony, which had a pagan origin. On St Peter's Day white-clad children bore rushes round the parish, then laid them on the floor of the church, where they remained for a year. By my time the rushes had been superseded by floral crowns for the girls and crosses for the boys. The little church of St Columba, where Lily had prayed, where Emmie had married Arthur Wynne, and where I had been baptized, was never free from this fresh, faded, rotting or desiccated vegetation. I was photographed in a floral group with Nanny's three nieces, the youngest of whom, Ella, was my first girl-friend.

The first theatrical performance I ever attended was

Cinderella in the Temperance Hall at Warcop: in this my mother played the principal role. The blacksmith and the shopkeeper were the Ugly Sisters, and I was much more struck by their green, purple and gold finery than with my mother's white and silver ball dress. When they bullied her, however, I cried; and Granny, who was sitting beside me, had to tell me it was all make-believe.

Lily Buckle did not let go of Garry easily. For several years she was torn between dwelling in the past and working for the future. She was Victorian enough to dramatize her grief to the utmost; but commonsense overcame morbidity, and gradually the demands of everyday life prevailed. In 1919 she had made a trip to France in search of Garry's grave, identified it wrongly and written a little book about her quest. In 1920, with Rose, she found the true grave and herself reburied the body. (It was later moved to one of the huge cemeteries.) At a farm in Devonshire she began to write the life of Garry, ostensibly for me but really, I think, as a healing occupation for herself.

After the Armistice Chris commanded the Royal Artillery at Cologne. But he was shooting at Warcop in September and October 1919, and in December with the Pembrokes at Wilton. He had been awarded the C.B. shortly after Garry's death, and since he already had the C.M.G. and was a Major-General Lily was confident he would be knighted. But the Honours List was very long; and when Chris was summoned to the War Office to discuss future employment, and refused the Gibraltar command or any other, he was crossed off. 'He was quite pleased, and got rid of his uniform as fast as he could lest he should have to attend dinners and functions.' Lily, however, was bitterly disappointed that there should not be another Sir Christopher Buckle after three centuries. (Only one of the four Buckle admirals had been knighted.) The sole trophy of Chris's forty years' honourable service was a box full of medals and orders to hang in the drawing-room: Companion of the Bath, Companion of St Michael and St George, Distinguished Service Order, Queen's Medal with three clasps, King's Medal with two clasps (South Africa), 1914–18 war medals with six mentions in despatches, Chevalier de la Légion d'Honneur and Croix de Guerre (France), Order of Leopold and Croix de Guerre (Belgium), Order of the Crown of Italy, Order of the Rising Sun (Japan).

Lily lost her last brother Braith in 1920. His wife Mary Campbell did not long survive him. They had no children and Mary left a large sum of money to charity, but there was £8,000 to be divided between Lily's daughters. In what may have been Braith's last letter home, he wrote:

September 3, 1919

My dear Lily

Yrs of 29th June came last week in it you say what a pity I can't drop in & have a yarn at the Cottage. It is just as well you cant call for a cup of Tea here as the Drought is Hell without sauce or trimmings of any kind. I noticed you are getting £36:0:0 for 11 weeks Rent of the cottage. If you were spending that on keeping starving stock alive *per week* with no prospect of it stopping for months on end until the bill becomes thousands & then they die on you at the finish is some of the joy of living in this land. We had 1 inch rain last May & 40 points last week Spring is here & no rain so there will be no harvest to speak of unless it comes very soon . . . Aunt Janey must be a marvel fancy her walking to Sandford & back with you. I doubt if I could do it in anything like decent time I am touching the $\frac{1}{2}$ century mark on the 25th of this month you must be nearly 100. Well we were gay dogs in our day you with the Parsons & I with the Poultry. Mary joins in love to you all

Yr affec Brother
Braith

Doris had been for three years at St Thomas's Hospital and determined to study medicine at University College, London; Tita was married to Eric Graham, Rector of Boyton, Wiltshire, and Dean of Oriel; Judith won an Exhibition at St Hilda's College, Oxford; and Christian was to go to Headington School nearby.

Just as old Mrs Turner had always set store by 'improving her mind', so had the aspiring Lily regarded the University of Oxford with reverent longing. Her first sight of Oxford had been in the winter of 1884–5, between Chamley's death and her engagement to Chris, when her mother had taken her on a visit to Dr Percival, President of Trinity College. Percival, a native of Westmorland and a pupil of Appleby's famous old Grammar School, had a daughter the same age as Lily, but the latter's only thought – though it was vacation time – was that she might somehow meet her beloved Douglas Terry, or at least see his college, Hertford. However, as she wrote:

> It was marvellous to lie awake and hear the chimes and bells: I put my lattice window wide to hear them better and shocked the housemaid when she came with the hot water in the morning and found a drift of snow on the carpet. Dr Percival was rather struck by my having read about the college before I came to stay and my knowing about its founder. He told mother I ought to go to Lady Margaret Hall and mother smiled and said that she would see. Oh, how I ached for such a thing to be possible, but I knew that every penny of the family income was needed for the boys.

Like Thomas Hardy's Jude the Obscure, Lily the not-quite-so-obscure had had her vision of the blessed city of learning which Hardy called Christminster, and heard the summons of its bells. Yet Dr Percival (whose grandson was in the Scots Guards with me) was a *successful* Jude the Obscure himself. The son of a small farmer at Brough Sowerby on Stainmore, south-east of Warcop, nine miles from Appleby, he had got his education by 'trudging to and from school in his clogs, with a blue linen bag of books over his shoulder'. More often, though, he rode a chestnut pony, with his red hair flying in the wind; and he sometimes broke the journey at Warcop to have tea with a Mrs Breeks who then lived at Eden Gate. Founding Headmaster of Clifton, Headmaster of Rugby and Bishop of Hereford, Percival, who never lost his northern accent, was one of the most high-minded and austere of Victorian educationists: but he incurred some ridicule by urging that boys should wear trousers fastened above the calf when playing football, lest the sight of bare knees aroused their sexual interest in each other. Because I know from experience the value of solitude, I often think of Percival's long walks and rides through the Eden valley, when he turned over in his mind the lessons of the day; and I pity the village children of the 1980s who are fetched and carried in boy-loud buses.

Lily was overjoyed that her daughters should have the opportunities at Oxford that she had missed: and she looked forward to a time when I should go up to the university. She took an old house in the village of Cowley, two miles from Oxford, where she and Chris would be near three of the girls.

> Village House had small rooms but plenty of them, and the drawing-room had a nice old conservatory out of it and the garden was delightful. But we had not moved in our furniture before the Oxford bus took to stopping at our door instead of up the road, and to coming every hour instead of every two hours. Before we had got straight it came every half hour, and soon two buses blocked our windows at lunch time and tea. Morris Works, five minutes up the road, enlarged enormously almost in a night, and before we sold Village House after three years it had become the centre of a new suburb of workmen's houses.

Working in the vegetable garden, though, had been good for Chris. He had rented some shooting and undertaken to manage the coverts of a local landowner, Harry Beaufoy, which he continued to do for years. Lily had lost her figure and dressed very dowdily in grey or black, with a felt or straw hat pinned on to her untidy white hair, and her buttoned shoes turning over sideways under her weight: but her white, smooth skin, her straight nose and dark eyes still held a hint of the beauty which had conquered Chris forty years before, and in which he had observed no change. On my visits to Cowley Lily read me chapters of 'my father's book' as I sat up in bed in the evening. I think my mother must have disapproved of the emotional wallowing which this involved. Lily took me down on the bus to Oxford on her shopping excursions. 'I do not think Dicky was more than five,' wrote Lily, 'when we walked up the High together and he was deeply interested in everything he saw. When we were coming back he announced that Mary Magdalen offering her pot of ointment over Magdalen gate was the nicest thing of all. "It was so kind of her"!'

I had learnt to read and write and it was time for me to go to school. There were no suitable schools in Westmorland, or if there were they were out of reach, for I must begin as a day boy. The south coast was clearly indicated, but my mother heard that there were schools on the coast of North Norfolk; some cousins had a house there which they used only in the summer, and they offered it to us as a base for operations. That this would be rent-free was an important factor. Rose decided to uproot herself and leave Warcop for this unknown region. From then on Warcop would merely be a place I went to during the summer holidays: but I never liked Norfolk and felt it was in Westmorland that I belonged.

With its flat, boundless fields and the up-tilted accents of its inhabitants, Norfolk was the most Danish of the English counties. Infinite windswept acres were planted with turnips to feed alike the cattle and the underpaid peasantry. Across this bleak landscape, where it was possible to see half a dozen plain church towers at the same time, gentlemen went shooting endlessly. From Sheringham to beyond Mundesley the low coast of North Norfolk rose into cliffs like a bastion against the North Sea. Cromer, the small capital of this colony of fishermen, a different world from the rest of Norfolk, was screened from the inland plain by wooded hills.

It was in the late eighteenth century that people had begun to take holidays by the seaside; and in 1800 the first *Guide to Cromer* was published. In 1816, in Jane Austen's *Emma*, Mr Wodehouse's indispensable doctor recommended Cromer. 'Perry was a week at Cromer once, and he holds it to be the best of all sea-bathing places.' The golden age of this strip of coast came, however, after the extension of the Great Eastern Railway to Cromer in 1876. The directors of the railway company sent Clement Scott, a popular and flowery journalist, to Cromer in search of publicity material. He saw the ruined tower of old Sidestrand Church, standing among cornfields on the edge of the cliff (which in 1916 would sink into the sea): he invented the labels of 'Poppyland' and 'The Garden of Sleep'. Tourists were lured by these names. In 1886 Tennyson stayed at Cromer and made excursions. The Empress of Austria put up at Tucker's Hotel at the foot of the Cromer cliffs in 1887 and went for walks without a hat. In 1892 Oscar Wilde wrote to Herbert Beerbohm Tree from Grove Farm, Felbrigg, which he had rented and where he was writing *A Woman of No Importance*: 'I find Cromer excellent for writing, and golf still better.' In 1897 Cyril Flower, the Liberal Whip, who married Constance de Rothschild (sister of my great-aunt Annie Yorke) and became Lord Battersea, commissioned Lutyens to adapt two existing cottages in Overstrand village and enlarge them into an odd rambling mansion with cloisters, called The Pleasaunce. In 1899 Lutyens built Overstrand Hall for our cousin Lord Hillingdon at the west end of the village, near the church. It was at this house that we came to stay in the winter of 1922.

We drove down the long drive (not quite grand enough to be called an avenue) and under an archway into Lutyens's circular courtyard, to be greeted in unfamiliar Norfolk accents by a slightly resentful staff of servants. I was impressed by the big staircase, panelled rooms, lattice windows and, above all, a sunken bath into which one stepped *down*. Rose might have been surprised to learn that she had come to a village which would be for forty years her home, of which, with her labours for the Church, the Red Cross, the old people and the young, she would become far more a part than her hospitable banking cousins had ever been, and where she would be loved, revered and relied on as much as the most benevolent of feudal landlords. Nanny, so kind and simple that she never looked beyond the sphere of our little household, could not know that she would be buried in a field opposite, which had not yet been enclosed as an extension to the churchyard. I could not guess that I should spend my formative years in Overstrand, reading, dreaming, and aspiring to paint or write.

It was during our year's stay at Overstrand Hall that I first received a sensation of excitement from works of art and that I went to school. The works of art in question were the contents of Tutankhamun's tomb, whose excavation was reported from 1922 onwards in the newspapers. I do not know if it was the thrilling thought of stumbling upon hidden treasure, the immense antiquity of the buried objects – which I could hardly comprehend – or the physical aspect of these inlaid and painted thrones, the golden leopards, the black and gold sentry guardians and the sarcophagi, one within the other, that stimulated my imagination. 'Ancient Egypt' became as much an inspiration to me as to the cabinet-makers of Paris after Napoleon's return from the campaign of 1798.

Cromer, with its tall church tower, its narrow streets of cobbled cottages and its two or three big hotels, lay two miles to the west, over the windy golf links. For the greater part of the year it was just a fishing village like Overstrand, only bigger. In the summer it became a town full of holiday-makers, and there was a concert-party at the end of the pier. Inland, towards the station, was a new suburb called Suffield Park. It was to Suffield Park School that I first went, in spring 1923, as a day boy. My mother took me on the back of her bicycle – along the drive of Overstrand Hall, turning right, up the hill, passing Risborough's farm, then down towards wood-girt Cromer. As we sped downhill I was crying and I put my new school cap in my pocket for fear that passers-by should guess the reason for my tears. At six I had never mixed with other boys before, or played games. To stand bewildered on a sportsground, with balls whizzing unaccountably around me, was an alarming experience.

My first children's parties were almost as daunting as going to school, but I usually gained courage before they were over and started to 'show off', as my mother called it, so that I had to be beaten with a hair-brush on our return to Overstrand Hall. The difficulties of bringing me up without a father to do the dirty work were beginning to manifest themselves.

Rose's Aunt May gave her a thousand pounds to build a cottage; and 'Steelbacks', dubbed with the nickname of my father's regiment, was planned and built in half an acre of ground on the outskirts of the village. It was a white rough-cast bungalow with a red-tiled roof. A garage, coal-shed, tool-shed, and at the back a hut for me, were added. The short drive in front, lined with rose bushes, divided a sunken garden with a sun-dial from a flat one in which half an up-ended fishing-boat served as an arbour. At the back there were lawns, crazy paving, an orchard and a lavender walk with more rose-beds. Beyond, fields stretched to the little local railway (long since closed), and on the other side of this could be seen, a quarter of a mile away, the low bracken-covered hills which secluded our coastal colony from the great Norfolk plain. Trees were planted, as well as privet hedges, to shield us from the road and from neighbours who were not slow to build on either side.

It was while Steelbacks was being built that I went to my second school at West Runton, a few miles west of Cromer. We were in lodgings near the Overstrand cliff, and I shall always remember Sunflower Cottage because of the agony of putting on for the first time a grey flannel shirt, which was an item of the obligatory uniform. It was so painful that I took it off again for a moment's respite. I soon became a boarder. My reports were glowing except for mathematics, science and games. Brilliant, but lazy, was the general impression.

Although some of Overstrand's freakish villas, built in its late-Victorian and Edwardian heyday, with their gardens running down to the subsiding cliffs, stood empty (at least for most of the year) – the long sham-Elizabethan mansion of Sir Edgar Speyer, one of King Edward's financial friends whose name made him unpopular during the war; the turreted house of Sir Frederick Macmillan, the publisher; the 'Danish Pavilion' transported from the Paris exhibition of 1900 by the solicitor Sir George Lewis – my mother had a few congenial or curious neighbours. There was old skull-capped Dr Beverley, with his two daughters, from the elder of whom Rose would eventually take over command of the Overstrand Red Cross. There were the Van Moppes, diamond merchants of Dutch origin, with whose youngest son I played. There was the vinous and, I think, homosexual Lord Wolverhampton, son of the popular novelist Ellen Thorneycroft Fowler; and Angel, the daughter of another best-selling lady, Florence Barclay of *The Rosary*. There was the half-Spanish Teresa del Riego, composer of sentimental songs such as 'Homing' and 'Oh dry those tears', and her actor brother; and, rather aloof at the far end of the village, the Honourable and Reverend Edward Lyttleton, former Headmaster of Eton, with his two daughters, distinguished by my mother as Delia Deaf and Norah Not.

At The Pleasaunce, which was surrounded by the cricket grounds she had given to the village, by rose gardens, Dutch gardens, and sunken Japanese water gardens populated with bronze storks; guarded by a guest-house, a gazebo and a watch-tower with a sea-pointing telescope; and served by secretaries, butlers, lady's-maids and gardeners, the aged Lady Battersea had just finished writing her memoirs. When I penetrated into this exotic bower, elaborated by Lutyens under the direction of her long-since-dead aesthetic husband who, with his pale noble features and auburn locks, had resembled (to judge from his portrait) a character from the *Idylls of the King*, I was as enchanted by the curtained doorways, the Burne-Jones paintings, the statues, the Oriental vases and the portrait of Edward VI over the chimney of the panelled dining-room as by the *châtelaine* herself, who wore exquisite lace pinned over her snow-white hair, a single strand of large pearls and an enormous emerald ring. The only time I ever saw Queen Alexandra she was leaving The Pleasaunce in a closed car on her way back to Sandringham.

My father in his youth had had so many homes, but Overstrand was my only home for years. Of course there were visits to Warcop, to the Buckles at Oxford and to my mother's relations. It was in the church of St Martin at Overstrand, however, that I grew accustomed to the Anglican service, first recited the Creed and sang the Magnificat and the Te Deum. The old clergyman, Canon Carr, was a singularly uninspiring priest, who pronounced 'Our Lord' as 'Our Load' and had a big affected wife with floating scarves, who did pastels of the cliffs at sunset. One day after church, during Sunday luncheon, I startled some of my mother's friends by asking what it meant not to 'abhor the Virgin's womb'.

I spent a year as a boarder at West Runton (where my mother paid twenty-five guineas a term instead of forty because my father had been killed in the war), loathing games and praying every lunchtime for rain. I enjoyed lessons in history, English and painting, ate bars of Sharp's Creamy

Toffee, was nicknamed 'Dorothy' because of my infatuation for Mary Pickford in the film *Dorothy Vernon of Haddon Hall*, which I had seen in Norwich, and under the influence of what book I do not know, began to write a play about the papacy in the Middle Ages called *The Duplicate Key*. A potent stimulus to my dreams were the adventure stories of Major Charles Gilson. These dealt with remote countries and lost civilizations. *The Lost City* was about the discovery of an 'Ancient Egyptian' kingdom surviving in the middle of the desert; *Treasure of Kings* was about a search for Inca gold; *The Silver Shoe* was about Chinese secret societies. A succession of crazes – for Egypt, for Peru, for China – turned me into a collector. At an antique shop in Cromer I was able to buy little Egyptian figures (possibly genuine) and Inca images in pottery. A different kind of shop sold nodding Chinese mandarins and incense-burners. One afternoon at school, having read about white men staining their features with walnut oil to pass for Orientals, I squeezed walnut juice on to my face and hid in some laurel bushes, hoping, if found, to be taken for a Chinese and to miss football. The school came to a sudden end in December 1925. We were told the headmaster had shell-shock and had been sent to a lunatic asylum: this was euphemistic. His liking for boys, which had made him a good schoolmaster, was also his ruin. Police came to Overstrand to question me; but I did not know what they were talking about.

We lived very simply, for my mother had to be careful over money. Rose had taken the awful decision of having her long hair cut off: she was shingled and her skirts only just covered her knees. Her chief temptations were clothes for herself and educational presents for me. Visits to my Sandford and Craven relations provided glimpses of luxury and glamour. Cynthia, Rose's second elder sister, had married in 1923 Captain Bobby Thomas, and I was taken to their wedding at St Margaret's, Westminster. The deepest impression I received on this occasion was of the appearance of Féo, Lady Alington, my Grandmother Sandford's first cousin, who had been a leader of the 'fast set' in King Edward's day, and in whose drawing-room Rose re membered hearing Melba and Caruso sing. She wore a lot of black make-up round her eyes, a gold lamé turban with an aigrette, and a long sable coat; and she carried a tall gold-topped stick with a tassel. When I got home I made a painting of her. In 1925 Rose's pretty twin, Violet, married Pat Kinnaird, the younger brother of a Scottish peer and a member of Barclay's Bank: she wore a knee-length waistless silver lamé dress by Reville with an endless veil of tulle. The house Violet and Pat moved into struck me as magical. It occupied half of the columned and pedimented building at the end of St Andrew's Place, a cul-de-sac at the south-east corner of Regent's Park. Every room was on a different level and the second front door in Albany Street was lower than the one facing the park. The first-floor drawing-room was Adam green with pink brocade upholstery and an Aubusson carpet. There were a chandelier, standard lamps and paintings of birds and fruit by Weenix and Hondocoeter. The dining-room below was full of Wedgwood urns, and there was blue brocade on the wide white-painted Louis XV arm-chairs. The pictures, collected gradually by Pat, who had a good eye, were Dutch. Everything about this house enchanted me – the food, the menservants, the sight of Violet, cool and made-up, sitting in an enormous bed after breakfast ordering dinner from the cook, and the fact that her scarlet lip-salve came out of a bottle and was applied with a brush.

My Grandmother Sandford had long been living in her large, ground-floor, Victorian flat, 25 St Mary's Mansions, Paddington, secluded between the Green, with its church and statue of Mrs Siddons, and the canal. The flats are still there, but the approach to them along the Harrow Road has given place to the overpass linking Marylebone Road and the highway to Oxford. When we rang the bell, the old bewigged parlour-maid would open the door. At the end of a long dark passage, in a sitting-room with two bow windows, Connie Sandford sat on her sofa by the fire, doing *petit point*, with a King Charles spaniel – later replaced by a dachshund – chewing a gold bangle on a cushion at her feet. '*Darling!*' She made a humming sound when she kissed us, as if savouring a delicious mouthful of food: she was always pleased to see us, but did not appear to mind being most of the time alone – although she never opened a book. Forgotten by the world, except for a few relatives, Granmumkie (as I always called her) was surrounded by relics of her worldly youth.

To me Granmumkie's parents, whose portraits stood on a table, were mythological. They had been 'the best-looking couple in England', but had parted company. Why? He had been 'the richest commoner at Oxford', but had 'lost three fortunes on the racecourse'. Why three? William Craven's father had been the second son of an earl and an actress, and had married Georgina Smythe, niece of Mrs Fitzherbert, the illegal but legitimate wife of bigamous King George IV. Georgina, whom the Duc d'Orléans, son of King Louis Philippe, had called 'the prettiest girl in England', was left a widow after only two years of marriage, then married the Duc de la Force and died in France. The tall dazzling William, most of whose money came from London property, married Lady Mary Yorke, youngest daughter of Lord Hardwicke. She was so beautiful that 'people used to stand on park chairs to see her drive past'. (This, of course, was said of many Victorian beauties.) The Emperor Napoleon III was attracted by her when she and William stayed at Compiègne. Some time in the 1860s William turned Mary out of the house. He had been consistently unfaithful to her, but things were not the same in those days for women as for men. Mary was banished to Paris, where she lived with a French lover, had a son, and died in 1890. Her children visited her and loved her, and Granmumkie remembered, on one of these visits, escaping from Paris before the siege, in the wake of the Empress Eugénie. My eldest aunt Eva told me years later that she could just remember, as a child, seeing Mary Craven on a visit to Connie and Francis Sandford in Rutland Gate. In youth Mary had had dark silken hair, but when Eva saw her this was dyed an outrageous red, and she was made-up like a clown.

It will be understood with what anxiety my Granny Buckle looked for signs of my 'Craven side' coming out in me. The eldest child of William's and Mary's disastrous marriage, Augustus Craven, married twice, had mistresses, got into the hands of money-lenders and sold the reversion to his inheritance, which his father bought back. None of the family had seen him for years. The second child was Granmumkie. The third was Caryl, known as Nunkie, an artistic bachelor. The youngest was Isabel March, of whom a painting stood on an easel behind my grandmother's sofa, and who had not lived long enough to become Duchess of Richmond. (Her husband was the son of Great-grandma Sandford's sister.)

My grandmother wore a *cabochon* ruby ring set in diamonds which the Prince Regent had given to Mrs Fitzherbert, and among the treasures on her table was a gold pencil-case which King George V had given her in his youth as a prize for beating him in a race. The whole atmosphere was as different as possible from that of Lily Buckle.

It was at my third preparatory school, The Manor House, Horsham, in Sussex, that I began to respond to nature and the arts, that I took part in theatricals and became stage-struck, that I was confirmed, in the fine old church at the bottom of the Causeway, by the Bishop of Madagascar, that I felt the first stirrings of romantic love (which came before desire), and that the breaking of my voice – just as I was about to triumph in the soubrette role of an operetta – proclaimed the arrival of adolescence.

Lily and Chris had moved to a larger and more attractive

house at Iffley, a village on the Thames which was later to be linked to Oxford by suburbs as Cowley had been, but which, in 1926, was still quiet and pretty.

Beechwood really did stand in a wood of beeches, or the remains of one. It was one of several Georgian or early Victorian villas built on a slope near Iffley Turn, where the Oxford bus stopped and the road turned right to the riverside village and its Norman church. From the stuccoed gate piers no house was visible, only trees. The drive wound uphill, sending an offshoot to the right, where there was a coach-house and cottage, then entered on its main stretch before dividing in two to enclose a circular lawn. The house was tall for its width, as if the sole survivor of a seaside terrace. Because of the slope it was higher in front than at the back and steps climbed to the front door, but in fact the basement was not used except as a cellar. Twin bows rose to the height of two storeys, and the windows of the girls' attics projected from the roof. The maids slept in a small wing, over the kitchen. The back of the house was quite common and ugly, because of a gabled extension, a chocolate brown con-servatory and a glazed passage leading to the kitchen. It was, however, at the back that one sat and had tea in fine weather. A lawn and a tennis-lawn were scooped out of the hill. On either side of these, paths, herbaceous borders and high walls ran up to the large vegetable garden and the piggery, which were screened from guests and tennis-players by a shrubbery and tall trees. There was a certain enchantment in coming slowly up the drive with Granny on a fine summer midday (after an excursion to the Oxford grocer Grimbly Hughes and the covered market, with perhaps a call at the Cadena Café for a gossip with old cronies, or a prayer at St Mary's), stopping from moment to moment to see how some wild flower, fritillary or Star of Bethlehem, which she had brought back from a picnic and planted, was doing, or to exclaim at a preening butterfly. I observed how pots of geranium, placed on either side of the steps, carried the drive almost through the open front door into the hall, to join the already visible lawns beyond. Granny would make straight for her deck-chair by the conservatory, and when I returned from taking parcels to the kitchen I would find her waving gently at the sight of my grandfather, in shirt-sleeves and tweed breeches, who came, laden with baskets of vegetables, down the hollyhock-lined path from the kitchen garden.

The house contained nothing beautiful. Lily was quite capable of admiration for handsome furniture and good pictures; but she would never have dreamt that she and Chris had arrived at a stage when they were justified in spending money on beautifying their own home. So, apart from inherited china, silver and miniatures, Beechwood held what was left over from the Buckles' years of military peregrination. In the drawing-room, with its black marble fire-place, there were tall baize curtains, not quite full enough, on rattling wooden rings, implacable blue armchairs, bamboo book-cases, Lily's bamboo writing-desk and two round brass Indian trays on folding stands. Over a hideous carved Victorian sideboard in the dining-room hung a crude portrait of Lily's Turner grandfather, whose ugly hands I fear she had inherited. Among the family portraits and photographs were a few old water-colours of Gibraltar or Westmorland. The 'Melbourne period' chairs on which we sat to eat and before which, along with the starched maids, we knelt every morning to pray, were what I liked best; and two of the eight had curly arms.

My normally gruff and staccato grandfather had a special way of reading prayers. His tone was curiously gentle, confidential and persuasive, and he made long pauses after each phrase and even between two past participles, which enhanced for me the beauty of Cranmer's Collects:

> Prevent us, oh Lord, in all our doings
> With Thy most gracious favour
> And further us with Thy continual help

> That in all our works
> Begun
> Continued
> And ended in Thee
> We may glorify Thy holy name . . .

It was from Beechwood that the first of Lily's several hundred surviving letters to me was written; and like some of those to Garry when he was at school it contains references to cats and cricket. *He* had been too interested in games, and *I* was not interested enough. My mother, whose modesty made her long for her own letters to be destroyed as soon as they were read, had the imagination to suggest that I should keep Granny's, and this I managed on the whole to do – for there are a few gaps – even throughout the second war. Although my mother's relations and all my friends called me Dicky and have continued to do so throughout my life, Lily and the Buckles, from the time I was about eight, never called me anything but Dick.

Lily was always sending me second-hand books she had picked up in Oxford. When most boys of my age were reading adventure stories by Henty I read and enjoyed all of Jane Austen, Thackeray's *Vanity Fair* and Charlotte Brontë's *Jane Eyre*. Not that I disliked stories of adventure, but I think a reaction against my military background made me averse to Henty's tales, with their themes of bravery and imperial expansion. Something mysterious like Rider Haggard's *She* held more appeal. My English master, who wrote on my third term's report 'Expresses himself well. He should be encouraged to write, for I think he has natural ability,' read aloud to us such poems as Masefield's 'Dauber' and 'Reynard the Fox' as well as the thrilling 'Raven' of Edgar Allen Poe; but the first verses I remember writing were a translation from Ovid.

Every day at Horsham began with a plunge into a cold bath, but in hot weather a horde of screaming boys girt with towels would scamper over the lawns to dive into a swimming pool two hundred yards away: so that was how I first felt the dew on my bare feet. Summer magic.

Certain pieces of music, such as Beethoven's Minuet in G or the Skye Boat Song, captivated me on first hearing; and it was on a winter's night, with the elements raging outside, in the long classroom which could be divided in three by folding screens, that the imaginative English master put on a record of Wagner's *Ride of the Valkyrie* and thrilled me with its savage sound. Next holidays I bought the overture to *Tannhäuser*.

It was in that same long classroom that a stage was erected for the performance of plays at the end of the winter term. The excitement which this feat of carpentry engendered was intensified by the glimpse of an artist painting hollyhocks, with rapid twists of a square-ended brush, on a piece of scenery standing in the barn. The mystery of the theatre had me in thrall. Then came the fitting of costumes and the indescribably exciting smell of grease-paint. In December 1926 I was only one of nine courtiers, but had romantic thoughts about C.M. (a future Labour Minister) who played the chief part. Later when I was promoted to leading roles, I played the Duchess in *Alice in Wonderland* and Minna in the operetta *Miss Hook of Holland*.

As Christmas drew near we would return from our walks, or from skating on the lake at Warnham, to find the shop windows of the twilit town had become bright shrines for fir-trees garlanded with tinsel, hung with red, green and golden baubles, laden with frosty glitter-dust and cotton-wool snow. This was winter magic.

It was the time of the silent screen. My very first visit to the cinema had been an excursion with my mother and Nanny on a bus from Warcop to Blackpool. I was later impressed by the terrible riders in *The Four Horsemen of the Apocalypse* and by the Babylonian orgies in Griffiths' *Intolerance*. *Under the Red Robe* drove me to Woolworth's to buy orange cotton and a diamond ring for an impersonation of Anne of Austria. I fell in love with Rudolph Valentino in *Son of the Sheikh* and with Douglas Fairbanks in *The Thief of Baghdad*. My mother took me to *Ben Hur* at the Tivoli Cinema in the Strand, but she must have seen it once already, for I had written to her in March 1927:

> . . . Mr Oakley [the English master] told me the story of Ben-hur, didn't you like the bit where the pirates tied the Roman prisoner on to the ram of their ship – and the Crucifixion?
>
> I have been reading *Beau Brocade* by Baroness Orczy, finished it yesterday, and got *King Solomon's Mines* out of the library, both are terribly exciting, the latter is by Rider Haggard and I have almost finished it.
>
> I have been drawing a lot lately, people.

When I returned from seeing *Ben Hur* I was so enchanted by the dark, lithe Ramon Novarro, by the helmet, muscles and metal armlets of Francis X. Bushman and by the jewelry of Carmel Myers, the vamp, who wore rings with long pearl-tipped spikes on every finger, that I painted a whole series of characters from the film and cut them out. (Only in 1980 did I learn that the costumes for this film had been designed by Erté, a White Russian exile, who was plump and middle-aged when I used to dance with him in queer night-clubs in Paris in 1938.) 'Ancient Rome' became an obsession, as 'Ancient Egypt' had previously been. *Quo Vadis?* by Henryk Sienkiewicz led me to associate the Eternal City less with St Peter's martyrdom than with sexual orgies. I grew interested in the emperors whom absolute power had corrupted, particularly in Nero and in those like Heliogabalus whose reigns were indecently short. The latter's rose-crowned revels were depicted by Fortunato Matania, God knows why, in the *Illustrated London News*. In The Pleasaunce at Overstrand, while Bishop Pollock of Norwich, gouty foot on stool, read me Macaulay's *Lays*, I pondered on the rape of Lucretia; and Lady Battersea gave me Walter Pater's *Marius the Epicurean*, which was above my head, though I lingered over the descriptions of White Nights, the villa in the Alban Hills, and of the death of Flavian. The suicide of exquisite Petronius seemed to hold for me a personal message, as did the love of Hadrian for Antinous. I began to collect Roman coins, which I bought from old Mr Savin, a kindly antiquary, the historian of Cromer.

A few miles away from Horsham, at the foot of steep, wooded Box Hill, north of Dorking, lived my great-uncle Caryl Craven. If I were seeking in my life parallels with Proust's *A la recherche du temps perdu*, my '*côté de Guermantes*' would be 'the Craven side' and Nunkie would be a milder M. de Charlus. Unlike the fabulous Baron he had never enjoyed great wealth – though to us he seemed very comfortably off. He had, in fact, been one of the first men in society to take a job in a shop; had worked for Maple's, advised people on the decoration of their houses, and helped Daisy Warwick to design her famous Louis-Seize ball in 1895. The work and the waltzing were over long ago. Nunkie had secluded himself in Boxlands, a two-storey early-nineteenth-century house, whose gardens sloped down to the river Mole, and which was connected by a drive with the London-to-Brighton road.

When Gibbs the butler opened the door I was immediately conscious of a luxurious smell, which I think must have been a mixture of Edwardian shaving-soap and Egyptian cigarettes, though perhaps wood-smoke played a part. A long hall stretched ahead to the glass garden-door; on the left a red-carpeted staircase crossed a tall window to reach a gallery above; on the right two small drawing-rooms with French *boiseries*, one white, one green, led to a larger, higher room which Nunkie had built on. Here, beneath a chandelier, there were full-length, life-size portraits of Lady Mary Craven in a black hat and crinolined walking-dress with touches of red, on an improbable beach, and of Aunt Isabel March in a white satin dress trimmed with fur, standing on a staircase to show her train, and looking wistfully over her shoulder. The re-arrangement in this room of smaller pictures, porcelain and objects in jade or crystal, necessitated by continual purchases, was Caryl Craven's principal occupation: but, just as his sister Connie in her Paddington flat seemed resigned to do nothing more engrossing than *petit point*, so would Nunkie sit for long periods staring into the fire or stand, looking sad and distinguished with his large eyes and white upturned moustache, gazing out of the window. Mention of the fire reminds me of how Nunkie rebuked me for putting a log on it myself instead of ringing for Gibbs.

It was by the marble chimneypiece of this room that Nunkie would receive us, chaffing gently, but quick to observe whether my mother, who had been so foolish as to marry a poor man, was properly turned out, and whether I, with my gushing Buckle grandmother, was showing signs of commonness. Nunkie's most Charlusian characteristic, apart from a love of beautiful objects and another which goes without saying, was snobbery. The higgledy-piggledy Craven family tree, with titles and estates passing from one obscure cousin to another, really offered little incentive – at least until the creation of the second earldom in 1801 (and the first earl of this second creation married an actress) – to such *folie de grandeur*, yet Nunkie dwelt in a dream-world of aristocratic immunity on whose defences the onslaught of twentieth-century ideas had made no impression. If the Cravens had been a really great and ancient family, he might possibly have been freer to concentrate on something else. However their crest, a gryffin on a cap of maintenance – which was in evidence even on the pats of butter, served on ice at our delicious meals – impressed me; I liked their red and silver arms; and much preferred the sound of their name to that of Buckle. It was only later that I discovered the Buckle arms were older.

We sometimes spent Christmas with Nunkie; and it was

during one of these cosy festivals, celebrated not only with chestnut-crammed turkey and incandescent duff, but with Strasbourg *pâtés* and Carlsbad plums, that the eldest daughter of Nunkie's disreputable elder brother Augustus, who had been living since her mother's death with friends of the family solicitor, came to join us. Ten years older than I, Violet Craven, the heiress of the Craven London estates, which were being held in trust for her until her coming-of-age or the death of her disinherited father, was on the defensive and shy of her unknown relations. Not the least alarming fact about her reception, she told me later, was that I was wearing a crimson silk mantle and a high paper crown, gilded by Nunkie. She thought she had come to a mad-house. It was arranged that she should live with my mother and me at Overstrand: the estate would pay an allowance for her keep. So Rose acquired an unexpected daughter and I an elder sister. Nunkie immediately began to amuse himself by dressing Violet up and buying trinkets for her, as he had done for his Sandford nieces twenty years back.

It was down the London-to-Brighton road, from which Boxlands was secluded by walls, lawns and trees, that the Regency dandies had raced on horseback or driven their four-in-hands a hundred and thirty years before. I had not yet visited Brighton, which owed its prosperity to the Prince Regent's passion for Nunkie's great-great-aunt Fitzherbert, nor fallen under the spell of its Royal Pavilion, but, being, like my great-uncle, interested in history and in dress, I was thrilled by a set of cigarette-cards illustrating historical costumes, and I knew from these and from Rowlandson prints which hung in the passage at Overstrand what Regency bucks had worn. Their sky-blue coats with brass buttons, tight white breeches and tasselled Hessian boots were a supremely smart outfit in my eyes. Fantasy and style in clothes and architecture, an appetite for the visual arts, a passion for collecting, the desire to conjure Xanadus from the earth and display my treasures in them, in fact the

Beckfordism which led to my experiments in the art of exhibition design and earned me some fame – though, alas, only after the death of my Buckle grandparents – would always be associated in my mind with the bachelor uncle whose interests I had inherited, and who was so closely linked to the princely patron of Holland, Nash and Wyatt, not only by Mrs Fitzherbert's marriage, but by that *corso* of cantering dandies, the London-to-Brighton road.

In the mid-1920s, because of my interest in Tutankhamun's tomb, my mother had subscribed for me to a magical fortnightly called *Wonders of the Past*, and I used to brood over illustrated chapters on 'Palmyra, Queen of the Desert', and 'Petra, the Rose-Red City of Mystery'. When this magazine came to an end and had been bound in three volumes we took in H. G. Wells's *Outline of History*. This was succeeded by *The World's Famous Pictures*. I thus became familiar with many masterpieces of painting before I had ever set foot in the National Gallery. At that time, though, I think my interest in them was literary and sexual. I liked the nudes best and rather preferred Albert Moore's 'Summer Night' and Herbert Draper's 'Fall of Icarus' to Giorgione's 'Venus' and Perugino's 'Apollo and Marsyas'. These illustrations were not, however, in colour.

I remember the seat in the small sixth form at Horsham where I received from a picture the first shock which could be called aesthetic. It must have been between the end of January and March 1929. My mother had visited the great exhibition of Dutch pictures at Burlington House, and she sent me a coloured postcard of Vermeer's 'View of Delft' – which Proust had thought 'the most beautiful picture in the world' when he first saw it at the Hague on 18 October 1902, and which he had seen for the last time at the Jeu de Paume, leaning on the arm of Jean-Louis Vaudoyer (whom I was one day to meet) in May 1921, shortly before his death. Something in the colour or composition of this picture, in its mellow tone and compact perfection, or in the glitter on its crust of paint, excited me, awakening a new sensation not unrelated to greed, but less easily explicable – like the urge I experienced to *lick* the rough and solid rose-pink grease, kept in tiny glass pots, with which women used to polish their nails. I at once began to collect reproductions of Vermeer's pictures, then went on to de Hooch, Terborch, Metsu and Jan Steen; then to Rembrandt. That year it was only the Dutch: but my interests soon expanded.

The first Shakespeare play I ever saw was an open-air production of *As You Like It* given in 1923 by the boys of Gresham's School, Holt, in Norfolk. I loved it. During the summer of 1929 my mother took Violet Craven and me to Stratford-on-Avon. The old Shakespeare Theatre had recently been burnt down and the new one (to whose building we subscribed) had not yet been built. Performances were held in the cinema. As far as I was concerned it would not have mattered if they were held in the public lavatory: I could not have enjoyed them more. We saw a play every night for a week – besides two matinées – *The Taming of the Shrew, The Merchant of Venice, Much Ado About Nothing, Hamlet, Richard II, Twelfth Night, A School for Scandal, Romeo and Juliet*; and after the Saturday matinée of the Sheridan play I went shyly round to get the autograph of George Hayes, who had played Hamlet, Richard and Feste, and with whom I had fallen in love.

Lily's eldest daughter Doris, who, out of rebellion, had decided to be called by her second name Eden, was married to Joseph Woodger, a biologist at the University of London, and lived on Epsom Downs, bringing up her family as agnostics and socialists, naked in the garden. Tita's husband, Eric Graham, was now Principal of Cuddesdon Theological College, near Oxford, and she was expecting a fourth child. Her eldest son John joined me in 1929 at the Manor House, Horsham. Judith had recently married Charles Thornton, who had been at Oxford with her. His family had interests in Argentine railways, and Judith's home was in Buenos Aires.

Christian was still at Oxford and would soon be twenty-one. I sat for and passed the entrance examination for my father's old school, Marlborough.

Beechwood,
Iffley, Oxford   20 November 1929

Dearest Dick

Hurrah! Bless you!! *And* what a relief! I *would* have liked to see your face when you got the news. I wonder if it were at breakfast. I am as glad as glad & hope you got a holiday.

Hardie has had a record shoot today. 418 head & his gun got too hot to hold. I wish I could trot off to see you, but I get too fagged & short of breath . . .

Miles of love & congratulations.

Friday 6 December 1929

. . . Aunt Jude sends capital descriptions of gorgeous moths & humming birds & of Catfish with whiskers 3 ft long which they catch up the Delta . . .

I do hope your rehearsals go well. Hardie is v. keen you should come for some covert shoots as Mr Beaufoy has invited you to stand by him & shoot, so I sent Mummie all the dates – Boxing Day is one – but if you spend Christmas Day at Boxlands I doubt if you could do it.

Your devoted Granny

I loved Lily and always looked forward to seeing her; but I was shy of my grandfather, which made me dread the long days spent tramping the woods with him, and I was not a good shot. Dressing up at Nunkie's was more in my line.

After Lily and my mother, my most regular correspondent was Dolly Sandford, who in more ways than just her diminutive size qualified for the role of fairy god-mother. Like Lily and Rose she was intent on my improvement; and pocket-money was to be offered as a bribe or reward. The improvement she sought, oddly enough, was linguistic – and perhaps, after all, it was only a pretext for giving me a tiny allowance and training me to look after the pence. There were certain words and pronunciations which were thought at that time to be common. Dolly, for instance, would never have referred to London as 'town', which Lily habitually did. Nunkie had snubbed me for speaking of 'taking' milk in tea. 'One doesn't *take* anything except medicine.' My mother never ceased to mock genteel people who accentuated the first or last syllables of certain words. You had to lose the 'ep' in S'ptember, and the 'ur' in Sandh'st. To sound the 'e' in 'poetry' was half-way to becoming Oscar Wilde: it was 'poytry'; and poems were 'pomes'. But the particular vice which Dolly discovered in me was pronouncing 'girl' as it was spelt: a gentleman said 'gairl'. She would give me half-a-crown a month and I was on my honour to forfeit threepence ('thrippence') every time I lapsed. I was soon cured. Because the postal order was timed to arrive on the first of every month it was known as 'Rabbits'; and it continued, slightly increased, even when I was a serving officer abroad. So I got at least a monthly letter from dear Dolly and she one from me.

Marlborough was reputed to be a tough school: since its foundation in 1843 it had been ravaged by rebellions and epidemics. I heard legends of torture and bullying; Lily had told me how my father hated it, though she tried to reassure herself and me that times had changed; and my mother, teasing no doubt, said that new boys were often thrown out of the windows of the special train from Paddington. The climate and the boys (many of them the sons of clergymen and therefore abnormally vicious) both appeared in an implacable light. But I went to Marlborough with my mother and my aunt Christian Buckle by car, thus avoiding defenestration on the Great Western Railway.

CHAPTER 7

Marlborough and Oxford, 1930–5

The morning of my departure for Marlborough – it was 17 January 1930, and I was thirteen – held new horror: for I had to put on the regulation school clothes which my mother had scrupulously provided. It was not the black coat and striped trousers I minded, or the striped shirt and stiff collar, but the thick, scratchy woollen underclothes. It was my old trouble. Strange that it never occurred to my mother or myself to make a variation in this invisible item of the school uniform! So, fearful, tongue-tied and itching, I was driven over the uplands, fed at Hungerford, and deposited at Marlborough.

Beechwood   4 p.m. Friday, 17 January 1930

Dearest Dick

I have been following you all the afternoon – 'Now they are at Wantage' – & *now* I expect those rather nervy interviews are going on. How I *do* hope you like your housemaster & find some congenial friend quickly – anyhow the sun has shone all afternoon & your artistic eye would see the old town & river at its best.

Do send me a long yarn & tell me if the dormitory is bearable & if you could sleep & if you ate a decent brekky – for I shall be fussing to know every minute.

Mind you find out quickly about exeats – & tell me if you found a smaller drearier person to look after – remember you look so nearly a man you must buck up & be what you look, even though it's not so. Well, I should like to bear every nervous or nasty moment for you, & a fine soft idiot that would make of any boy. Remember it's facing up to the hard things in life that is one's real business – when you are in Chapel remember your father & be the son he would wish.

Your devoted Granny

A master at Horsham (who later committed suicide) had warned me that even if I was unhappy during my first days at Marlborough I must not write home about it, because it would worry my family to death. Two days after my arrival, a Sunday, miserable as I was, I replied to Lily's letter.

19 January 1930

Darling Granny

Everything is going very well so far, and everyone is very nice. I am going for a walk in Savernake Forest this afternoon. I do hope Aunt Chris will be able to motor me over to see you some Sunday soon, as there is such a lot to tell you.

There is no half term exeat.

I can get off on Sundays from about quarter to twelve until about 5, I think but I am not sure. The Chapel is awfully nice, so are the Hall and the Memorial reading room.

Will write again soon. We play hoccey only this term.

Very best love

Dicky

Dormitories and masters are all awfully nice.

That afternoon I walked alone to Savernake Forest, and was so ashamed to have no friend with me that I hid in hedges when other boys came by in pairs. The trees on the edge of the forest were scarred with initials which I imagined to be those of past Marlburians. I spent some time looking for my father's – in the expectation, I suppose, that if I found them I should feel less alone in the world.

Above: Dolly Sandford sketching at Flatford ('Constable's country'), 1914.

Right: Garry Buckle with Dick, Square House, Wilton, 1917.

Below, left: Mrs Sandford with her great-grandson, Dick, on the day after her ninetieth birthday, Hamilton Gardens, Park Lane, London, June 1921. Photograph by Rose Buckle. *Below, right:* Rose Buckle with Dick at The Fox, Warcop, 1921.

THREE WATERCOLOURS OF WARCOP BY DOLLY SANDFORD

Above: The Fox, with Middle Fell and Helbeck beyond, 1921. *Below, left:* Rose in the lane between Warcop House and the Old Cottage, with Smithy Hill beyond, 1916. *Below, right:* Warcop Bridge over the Eden, 1921.

Dick at Overstrand, probably 1928. Photograph by Rose Buckle.
This was taken when the author was at his third preparatory school, before
going to Marlborough in 1930.

Derek Hill, about 1940.
Photograph by Cecil Beaton.

Right: Ursula Tyrwhitt when
she was a student at the Slade
School, about 1895. Drawing
by Augustus John. Collection
Mrs Brenda Z. Seligman.
This was probably the first of
several drawings made of
Ursula by John, who loved her,
thirty odd years before she
became a close friend of the
author's and took him on his
first visit to Paris.

My letter had the desired effect on Lily, who wrote that she 'could have shouted for joy'. She went on:

> . . . I think it must be nicer for you than for some new boys because you are so big – but I suppose the ideal thing is to come with a great friend. I hope you will make one soon.
>
> I have been allowed into the conservatory today, & to lunch in the dining-room, & tomorrow my hair is to be properly cut, so I am getting on.
>
> God bless & keep you – the angels must be tired of passing on my prayers for you & be saying to each other 'Old Mrs Buckle sending *another* up for Dick – really it's too much!'

That Easter term icy hours were dragged through in games of hockey on the downs, waiting for the whistle. Life was not wholly unendurable, however, for I was naturally resilient and could always think of something to look forward to, if it was only reading a book in bed, a fried egg with Heinz baked beans (a new and thrilling discovery) at Duck's shop, or Saturday afternoon; and it was a positive joy when rain cancelled games. I was in the Shell form and a clergyman called Daddy Lane taught me English, history and divinity. For Latin, mathematics and music I went to other masters. The Greek master frightened and muddled me, and put me off the language of Homer, to my permanent regret.

I was more alone than other new boys, partly because I did not like games or ragging – preferring to read or paint – and partly because I was old for my age. I had already reached almost my final height of 5 foot 9 inches, my hair was brushed smooth, I was tidy and my clothes sat on me like those of a grown-up rather than a rumpled child. I looked and behaved like a young man of fifteen – that is to say, two years older than I was, a tremendous difference in the eyes of schoolboys. This attracted notice, caused comment and aroused indignation not only in 'A'

House but throughout the school of seven hundred and fifty boys.

At Marlborough boys went first to a junior house, then after a year or so to a senior house. Shortly before they left, a few, through athletic prowess, through being prefects or through some distinction of personality, became accepted as 'bloods'. I suppose it was like being in 'Pop' at Eton, except that there was no formal election. Bloods had certain privileges: they could wear light-coloured trousers and put their hands in their pockets in a different way. Through no plan of my own, but just by being what I was, I struck the whole school as having pretensions to behaving as a blood – and this in the very first weeks of my first term. Older boys in other houses would stop and point me out to each other and laugh or shout an insult. I was taken by surprise and had no weapons to defend this 'image' of myself which I had been at no pains to create. (I later acquired a defence in the form of a mask or pose.) So I was known as 'Bloody Buckle'.

It may have been because of my apparent sophistication that my housemaster, a big hearty man with a red moustache and a schoolboyish mind, when he sent for me to talk about sex managed to avoid doing so on the pretext that a boy who looked so grown-up must know all about it. 'I think we're both men of the world?' 'Oh, yes, sir.' 'Well, I just thought I'd say that I hope you won't – I'm sure you won't – get into any childish habits.' 'Oh, no, sir.' (I had no idea what he was talking about.) 'Last summer we had a bit of trouble with a few silly young fellows who used to go up into the bushes on Granham Hill and try forcing the stuff out of themselves.' Sick with horror at the idea of this excavation, which I assumed to have been performed with sharp instruments, probably dividers, I came away with a distaste for sexual experiment, and my flowering was retarded by a year.

Lily's health was steadily deteriorating: she had angina and colitis, hated money being spent on herself and genuinely thought she would be better out of the way. She described the process of being X-rayed with interest and at length. 'They found out one thing directly – that I have a dilated heart, so that they won't operate whatever else is wrong – that *does* please me – I abhor operations & the fuss & cost thereof.'

Lily's letters reported the death of Admiral Claude Buckle, a Crimean veteran, and celebrated the arrival of spring. 'I can hear the tits saying "Me. Me. Me!" and the crocuses begin to shine in the grass. Do you know the Great Tit's note? It's exactly like the noise of a small saw – he doesn't say much except when in love.' She recalled that on St Valentine's Day in her youth 'extra postmen were put on and the door-knocker seemed to sound all day'. Would I look up for her 'the beginning of baronetcies and the end of hereditary knighthood'? I did and it was my first job of research. '*Well* played & you tell me exactly what I wanted,' wrote Lily. Christian had a friend who was descended from Sir Thomas More. 'I like to think of all those fine old Buckles behind you & your Father who did better than any & now you to come on & valiantly do your turn – so pray "water fag" in the most knightly style!' Woollen gloves were fatal for chilblains; one must wear silk ones underneath. 'How jolly to have a keen drawing master!' She was 'deep in a new book on *Hell*! – all the old legends & pictures & horrors (which it *paid* the Church to spread as it got all the money for the masses for the dead) . . . it was not Christ's teaching at all . . . When my favourite brother Chamley was drowned I went nearly crazy with terror lest he was in Hell – because he wouldn't go to Warcop Church, where the Parson was often tipsy . . . When I was so ill at Christmas I saw Chamley quite plainly with my Father and your Father. There really is *nothing* in death.' But she was grieved that her dear Sybil Rogers (wife of

Garry's schoolmaster) had died at Bath. And at Warcop, Aunt Janey was dying. There had been a stirring sermon from the Bishop of Pretoria in St Mary's, Oxford. From Buenos Aires 'Aunt Jude sends lovely letters about humming-birds & vast yellow toads, weighing over a pound, who sit under the el. light in her porch & swallow all the flies that come to it – & great beetles that scuttle along, the size of mice.' Christian had fallen heavily for the Oxford Group 'Moral Rearmament' campaign and was addressing meetings of three hundred people in Edinburgh when she ought to have been working for her Finals. John Graham was often top of his form at Manor House, Horsham. Lily had entertained his younger brother Peter in the Cadena Café the other morning, but Aunt Tita had reminded her that he didn't have cakes or sweets in Lent. 'As he sadly ate a plain biscuit I said, "Would sixpence be any use to you, Peter?" He did not smile, but answered that all his pennies now went to the missionaries . . . I don't think people under ten ought to support missions *or* fast – but then I am a bad old – Granny!'

Lily had hardly tried me out on poetry, and the Masefield poems Mr Oakley had read aloud at Horsham were of the narrative kind. One day in June when Mr Lane was indisposed, the Master (i.e. Headmaster), George Turner, came to take our English period. He was a short, quiet man with a demure manner but a commanding eye. Without any introductory explanation he walked to Mr Lane's high desk, opened a book he had brought with him and began to read.

> In Xanadu did Kubla Khan
> A stately pleasure dome decree
> Where Alph the sacred river ran
> Through caverns measureless to man
> Down to a sunless sea.

Coleridge's incantation worked on me like a spell. Mr Turner read it through to the end, closed his book and told us we could have the rest of the period to ourselves. As he made for the door we must have stood up and the boy nearest the door would have jumped proudly to throw it open. I am sure I envied him the privilege, but I was behind a long desk on the east side of the room backing on two windows which looked towards the High Street.

Was it, as I think, about a week later that the Master surprised the form by coming again, to read *Wordsworth* to us? Did he come deliberately, brushing aside the Reverend Mr Lane (who was perhaps as fit as a fiddle) without an explanation to anyone and conceding no more than a bare glance in my direction, to read Wordsworth *to me*? After the fantasy of Coleridge did he reckon on the simplicity of Wordsworth aiming straight at my soul? If so, his reading had the desired effect.

> No nightingale did ever chaunt
> More welcome notes to weary bands
> Of travellers in some shady haunt
> Amid Arabian sands.
>
> A voice so thrilling ne'er was heard
> In springtime from the cuckoo bird
> Breaking the silence of the seas
> Among the farthest Hebrides.

That summer I went abroad – to Germany, where nearly two-and-a-half million men were unemployed. Our goal was the Oberammergau Passion Play. Tense with excitement, I felt the throb of a ship's engine for the first time; caught my first sight of Europe at Ostend; stayed in a *pension* at Brussels; admired the elephantine Palais de Justice; visited the cathedral; went to the Musée des Beaux Arts, where the painting by Nicholas Maes of an old woman asleep over her Bible reminded my mother and me of Granny; saw the Rhine at Cologne by night from the windows of our train; and arrived at Munich.

We were an odd little party at our *Pension* in the Theresienstrasse: my mother, Violet the heiress and I, with hardly a word of German between us; the elderly Miss Scoones, an Overstrand neighbour (daughter of a formerly celebrated crammer) who had given me the letters of many famous men for my new collection of autographs and coached me occasionally in French; and a mysterious friend of hers who arrived suddenly, a Professor Maxse, with a waxed moustache and a red wig. Looking back, I realize that Scoonie was in love with Maxse, and that Maxse (who probably sponged on her, poor as she was) was in love with me. Scoonie, who had always been fond of me, suddenly turned spiteful and continually found fault. I was bewildered. Maxse's strategy was the pretext of improving my drawing by taking exact measurements of my body in the nude. I suppose I responded with a kind of coquetry, as boys do.

Besides visiting the Alte Pinakothek and the Greek sculptures of the Glyptothek, I had intoxicating thoughts of outer space in the Planetarium; and I heard my first opera, *Die Walküre*, at the Prinz-Regententheater, where Diaghilev, a future hero of mine, had heard *Tristan* and *Die Meistersinger*, on his way to dying in Venice, exactly a year before.

The *Pension* at Oberammergau was of course a Hansel-and-Gretel house with carved gables. We sat through the day-long *Passionspiel*, but what made more impression was seeing St John, with his long fair hair, playing an accordion in a *Bierkeller* the same evening. We visited the mad king's Linderhof, but alas! not Neuschwanstein, which appealed much more to my imagination. On the way home we stayed two nights at Nürnberg, where I was anxious to see an implement of torture called the Iron Virgin. From the castle battlements we looked down on the ruddy roofs of the accursed town, then visited Dürer's house. We ran short of money and rationed our meals so as to buy postcards. In Munich we had seen the film *Die blaue Engel* with Emil Jannings as the respectable old schoolmaster and the about-to-be-world-famous Marlene Dietrich as the cabaret singer with whom he fell in love. Our communicating rooms at the poor little Nürnberg hotel near the station gave on to a well, across which stood a cinema where this film was showing. At night my mother and I would lie awake following the sinister story of the unseen movie, and as the moment approached when Jannings went mad and crowed like a cock Rose would tap on the wall and exclaim, 'I *can't* bear it!'

We spent the rest of August at Warcop. Lily had rented Haybergill, a hideous house in a heavenly situation on the way to Deepgill, which Emmie and Arthur Wynne had built after the war and which they had given to one of their sons when they moved to Camberley. I shot rabbits in Deepgill with my grandfather and bathed in the Hayber beck.

During the last year I had become aware of the beauty of weather and landscape, and I rediscovered Warcop and the Eden valley. Familiar corners and views now meant much more to me than before: it was as if they had been inside me all along, waiting to be revealed. I felt I had always belonged to this landscape and it to me. I began to take note of historic remains. The greatest character in Westmorland's history had been Lady Anne Clifford, heiress of the Earls of Cumberland, who had married in the reign of James I the Earl of Dorset, then in the reign of Charles I the Earl of Pembroke and Montgomery. Twice widowed, she returned north to restore her five castles and rule her wide estates. Her descendant, Lord Hothfield, lived at Appleby Castle. In Appleby Church was her explicit armorial tomb. When we drove to sports or sheep-dog trials by the lake of Ullswater we passed a column to the left of the road between Appleby and Penrith, which commemorated Lady Anne's last parting from her mother, Margaret Russell, Countess of Cumberland. When I went to spend the day with my cousin Anthony Brougham (a grandson of the spectacular Lady Alington) at Brougham Hall we passed the red ruins of Lady Anne's Brougham Castle on a bend of the Eden.

It will be remembered that Eden Gate, by the river, was the last house in the village of Warcop. Passing its entrance on the right, one plunged down a steep hill between walls, through a dark tunnel of trees, to the old bridge over the Eden. The road here was always muddy and thick with cow dung because of a farm opposite the entrance to Eden Gate. This farm, Warcop Tower, was on the site of the former castle of the Norman Vieuxpont or Vipont family, whose last heiress had married a thirteenth-century Clifford ancestor of Lady Anne's. On the walls of a barn at Warcop Tower, visible from the road, were carved two shields; apart from earthworks and the church, these were the oldest bits of history to be found in Warcop. One of them bore the arms of Vipont, six annulets (rings), three, two and one (the red and gold had to be guessed at). It is curious that these arms, which seemed to me a romantic vestige of feudal times, are the same which Proust gave to his imaginary family of Guermantes, who embodied all his dreams of the Middle Ages, and which, because he had borrowed them from the real family of the marquesses of Illiers, I would see many years later in the church at Illiers-Combray. I did not know in 1930 that I was descended from the Viponts and Cliffords. When I discovered this, long after Granny's death, I felt all the more a part of Warcop.

On the return journey to Overstrand we stayed a night at Liverpool to see a friend of Violet Craven's acting in *The Importance of Being Earnest* at the Liverpool repertory theatre. While there we read that a new Noël Coward play was being tried out at Manchester, and my mother decided we must see it. This was *Private Lives*. Curious that the first modern play I saw should have been such a masterpiece of comedy. The immaculate production set me a standard for life. Coward's subtle timing, the glamour of Gertrude Lawrence, *his* dressing-gowns, *her* sun-tanned back framed in the low-cut oyster satin Molyneux dress, the wit, the sin, the song, the luxury, the magic!

Beechwood   9.15 p.m., 30 October 1930

Dearest Dick

I hope you are going off to sleep after a good day. It has been lovely here – a real Devon wind coming up from the west with a tang of Lundy [Island] about it which bucked me up & made me enjoy walking up the High & watching the whirl of yellow leaves near Magdalen. But the old heart hasn't given me much peace since. How jolly to be like the Bishop of Worcester – well enough to go up to town & do all his work, & then just get one bad pain as he was crossing Palace Yard & find himself on the Other Side – no illness & no fuss. I've been trying & trying to write just lately. I did two scraps & showed them to Aunt Tita & she vowed they were good – but they aren't – my sentences go skeweye – my matter is poor and my style worse. I tell myself that Lady Harriet [Lindsay] will like *anything* I write & Dick may be interested, but I hate piffle & I can't avoid it . . .

3 November 1930

. . . Fancy – *I* am writing again! Furiously, forgetting all time & space in the dear old way . . . oh dear, how I should *adore* to do something even slightly decent before I go hence, & to distract my feeble mind from my tiresome old body. And writing – once you break through & begin to get into it – the effort almost makes me bleed – is so heavenly, because you can get the swing of a good sentence even in bed in the weary small hours – & jot it down if you like, too! I think it's almost like another sense . . .

Lily was 'enormously pleased' at my sending on a penny stamp after forgetting to put one on a postcard. But one of her last letters of 1930 contains a phrase prophetic of later academic disasters: 'Don't let your work go off because of the play.'

I wrote to Lily that I was producing a sketch for the house concert, that the library walls were 'blazing' with my paintings, and that I had got 'a new friend – a very artistic boy in Upcot (called Hill)'. She was pleased about the new friend – 'exactly what I wanted for you'.

Derek Hill had divined in me a kindred spirit and sought me out. He was tall with long lustreless dark brown hair and brown eyes. His features did not quite belong to each other. The big square head and strong chin were at variance with the delicate upswung Modigliani nose, which was much admired by older athletes, and the little petulant mouth which turned down at the corners when he was left out of some gaiety or if someone tried to steal credit for his work. He was a funny mimic and storyteller. He must have found me a great deal more naïve and innocent than he expected. I had never heard of T. S. Eliot or D. H. Lawrence or Cecil Beaton or Matisse. Besides introducing me to *The Waste Land, Pornography and Obscenity*, the world of *Vogue*, and Wilenski's book on modern painting, Derek taught me the facts of life where Mr Chilton had failed. He also made clear to me that although we were in junior houses, we were nevertheless Aesthetes, like Christopher Bailey with the long lock of hair in C.2, and like another rebel who was expelled soon afterwards. With these older boys Derek was already acquainted: his social prowess was dazzling.

So I was an Aesthete! What a relief! As long as there was a name for a condition there could be no harm in being in it – one could even defend it and be proud of it. I was no longer an outsider and inferior to other boys because of preferring art to games: I was probably even superior to them. I could jeer back and make the most of myself. I ordered some silk bandanna handkerchieves. Self-confidence was restored.

1931 was a crucial year in my life, although no one realized this at the time. On the one hand, as my appreciation of the arts grew wider, so were my energies dispersed and my academic studies neglected; on the other hand, new ideas of atheism, pacifism – which was not wholly idealistic, but derived partly from anti-militarism – socialism and antipatriotism were bound to fill my mother and Granny with dismay. From 1931 until the outbreak of war, every year – at Marlborough, at Oxford, in London, in Paris and back in London – was, or appeared at the time to be, a downward step on the primrose path. Quite early in my schooldays I had told Lily about my infatuations for other boys, and she had brushed this aside as something quite normal at my age. At her own school in Upper Baker Street she had been in love with first one then another of the mistresses. Only a vague reference in a much later letter suggested that she might have suspected that I was in danger of being stuck for life in a homosexual rut. Many times Lily must have been tempted to give me up for hopeless as a scholar, as a Christian, as an Englishman or as a Buckle; and yet she persevered.

My friendship with Derek, who explained so much to me (although there was never any romance between us), my dabbling in poetry, painting and theatricals, had given me a sense of creative potentiality. I did not know what I should become – and the early indecision whether to be a painter or a poet was replaced in the late 1930s by theatrical ambitions, though I could not then decide if I should be an actor, designer or producer – but I was sure there would be no difficulty in becoming it. Even the fact that I passed the School Certificate (the equivalent of today's O Levels) with six credits in the summer of 1931 only confirmed my belief that for a genius life was easy. This was a mistake. I would never pass an examination again. My euphoric self-confidence, combined with the indolence and love of pleasure which came from my 'Craven side', stopped me working at anything that did not interest me. But I was not, as I believed, cut out to be a youthful prodigy. I would develop late, and only after many trials and errors, misdirections and delays (including a five-year war), start to produce work of merit in middle-age. I had to fail before I could achieve any small degree of success, and that would only be after Lily was dead. It was in 1931 that I began to be a failure.

This was not at once apparent. 'How you do surprise me!' wrote Lily in acknowledgement of a little leaflet of poems I had vaingloriously paid to be printed in Marlborough. 'And the poems are original in theme and gracefully put – except that the last word of Cleopatra comes rather as a shout. *Go on* . . . Granhardie asked to read "Cleopatra" & said "*Amazing!*" when he finished it.' In July, after the Speech Day, when the products of our art school were exhibited in the gymnasium, she wrote: 'Mrs M. . . . delighted me with praise of your pictures – after she had admired them & passed on, she said, 'There's another clever picture' & when she looked at it, it was another of yours! . . . I had to fill in a long form for Burke's *Landed Gentry* yesterday, & after putting in 'P. N. Graham, M.A. Oxon, Judith St J. Thornton, B.A. Oxon, – & leaving a gap for Christian, B.A. Oxon – I longed to add, "This family has ceased to own estates but has improved in brains!" I wonder what will go in after your name in ten years' time.' (Christian got a Second in English.) On my birthday Lily wrote from the Lakes, ' "Love justice, do mercy & walk humbly with your God" is the finest guide I know – & that was my father's motto in life. I can't fancy you unjust or unmerciful – your temptations are more likely to come in the last precept – & so I fear have mine. Well, we must just fight them.' On 3 September she wrote about the results of my School Certificate examination: 'You may be sure I pranced up the High when I saw you had *six* credits.' Chris wrote at the foot of her letter, 'Well done, Dick. Six credits is splendid. CRB.'

That autumn I moved across the Court to a senior house. On my first afternoon in Mr Cornwall's house I suddenly decided in the changing-room that I would not play games. I had been put down for a game of rugger and I did not turn up. I was beaten. Persevering in my decision, I took another beating next day. After this Mr Cornwall must sensibly have

The gates and court of Marlborough College.
Drawing by Christopher Hughes for a book-plate given to prizewinners.

decided that I should not be made to play games again, and I never did.

Evenings were spent in the art classroom under the tuition of Colonel Christopher Hughes, a painter of ability and a local historian. I began to draw from casts and from models recruited in the town. I drew from a cast of Michelangelo's most languid Slave and made a large copy in water-colour of the head of Botticelli's Venus. I began to paint in oils and, in the course of time, underwent the influence of Van Gogh. Happy winter evenings with the smell of turpentine, an old man posing on his throne under a bright, shaded light, a few of us at our easels, and the rest of the room cosy, mysterious and dark!

I was now in the 'Upper School' and could specialize: I chose Modern Languages rather than Classics or Science. For French I went to the urbane Mr Titley in a fine panelled room on the first floor of the old Castle Inn, looking down on the lawns, huge cut yews and towering trees of the Master's Garden. Tennyson, staying at the Master's Lodge in 1866 and looking out on these yew hedges, had begun a poem. For German and English I went to Mr Bain's classroom in the Museum Block (by A. E. Street and A. W. Blomfield, 1882–3), with a view down on the Court's lime-tree avenue. Bain was small and ironical with George Robey eyebrows, a check suit and a buttonhole; and the more sophisticated among us liked him because we felt he took his profession lightly and would rather have been an actor. With him I first read the plays of Shaw, Ibsen and Galsworthy. My mother had taken me to *The Apple Cart* on our way through London during the previous winter, and I had adored the sight of Edith Evans in cyclamen pink velvet rolling on the floor with Cedric Hardwicke. (Returning my copy of the play, Lily had written, 'I can't like it. Such horrid self-seeking people and everyone at variance. My old ideas of proper politicians are people like Lord Salisbury, who simply live to serve the country & rightly administer large estates.') Shaw went to my head. I wrote an imaginary conversation between G.B.S. and Cleopatra, which was praised and which delighted Lily. ('Cleopatra wd be amazed,' she wrote, 'at no slavery, hospitals for all sick, kind asylums for the insane & all that Christ's teaching has brought us.') I even became involved at one remove with Shaw himself in a magazine correspondence about the teaching of English and he wrote of me 'Blessings on this level-headed essayist!'

While eager to encourage, Lily strove to perfect me. 'Dick, I want you to begin to write rather a tidier hand & less sprawly – if you are going to be a literary genius it's most important. Your present script, beloved, is not impressive . . .' She worried about my shallow knowledge of English literature. 'For instance, do you know who Little Nell & Mrs Jarley & Uriah Heep were?' A constant refrain was, 'Do always date your letters.' It is shocking that I could not even do *this* to please my grandmother: hardly a letter is dated before I went abroad in the second war.

The *Marlburian* published some of my poems, most of which were in free verse. Then, lusting for wider fame, I brought out a magazine called *Light and Shade*. The first number contained a satire on the local Member of Parliament; the Master disapproved; he exchanged letters with Lily, and the second number was the last. 'Two letters from your Headmaster in one day & four visits from doctors . . . If your heart's desire must go,' wrote Lily, whose own heart had nearly ceased beating twice within a month, '*let* it go, as a gentleman should – & don't crab your CO or let the other boys crab him in talking to you. It's his show to run the college, yours not [just] to obey as a matter of necessity with a bad grace, but to hurry gallantly to meet his wishes. That is the Montrose touch . . .' There was a general election that October and the National Government was formed, with Ramsay MacDonald as a token Prime Minister and Stanley Baldwin as his powerful second-in-command. '*Hasn't* it been a fine election!' wrote Lily. 'More for country and less for self.' How did our family react to the country's plight in those years of economic breakdown, failing dividends, unemployment and depression? Apart from shooting game, my grandfather worked very hard in his garden and sold the produce ('quite £75 this year'), while Granny 'screwed', as she called it, for her children and grandchildren. Doris Eden had sold all her investments to build model houses for workers, and she boasted to Lily that her rents came in where Chris's dividends had failed. Christian was working at the Greyladies College in East London, running a club for recalcitrant girls, who came from houses where all the furniture was in pawn except the bed – which sometimes had to accommodate six people. (Lily thought Christian was 'like a racing colt drawing coal carts' and wished she could 'marry a really A1 young Bishop'.) Rose, who was wonderfully good at looking after Lily when she was iller than usual, did annual duty with her Overstrand Red Cross detachment, at Yarmouth, tending the fishergirls. It must be admitted that most of my Sandford and Craven relations thought of the lower classes as brutish creatures with no rights at all. I was sent with a party of Marlburians to spend two days of the Christmas holidays in the East End of London, to see how the poor lived. We stayed at a hostel in Wapping, visited slums, clubs, docks and Barclay & Perkins's Brewery. I was afraid of the working class, aware of their grievance.

We spent that Christmas in Westmorland, and Lily wrote to my mother:

Beechwood   5 p.m., Christmas Eve 1931

My darling Rose,

I long to wire & ask about your cold, for it rather gnaws at my heart that you went off pale & hoarse & worn out with all the trouble I had given you – & I do *so* hope you won't be ill for Christmas.

Dear brave daughter that you were – & oh! you have got your work cut out with your son, my dear, & no one else can do it for you. He seems to me just bursting with brains & ideas & extravagance & careless youth. May God be with him as He was with his father – but these big natures seem to have much to go through, which lesser people would never stand, to make them perfect – & I wish I could bear it all for you both.

I am rather better & crowded out with flowers & pots & pots beyond anything I ever had – it's a kind world. But your tender kindness & patience has been my chief gift & I shall never forget it & I think Garry must know about it & be glad.

All Christmas love & wishes

Muddis

P.S.

I listened to carols on Miss M's wireless this afternoon – quite heavenly – but the chorister reading the lesson made me laugh until I cried – the cheeky tone of his voice & a touch of Dick in it quite bowled me out.

Wishing me 'Everlasting happy New Years' on the first day of 1932, Lily urged me, 'to begin to take on the future head of the family duties . . . to repay Granhardie.' 'Write to him sometime in your best man's style (i.e. *date* your letters & don't scribble!) . . . Begin to keep accounts as a man should. Say your prayers even when you don't want to – And still love that old hag – Granny.'

My religious doubts were encouraged by reading an essay of Bertrand Russell's. Since Man had been in existence for so brief a time on this minor planet it was absurd to think of him as the centre of the universe. Looking at the stars one night I felt inspired at the thought of my insignificance and was convinced that there could be no God to take a personal interest in me. Thomas Hardy confirmed my view.

'Did you say the stars were worlds, Tess?'
'Yes.'
'All like ours?'

'I don't know; but I think so. They sometimes seem to be like the apples on our stubbard-tree. Most of them splendid and sound – a few blighted.'

So Life was just a rash on the earth's skin. This freed me from many obligations, I supposed. Nothing mattered. I was nothing.

I must have blurted out a little of what was in my mind on my visit to Beechwood on the way back from school, for Lily wrote out for me extracts from a sermon of Dean Inge. 'Faith has been well defined as *the resolution to stand or fall* by the noblest hypothesis . . . *It is the determination to believe,* to behave as if certain things were true, hoping and believing that they are true, but not necessarily feeling sure about them . . .' Lily added, 'And the gist of it is – never mind about doubts – of whom the devil is the father. He *always* sends them to try the pick of the young men & girls – but just stick to Prayers & Communion & doing the just & merciful thing & they flee . . .'

But the cinema had focused my thoughts on the delights of this world, and I cared nothing for bliss in the next. During holidays at Overstrand the friends whose company I most enjoyed were two middle-aged sisters who kept a shop in Cromer where my mother bought most of her clothes. Bertha and Hilda Hughes were big, dark, bosomy, highly-coloured and spectacular women. It was hard to imagine them, before they forsook the shade of the greenwood tree for the feathers and finery of London, as country girls from a village near Weymouth, who had spoken to Thomas Hardy as he leant on his bicycle in a Dorset lane, for they seemed queens of the rag trade in a hereditary – almost Jewish – way, exuding scent, cigarette-smoke, sophistication and know-how, with an eye alert for any smart customer who might try to take them for a ride, but never averse to one more for the road. It was with them that my mother and I, and sometimes Violet Craven, would see at the little Cromer cinema (whose flattered and winked-at manager always reserved for Bertha and Hilda the best seats in the front row of the circle) the latest romances of Greta Garbo, the comedies of Myrna Loy and William Powell, the dazzling dance cadenzas of Fred Astaire. After the movie, which held me spellbound, but during which the sisters never failed to note that such-and-such a local magnate had brought a party, that Mr X was sitting with the manageress of the such-and-such Hotel, that the awful woman Y was looking twice her age in a very flashy dress probably bought at that new shop in Sheringham, and that the Z girl had been behaving outrageously with an unknown man in the back row, we all repaired for supper to their flat over the shop. This struck me as the height of glamour. Two narrow streets of fishermen's cobble and brick houses converged at the spot where ramps led down the cliff to the pier. The Phoebes' corner house – we always called them by the name of their business – was thus shaped like a slice of cake. The shop-door was contrived in the acute angle, and the turret over it was part of the sitting-room, with a tiny semi-circular window-seat. At some point in the 1930s this sitting-room was transformed from what I think may have been a stuffy Oriental Poiret décor, perhaps black and gold, into the purest Art Deco, as it is called today. The rough-cast walls were primrose yellow, the jade-green carpet wall-to-wall. (Wall-to-wall carpeting was a novelty in those days and considered 'common'.) The backs of the expensive rectilinear limed-oak arm-chairs, upholstered in jade-green tweed, were stepped up like the Cenotaph or the tower of Shell-Mex, and the low, heavy, two-tiered glass-topped limed-oak coffee table had blunted corners. On top of the glass-lined limed-oak bar cabinet stood a tank of artificial velvet-covered bulrushes. In this would-be Noël Coward atmosphere, to the sound of Cole Porter's songs or Paul Whiteman's band on the long-playing limed-oak gramophone, and in the company of two immense impervious Blue Persian deities, of whom the Phoebes deemed themselves the privileged slaves, I sipped Gin-and-It or *crème de menthe* from much-admired cubistic glasses, thinking I was Robert Taylor or Tyrone Power.

My great-aunt Dolly Sandford also adored the cinema. She spent one afternoon a week at the Picture House, King's Road (later known as the Chelsea Classic, now destroyed); basked in the beauty of Garbo and was madly in love with Adolphe Menjou. It was startling to see this tiny Victorian lady, under the influence of some gangster movie, twist her mouth into a sideways snarl, chew imaginary gum and spit out the words, 'Gee, ya dumb broad, no kiddin', Ah'm gonna bump-ya off.'

And I was lost in dreams of the South Seas. The only breaks in the monotony of our life at Overstrand were expeditions in my mother's car to Norwich, twenty-three miles away. This interesting brick capital of our flat county was built on as many hills as Rome. I loved invading it and, while Rose was at the hairdresser or dressmaker, scoured the bookshops of Elm Hill, returning with my loot to long evenings of reading on the sofa by the fire. Rupert Brooke had been my latest discovery and it was his South Sea Island poems which moved me, as the wind roared round our little house and the waves beat against the cliffs, to envious dreams of love-making in a tropical paradise 'a long while since and by some other sea'.

Indeed, I was a Romantic in the sense that what I liked best in the Romantic poets was their living in, writing about and dying in Italy or Greece. André Maurois' lives of Shelley and Byron were easy reading. I dreamed of disporting myself in Mediterranean landscapes. An indispensable attribute of a poem was that it should contain the word 'blue'; and the book-box with a sliding front which I ordered from the carpenter at Overstrand to carry my favourite poets from Norfolk to Wiltshire every term and back again for the holidays was a substitute for the treasure-crammed travelling carriages in which Byron made his state progresses.

For the time being I had to be content with more limited travels. In October 1930, Lily had been driven over to Marlborough for a picnic in Savernake Forest by a neighbour, Ursula Tyrwhitt, the first of many painters who were to be my friends. Ursula had been at the Slade with John, Orpen and McEvoy. Augustus John had loved her and Gwen John was a close friend. She appeared a typical English old maid, neat, prim-looking, apple-cheeked, with bird-like darting movements and a precise fluting voice. Yet she was a rabid bohemian, detesting regular hours, conventional meals and the restrictions of society. This gipsy quality appealed to me as much as her passionate feeling for Nature. 'I sometimes drive out of Oxford and stand in a field and shout,' she told me. 'What do you shout?' 'Oh,' with a little gasp of laughter and convulsive shiver of the shoulders, 'I don't know. "Hullo!" or "Hurrah!" ' She had married, after several askings, her second cousin, Walter Tyrwhitt, who painted large elaborate academic water-colours of Oxford or, on their tours together, of Italy, Sicily and the Middle East. Her own paintings, which she exhibited at the New English Art Club, were mostly of landscape and flowers, though she did a few portraits. In contrast to her husband she valued speed, attack, immediacy. To rush at a canvas or sheet of paper and make just the right marks, then leave it alone! She seldom satisfied herself and, I fancy, thought of her best water-colours as something that might be held up for a moment to catch the light and make their fleeting impression before being flung across the room and shut away in a drawer. Walter Tyrwhitt died early in 1932, and as Ursula had taken a liking to me it occurred to her to celebrate her new incarnation as a widow by spending a holiday with me abroad. 'Mrs Tyrwhitt was here yest^y' wrote Lily on 14 February '& Spain is "off" because her cousin in the Foreign Office says it's seething with revolution & unsafe for people who don't want to be detained there for months – but she still thinks you could do Paris & pictures & go down to the Aisne for a day or two [to visit my father's grave] & put in a fortnight with her . . . It was settled. Ursula and I were to go to Amiens for a night, visit my father's grave, stay at Laon, then spend ten days in Paris. Lily had been 'extra ill lately & a complete worm, in bed, almost always in pain' and wishing that there were 'definite instructions in Holy Scripture for putting old people to painless death', but she wrote to me: 'It's all fixed & lovely about France – you come here from M. & I *think* Mummie drives you to town on the Wed. Anyhow you meet *Aunt* Ursula (she is to take you on as nephew for the trip, but she's such a pet *I* should stick to her for life if I were you) *11. a.m. Thurs at Victoria,* cross from Dover & stay at Amiens, just as I did; you get there at tea time . . . I can see Amiens so plainly – the nice open market in the square & the cathedral towering up – & its marvellous rose window & the strangely haunted garden in the hotel where the band plays & the fountain sparkles & the great plane trees hang over the lawn & yet you feel anguish is *still* there – all the hundreds of officers who went there for their last night before their last trenches. Somehow their pain soaked into that little lawn as I never felt pain before . . .' Unfortunately I arrived at Beechwood with my hair slightly longer than usual; there were remonstrations and silences; and my mother was in a disapproving mood when she handed me over to Ursula at Victoria Station.

To travel with Ursula was a delight: she reacted with such glee to every experience. Duncan Grant was on the boat, standing on deck with strapped bundles of canvases, and she introduced me to him. She and I entered the cathedral of Amiens at dusk and saw worshippers in a glimmering side chapel. My father's remains had long since been moved to one of the immense British cemeteries, which we found with difficulty, and Ursula wept at the parade of graves. I took a photograph. We arrived at the hill-town of Laon in the dark, putting up at L'Hôtel de France et de la Hure; I was delighted with the magenta, black and silver modernistic wallpaper of my bedroom, which made me feel like a film-star; and even more next morning with the unguessed view over a wide plain with straight white roads fanning out to the horizon. In Paris we stayed, I don't know why, at a somewhat characterless hotel in the Avenue de la Bourdonnais, near the Eiffel Tower.

And so I saw the grey city on the curving Seine; tasted new food, drank wine, smoked cigarettes, felt grown-up, was un-criticized by Ursula, bought a *béret*, visited Montparnasse, crossed the Pont des Arts among a crowd of students, entered the Louvre.

What an experience to climb the stone staircase and see the 'Winged Victory' for the first time! I was transported to the Isles of Greece. The same breeze that caught the draperies of the angelic figurehead, flattening them against her thighs and curling them in the air around her, filled my lungs and soul with the wonder of a Mediterranean world I had never seen. Nearly thirty years would pass before I felt physically a sensation equivalent to that which I then experienced in my imagination as I gazed at the 'Victory of Samothrace' on the prow of her stone ship: and that would be in a speed-boat, warmed by sun and fanned by breezes, parting the waters of the Venetian lagoon.

Botticelli's two frescoes, which were the next works of art I set eyes on, pleased me hardly less. I loved and envied the serious yet elegant young man with his long hair and perfect profile, being led through a dark wood – *una selva oscura* – by the modest lady personifying Grammar, to be presented to Wisdom and the Liberal Arts.

Enraptured by my first feeling of bohemian life – although it consisted merely of sitting on the *terrasses* of cafés, lunching off red-checked table-cloths in the Place du Tertre at Montmartre, talking about pictures, and being caricatured on the top floor of the Eiffel Tower – I can have read Lily's next letter with nothing but impatience.

Beechwood   1 April 1932

> Dearest beloved, be sure you have your hair cut before you come away from Paris. Mummie minds its being long *so* badly, & considering all she has suffered & all she has done, & that you are her one & only pride & joy, you must be ready to wear a *pigtail* if it would please her *or* a convict's shave – until you are of age. It did really cut me to the heart to see her so upset about it. The cleverer you are the finer it is to render honour where honour is due – & all yours is due to her. And Dick, *you mustn't judge her;* she never had $\frac{1}{4}$ of your education & care, but she has given you the best she could of everything & she has had a hard & lonely furrow to plough ever since you were born. Also, she *does* know a lot more than you or I on many subjects, & dress & manners are among them. Here endeth the first lecture!

But blows began to rain on Lily thick and fast. Back at Marlborough in April, bored by a wet Sunday, I arranged to attend an evening lantern lecture in the Memorial Hall (our theatre), dressed as an imaginary Egyptian aunt of Derek's, turbaned, befurred and skirted, in full make-up. I made my entrance late, just as the lecture was about to begin in the presence of the Master, leaning on Derek's arm, gabbling gibberish, followed by two boys carrying cushions. I was of course recognized and all four of us were beaten. Lily tried hard to maintain her faith in me, writing on 2 November, 'I love you and feel more and more that you will help the world along'; yet, later that month, during a week-end at Beechwood, I had a defiant outburst, so that she was stirred to write: 'I thought a great deal over the teatime argument & feel *certain* you would jump into a river to save anyone – idiot or otherwise – just as your father did for Sandy Lokko [an African he had failed to save from drowning]. One can't sum up other people's value, & anyhow it was to save rotters that Christ died. Granhardie says he must read *Flowering Wilderness* before he can judge about turning Moslem . . . Square miles of love. Y.D.G.' In January 1933 (the month in which Hitler became Chancellor) fell THE BLOW, and I do not know what it was. Did I write that I finally renounced God, King, Country and Family, believed in Free Love and intended to open a brothel?

Tanton's Hotel,
Bideford   5 a.m., Friday, 12 January 1933

Dearest Dick

I wrote what I meant to be a nice letter after the blow, & got such a horrid answer a week later that I tore it up at once lest I should read it again. I thought 'I *must* forget it & he will write next post & say he didn't mean it', but it's over a fortnight & not one word! I came down here feeling awful next day & have been having doctor & nurse & heart attacks almost every day – some not so bad, others desperate. Hardie came & goes home today & the doctor told him yesterday that I have a thing called coronary atheroma – I may go on years, losing sight & memory, or I may die any moment from heart . . . I look 20 years older in this fortnight . . . The river under my window here is my joy & solace . . . Try to love me a little still.

Y.D.G.

Next, I began cutting parades of the Officers' Training Corps, and, on the pretext of pacifism, missed a Field Day. I was allowed to leave the Corps, so long as I soldiered on till the end of term. Thus I contributed in my small way towards the rise of Hitler – like those members of the Oxford Union who, that year, passed the celebrated resolution 'That this House will in no circumstances fight for its King and Country', and of whom Winston Churchill later wrote: 'It was easy to laugh off such an episode in England, but in Germany, in Russia, in Italy, in Japan, the idea of a decadent, degenerate Britain took deep root and swayed many calculations. Little did the foolish boys . . . dream that they were destined quite soon to conquer or fall gloriously in the ensuing war, and prove themselves the finest generation ever bred in Britain.' In my uninformed way I professed a kind of socialism, declined to wear a dinner-jacket and remained seated during 'God Save the King'. My mother had to write to my housemaster about this too.

Luckily my grandmother had other sources of interest and objects of affection besides my wayward self. With the births of Judith's first child, a son, in May and Tita's fifth and last in December 1932, she now had twelve grandchildren. There would be two more to come. She had celebrated her sixty-seventh and Chris his seventieth birthday that winter and they had been married forty-six years. *Cottage Pie*, her last little book of stories, which was published at her own expense in 1931, had made £15: this paid for Mowbray-blue baize to cover the inner swing doors in St Mary's, the University Church. At Beechwood Lily's pet robin came to feed from her hand 'several times a day' as she sat in the garden, and perched on her knee, 'singing like an angel'.

I took no interest at this time in public affairs and, despite Granny's incitement, seldom opened a newspaper: but Hitler's July 'purge' and the assassination of Roehm struck me as so sensational that I began to follow the exploits of the Nazi gangsters as if in some horrific serial which bore no relation to real life, but of which I longed to know the bloody outcome.

That summer of 1933 I won the Art Cup and the Furneaux Prize for a poem on 'Flight' in elegiac couplets, and designed the scenery for a production of *Julius Caesar*. Lily wrote:

Beechwood   3 July 1933

> *What* glories! . . . I had a lovely Sunday morn^g, Hardie took me out to the [location of the] shoot in his new 2nd hand shooting car; took the seat out & put it in a lovely ride where he had seen a Purple Emperor butterfly.

We didn't see that marvel — they nearly always live on the tops of oak trees — but a White Admiral sipped bramble blossom nectar close to me & I had not seen one since your father & I caught one in I. of Wight when he was about 10; & the whole place was full of butterflies & lovely high meadow grasses like tropical trees in miniature & wild flowers which never grow at Iffley. I couldn't see anything clearly unless quite close to it, but I saw enough. Before we came away Hardie & I said the Lord's Prayer together, hand in hand, & kissed each other.

There had for some time been talk of a Modern Languages scholarship for Oxford. I was in the sixth form and under the frenetic guidance of a transient young German, Herr Friedrich, who had a Byronic profile but no back to his head, who made clutching gestures in the air when he recited, who would sometimes slump despairing over his desk, head in hands, and who explained to me at some length the noble aspirations of Adolf Hitler. With him I made some progress with Goethe, got to admire Hölderlin and Rilke, even translated a few poems. Under Mr Titley and with some hints from Lytton Strachey I read most of Racine, a lot of Molière and a number of plays by Hugo, Musset and Rostand. Corneille was too austere for me. I loved Hugo's *Légende des siècles,* Ronsard, du Bellay, Baudelaire and Verlaine. La Rochefoucauld was my favourite philosopher — my only one, I might say. I had a new great friend, Charlie Colville, a quiet and studious type with whom I shared a study and whom I infected with my passion for French poetry. Lily wrote: 'I told Ursula that your scholarship was 7 May & if you missed it I supposed it would be Barclay's Bank for life for you. But she said "Oh no — he can make a start there & earn his bread, but then he will jump off".'

I had a new interest. On the way home from school that Christmas the dustjacket of a book had caught my eye on W. H. Smith's bookstall at Liverpool Street Station. It was the biography of Nijinsky by his wife. I had never heard of ballet, of Nijinsky or of Diaghilev. The strange pose of this muscular little man in the photograph dressed in rose petals – its sculptural perfection as well as the mysterious atmosphere which emanated from it – affected me as strongly and immediately as had the postcard of Vermeer's 'View of Delft' in 1929 or my first sight of the 'Winged Victory' in 1932. I longed to know what it was all about, but desisted from buying the book because I sensed it might contain something to shock my mother. Yet when I arrived at Overstrand there was the book on her table by the fire. When I read it a new world opened before me. It was to affect my life – though this was not at once apparent – as the 'book bound in yellow paper' did that of Dorian Gray. Before I ever saw a ballet on stage I fell in love with the idea of a travelling troupe of artists who performed in cities such as Monte Carlo, Rome and Paris, creating masterpieces *en route*. It never occurred to me to want to dance, though I did think that if I became an actor it would be nice to wear different coloured silk shirts, as Nijinsky did, for rehearsal. During the next summer I was to find a handsome pamphlet in the modern bookshop in Norwich's Elm Hill, *Les Ballets Russes de Serge de Diaghilev*, with coloured illustrations of designs for *Coq d'or, Pulcinella, Les Fâcheux* and other ballets. I immediately began to splash imitation Gontcharovas, Picassos, Braques, Rouaults and Tchelitchevs on large sheets of cartridge paper. Then came the publication of Haskell's *Balletomania*, which I gobbled up. During the winter of 1934–5 I would see my first ballet, *Giselle*, with Markova, at Sadler's Wells; and shortly afterwards visited Covent Garden for the first time to see the de Basil Ballet, with Massine and Danilova in *Le Beau Danube*.

In preparation for my scholarship exam I now had private tuition in English literature from an encouraging young Australian master, Bernard Hone. When I walked on winter evenings to the house where he lodged up a hill on the way out of Marlborough, the curtained windows of secretive suburban villas gave me a feeling of cosiness. Hone did his best to drag me out of my Romantic rut. He made me read Milton and the metaphysical poets, as well as Tennyson, Browning and Hopkins. But I failed the scholarship. The chief preoccupation of my last term at Marlborough in summer 1934 was a production of *Twelfth Night* which I directed and designed. I was convinced that Shakespeare should be got through at top speed (and this I explained in a programme note), with no waits and with as much music as possible. There was an apron stage and the sets were hessian curtains and swivelling flats painted with linear designs of trees, fountains and architecture. I played Orsino in black and silver, and my languid court was dressed in mauve, emerald green and cyclamen pink. Feste wore white all-over tights, a huge white ruff made by my mother and a spangled skull-cap. My mother, rather a good actress, was always embarrassed by my appearances on stage.

There was not enough money for me to go up to Oxford without a scholarship. It was therefore decided that I should stay at Beechwood and work with an Oxford coach until the following May, when I could have another shot.

Lily had another sorrow that summer of 1934.

Beechwood   14 July 1934

I have been bowled out beyond anything since 1918 by Christian suddenly telling us that she wanted to go into the convent at Wantage: & Hardie has been seldom dry-eyed. Now, I have been to see all sorts of people who know all about the life & a good deal about Christian, & when she comes back tonight from town I have a hope she will consent to take no steps for at least a year . . . I don't want anything done for my sake – though life without her looks black, but I don't mind any sake that gives her longer liberty to enjoy life in freedom.

I had hardly arrived at Beechwood to start my autumn and winter coaching when the thought of the University reassembling without me spurred Lily into action. She took the bus down to Balliol, interviewed the Master and the Senior Tutor, asked if my scholarship papers had not been good enough to qualify me for admission to the college without further preliminaries, was told they had, decided that money must be raised to start me off as a Commoner on the understanding that I should get the scholarship a year later, and dispatched me across-country to Dorking to ask Nunkie for a hundred pounds. This embarrassing mission was successfully fulfilled; my grandfather opened my first banking account; I was introduced by Christian (who had agreed to postpone taking the veil) to the English don at Balliol who was to be my tutor, the Reverend M. R. Ridley, editor of the Temple Shakespeare (whom I never set eyes on again); and I dined in Balliol the next night.

Although I was supposed to be reading English – and did in fact attend a few lectures on literature and on Anglo-Saxon – the university decreed that undergraduates should pass a simple general exam called Pass Moderations at the end of their first term. Why I had to study for this the chronicles of Philippe de Commynes I cannot recall: I could make no sense of their medieval French. We freshmen also had to read an essay once a fortnight to the Master of Balliol, that formidable Scotsman and socialist, A. V. Lindsay. For my essay on Sir Walter Scott I mugged up David Cecil's short book, but I failed to deceive the Master, who at the end of my reading asked, 'Have you ever read a novel by Scott?' Apart from *Ivanhoe*, in childhood, I hadn't. It will readily be guessed that I did not impress the Master; that I neglected my work and failed Pass Mods at the end of the term. Oxford offered so many delights and distractions.

There was the new freedom and lack of supervision. There was my small bank account. There was society and the possibility of entertaining friends in a room of my own. There was the Oxford University Dramatic Society. There was Oxford itself, so perfect a background for a life of elegance and art – and I was at a stage (never entirely outgrown) when backgrounds meant more to me than the action which took place in front of them.

Lily had given me a penny notebook and made me undertake to keep accounts. These did not survive the purchase of my first picture, a landscape, at an exhibition in Ryman's Gallery in the High, for I was struck by the absurdity of a sequence of entries such as: 'Matches, 1d. Stamps, 9d. Violets, 6d. Painting by Steggles £8.' New friends burst in to drink sherry in my little sitting-room in the Garden Quad, over the Junior Common Room, and for the first time in my life I had the fun of planning and giving small parties. I got drunk for the first time at a fireworks-party, but I missed the fireworks and reeled back up St Giles's to Balliol to be sick.

One friend whom Granny particularly resented as a distraction from my work – and from Beechwood – was Olivia Cooke, an American living apart from her husband in a rented Cotswold cottage at Oddington, near Stow-on-the-Wold. It was Ursula who had introduced me to Olivia, but whereas Lily could accept and even understand Ursula, Olivia was so different from Lily in her overt bohemianism and so like her in her all-embracing warmth of heart as to constitute a more dangerous rival. I fell in love with Olivia's fair-haired daughter, Priscilla (whom Ursula painted in hunting kit), and when she declined to take me seriously – although I dreamed of sylvan orgies and of showing off my new mistress to old friends at Marlborough – transferred my affections to her brother. Getting nowhere in this direction either, I settled, in a Platonic way, for Olivia herself. She encouraged my oddities and excesses, and my personality was allowed to burgeon by her log fires as it could never have done at home.

The privilege of being in and belonging to the ancient, holy city of learning – one which even Shakespeare never enjoyed – did not leave me cold: but I was aware of it mainly in an architectural sense. The curve of the High Street, with the cupola and pediments of Queen's contrasting with the crocketed spire of St Mary's; the Augustan rotundity of the Radcliffe Camera; the calm quads of Oriel and Merton; the grandiloquence of the House; the deer park of Magdalen; the expanse of Christ Church Meadow, 'rook-racked, river-rounded' – all these composed the ideal, historic, princely setting for genius to flower in. And yet how trivial and silly were my days at Oxford! If, at eighteen, Shakespeare was tumbling in the hay, at least he was writing verses.

Even the theatrical adventures, which soon absorbed me, were a waste of time – unless it is true that anything one enjoys enriches one's life and may bear fruit in later years. At the end of that first Michaelmas term plans were already afoot for an OUDS production of *Hamlet* at Easter. Nevill Coghill of Exeter was to direct it and John Bryson of Balliol, who had heard from Bernard Hone – a former pupil of his – about my stage work at Marlborough, suggested to Coghill that I might design it. Nevill came from a family of Anglo-Irish squires; he was a big man, bursting with energy and enthusiasm, a Chaucerian and Shakespearean scholar, already known – but later to become even more renowned – for his theatrical productions, which supplied in gusto what they lacked in perfection of detail. I think that if I had had *him* for a tutor, or perhaps the fastidious Bryson from Belfast – an aesthetic all-rounder, who later became a close friend – I might have studied profitably, and even qualified, as Granny so hoped I should, for an academic career; and my life would have been very different – possibly blighted. Coghill took me on, and over Christmas at Boxlands I was designing *Hamlet*.

But Christmas was dampened by my failure in Pass Mods. Then, I was no longer the favourite with Nunkie that I once had been. It was not just that I had let him down after begging the college fees off him at Granny's instigation – though he thoroughly disapproved of Granny and all her ways. I was not turning out the sort of man he most admired. If only I had been tall, beautiful and athletic I could have run up debts and he would have paid them gladly – and probably made a will leaving me everything he possessed. That I had some of his artistic propensities was not even in my favour – and he could see nothing in my 'modernistic' designs for *Hamlet*. Besides, I had become bumptious and affected, and consequently middle-class.

How different were Lily's feelings for me! The affection of a parent or grandparent for a son, daughter or grandchild is more like that of a jealous lover than is usually believed. The worse I behaved, the more exams I failed, the greater was Lily's love for me. When I was with her we always got on very well. Not to write regular letters when I was absent from her was the only crime – worse, though she would never have admitted it, than 'slacking' and denying God. As the years went on I wrote less regularly and was almost supplanted in her affections by Peter Graham.

I still held the theories about stage design which had dictated my *Twelfth Night* at Marlborough; one of them was that painted scenery should be linear or in flat colour, as perspective and contour distracted attention from the actors. The big New Theatre had just been built in George Street, and I suspect that my décor for *Hamlet* was as much of the period as the New Theatre's super-cinema style of decoration. It was a great excitement to see my gaudy costume sketches realized by two old sisters in Soho; and I was uncritical of cut or fitting. (It was on the way back from a visit to these costumiers, in the tea-car of the 4.45 from Paddington, that Nevill Coghill introduced me to John Betjeman.) Peter Glenville of Christ Church, son of a famous theatrical couple and later a celebrated director, was Hamlet. I played Rosencrantz, mincing outrageously.

Lily was too ill to get to the theatre.

Bed   12.15 p.m., Friday [1935]

Dearest dear

So nice of you to write . . . Have been having Twylight Sleep & all sorts of new things. In conservatory yest^y, but had two hypodermics for breathlessness this morning so am in bed today. Don't buy me any more flowers, but come on & get a nice pot for self as there are lots now in conservatory. I'd rather see your face for two minutes than the finest flowers that blow – & you *must* get fresh air – you looked really ill the other night. No good killing yourself at the first fence. Have been trying to make Hardie see how much more cheaply & nicely he and Christian can live if I can be quick & go, but he says 'It will be no economy at all!' . . . Did really think my last breath was near about 10 this morn – had windows flung up – said a brief prayer – but Heaven sent back my breath & here I am, full of atropin & pituitrin injections!

Ursula, however, saw *Hamlet* and went to Beechwood to rejoice Lily with 'high praise' of my designs. Even my grandfather made the effort, with a visiting cousin from Cheltenham. 'Granhardie took May Griffiths to OUDS yest[y] & said he enjoyed *every minute*. Dresses & decor wonderful . . .'

The summer term which was to be my last at Oxford – because, naturally, I failed the awaited scholarship exam – was marked by a romance with Hazel Terry, whom I met through Michael Rufus-Isaacs and Virginia and David Parsons (grandchildren of Sir Herbert Beerbohm Tree). There were also rehearsals for *Julius Caesar,* in which I overplayed the 'cameo role' of Cinna the Poet and was torn to pieces nightly for a week in the cloisters of New College by a crowd of maddened undergraduates.

I had learnt nothing, I had achieved nothing, I was equipped for nothing and apparently good for nothing. It was a depressing time for my grandparents, but even harder for Rose because she was so loyal to me that she would not listen to criticism of my behaviour even from her closest relations, and was thus condemned to brood in silence. Whatever rows we had in private, she was always a tigress in my defence against the world.

CHAPTER 8

◆●◆

London – Paris – London, 1935–9

If I were to force an entry into the theatre it seemed possible that I had better start as a designer. To further this aim it was decided that I should go to an art school and learn to draw. A neighbour of Violet and Patrick Kinnaird in St Andrew's Place was a painter whose sister designed Cochran revues. She recommended Heatherley's, an old but rather genteel art school, on the top floor of a building in George Street behind the Wallace Collection. While attending Heatherley's I should live at the Kinnairds'; so I returned from a stay in the Outer Hebrides and from attending Violet Craven's wedding to Tom Wimbush in Norfolk to take up residence in St Andrew's Place. It was the time that Mussolini was preparing to invade Abyssinia.

Pogson, the butler, had started life as pantry-boy in the house of my Sandford grandparents, then rocketed socially on making a startling marriage to Crootie, the lady's maid, who was old enough to be his mother. He thus became a butler, and continued to be one after Crootie's retirement and after my grandfather's death. 'Such a common man!' Granmumkie used to exclaim, expecting I know not what degree of distinction in an upper servant. She also said he had killed my grandfather. 'How?' 'He kept a store of Wincarnis – a sort of invalid port – in a barn, and used to smuggle bottles of it in to Francis after he was forbidden drink.' I did not always believe what this grandmother said. On Aunt Violet's marriage, Pogson had come to work for her. I do not think he got on with Violet, and his footmen could not have got on

155

with him, for they changed frequently. He was interested in the Turf. The only things I learned from him were how to roll an umbrella and that in Cockney language girls were 'birds'.

Our days were regular. A footman brought me tea at half past eight. I breakfasted at nine with Patrick, while he read the papers. He always sat facing the big window and the Park; I faced the chimneypiece surmounted by Wedgwood's neo-classical urns and a brownish painting by Brekelenkam of a bearded man in a tall red cap doing something in a kitchen. Breakfast was profuse, with porridge and cream, fish as well as bacon and eggs or boiled eggs, and home-made scones as well as oatcakes and toast; in summer we had salmon kedgeree and strawberries. Violet, meanwhile, was sitting in bed with her letters, tea and an apple. She received first Pat, who went to kiss her before leaving for the bank, then me, with whom she made plans for the evening or several evenings in advance, then Mrs Stanbra for long conferences over food, with notebooks. If Pat and Violet were dining alone or with two or three people I was welcome to join them; and the dinners were delicious, always ending with a savoury, which I liked – Mrs Stanbra must have had a repertory of at least two dozen. If they were eight for dinner to make two tables at bridge I was expected to go out, and was free to go to the ballet or a cinema or to make disreputable friends. I had a small allowance of about a pound a week, which Pat doubled, and London was open to me as Oxford had been a year before.

Carrying a tiny cardboard suitcase containing my lunch, I walked daily to Heatherley's. I learned a little basic drawing there. Not only were we expected to build up careful studies from the nude models over a week or two: every afternoon we had to do quick sketches while the model held different poses for five minutes, perhaps ten in an hour. My chief teacher was the brusque and horsy-looking Bernard Adams: he taught me how to block in a figure drawing, first getting the proportions and masses right before putting in detail. But I did not learn anatomy from the inside, was mystified by the principles of composition and made little headway in oil paint. I not only preferred drawing young men, but found it easier to discern the structure in male than in female bodies; and when a fat girl was posing tended to retire to the back of the room and design costumes for imaginary ballets about Montezuma.

Meanwhile Lily was consoling herself with the company of my old Marlborough friend, Charlie Colville, who had gone up to Christ Church.

Beechwood   7 November 1935

. . . Charley C. is good-looking & seems to be doing all the things I hoped you would do & being most careful about expenses etc. Yet I feel you had it in you to be the bigger character – you have more original wit & insight & a quicker brain: it's laziness & vanity you must get to grips with, Dick, if you want to make what you could of life. I haven't had to fight laziness, but I *have* always had to fight a love of praise & consequence, & showing off is as natural to me as to any old barndoor cock although it is a sin I *hate* – & I had a pack of brothers & elder sisters to keep me in my place. Don't give in to it, beloved: let other people love Dick Buckle, but do you keep him under & tell him he must serve the world & not swagger about its surface.

Your sinful old

Granny

6 p.m., Armistice Day 1935

. . . It was perfect of you to write me such a nice Armistice letter in return for my sermon which, after posting, I rather repented lest I should vex you . . . Aunt Chris & I listened to the service on the wireless. I like Reveillé & the clatter of the arms the best. It's a fine end – death in battle & good to go before the least touch of failing power comes . . . When you walk up Regent's Park – where I walked to school in Baker St every day for three years – look at 24 Cumberland Terrace where we lived. What fun we all had there sometimes when my handsome brother Chamley came up from Aldershot.

13 December 1935

. . . Everyone has been v. kind over my 70th birthday & 49th wedding anniversary. Uncle Arthur burst out with a bottle of best Brandy! and I gave myself a new Shetland shawl as Hardie never remembers to give me anything . . . Fancy being seventy – the whole gamut of life run! I feel I had so much & did so little with it . . .

Christmas Eve 1935

. . . I wish I could see you all at Mr Craven's, but I should feel very out of the picture if I were there.

You – with a piece of me in you & a piece of your father – have the other part Sandford & Craven, so should find some common ground . . .

I had a scene with Nunkie that Christmas. I remained a night or two at Boxlands after my mother and other guests had left. Nunkie had just made a present of some diamond earrings to Lady Byng, whose houses my Aunt Eva Sandford helped to run; and one evening he began to ruminate whether he ought not to make an allowance to 'poor Mimie', one of his two Gordon-Lennox nieces, who was not very well off. The fool Dick rushed in where angels would fear to tread – just as Granny would have done – and staked a claim for Rose Buckle, who was very badly off indeed. Nunkie was furious. 'Your mother had no business to marry your father. He had no money. I was always against it. And who are the Buckles, anyway?' I said that if my father had not been killed in the war we should probably be comfortably off; and that the Buckles were as old a family as the Cravens. This was not the best way to ingratiate myself with a rich great-uncle from whom I had expectations: but, to my surprise, when I described the exchange to Pat and Violet, back in London, their sympathies were with me. 'Good for you,' Pat said.

After a miscarriage, Violet had been advised to have the operation which prevented further childbirth. This was a tragedy, because she loved children. (If she had had a son who survived he could also have saved the Kinnaird peerage from extinction.) She tended to think that I belonged to her as much as to my mother, and made mocking references to 'Mummy'. My relations were all so different and so at variance with each other; and I played up to them all in turn. Pat was the kindest of men – which was the reason that Prince Henry (later Duke of Gloucester) and Prince Leopold (later King of the Belgians) had been allotted to him as fags at Eton. When my Grandmother Sandford came to dinner Pat always drove her back to Paddington, which she appreciated. 'He's a dear,' she said, 'but he hasn't got *it*. Now, Bobby [Cynthia's husband] is much more attractive as a man.' By 'it' she meant sex appeal. 'I've got it,' she informed me. 'You've got it; and your mother's got it. Pretty as she is, Violet hasn't got it.' One day she gave me some advice that would have astounded Lily if I had repeated it to her – which I was quite capable of. 'You sow your wild oats, darling.' 'Whatever do you mean?' 'So much nicer for your wife when you get married.' 'How would it affect her?' 'Oh, I'd much rather marry an immoral man than a moral one, because they know the ropes and they don't maul you about so.'

King George V died in January 1936, and I was sent with Pogson and Violet's maid, very early in the morning, to file past the coffin as the King lay in state in Westminster Hall. I also drove down on Sunday with Pat and Violet to Windsor to see the flowers which filled the approach and courtyards of the castle. 'Never was a king so mourned,' wrote Lily. 'His last hours seemed to draw the whole nation together.'

Great-uncle Arthur – General Sir Arthur Wynne, G.C.B. as he had become – at whose Warcop wedding to Emmie Turner Lily had been a bridesmaid in 1886 and from whose house she herself had been married, died that February; and Chris travelled to Warcop for the funeral. Lily would miss Arthur's letters – 'twice a week this last six months right up to a fortnight ago, bless him . . .'

'Write, I say, & again I say write!' 'I would still rather see your handwriting than any other – sinful scrawl & undated as it is!' This was one constant refrain in Lily's letters. Another was the perpetual question of my career. She was pleased with a recent photograph of me. 'Put your hand over the lower half of it & it is your father again, also my father & me; i.e. you will be worried with bits of our ideas and consciences all your life – even if you turn into a Film Moon – I don't suppose a Star would be big enough to suit you.' 'You won't always be a rascal,' she wrote, 'it bubbles off in nice people about twenty-one or twenty-two.' She was over-optimistic. Meanwhile she was praying for another scapegrace – the new King – 'even oftener' than she did for me. Our interest in the affairs of King Edward VIII prevented us from noticing that Hitler had re-occupied the Rhineland.

Easter 1936 was the Buckles' last at Beechwood. They were returning to the Old Cottage at Warcop in May. 'Ursula has been here, very nice & dear & kind. I *shall* miss the kind Oxford friends.' Chris was 'miserable' about giving up the shoot – and the handing-over would necessitate several journeys up and down: but Beechwood had served its purpose, and the Buckles were much worse off than they had been ten years before.

The Old Cottage, Warcop   9 May 1936

   . . . Warcop seems completely unchanged & quite lovely – same curlews calling at night – same kingcups in the Crooks – same beloved old fells – & a great many of the same kind faces. The Cottage needs re-doing up in every room, but some is done, & I have put the little drawing-room back into plain cream & shall soon get Dent to do the rest. I am so glad I improved the kitchen & made the outside rooms & bathroom, for it really is quite a dear little place now – for the summer at any rate – & I have had an el [ectric] fire & kettle put in. I hope to get part way to Deepgill soon, so far I find Church or Row End far enough . . .

Lily's verdict on her neighbouring relations veered between 'kind' and 'dull'. Of course most were both. Since Arthur's death Emmie Wynne had taken a farm called Row End at the south-east extremity of the village, on the road to Musgrave and Kirkby Stephen. Lily had never really got on with Emmie – she much preferred Uncle Arthur: while Emmie, who thought Lily odd, tended to humour her in a condescending way (much as Violet Kinnaird did my mother). Lily's cousin Janet Irving, whom she had displaced from the Old Cottage, was a kind, bustling, sociable, deaf old maid, who ran the Women's Institute and was much involved with village affairs. Two other old cousins, Nellie and Millie Hill, daughters of the clergyman who had married Nellie Turner to Willie Birdwood at Christ Church, Albany Street, lived in lodgings near the smithy, but were seldom on speaking terms with each other or anyone else. Millie may have been kind, but Nellie 'drank' and was not. At Warcop House opposite the Old Cottage lived the principal cousin, Tim Chamley, in place of Uncle Tom. He was exceedingly kind, always coming over the road with baskets of vegetables or hothouse peaches, but undeniably dull. His wife Mabel, stout, with popping eyes, was so very pleased to be Mrs Tim Chamley of Warcop House, in active opposition to the Wilds of Warcop Hall, that it was quite comic, like something in Jane Austen. In fact, Lily got on rather well with the sardonic, misanthropic squire, Jim Wild, and his wife Alice, with whom my mother had been friends (and dubbed Jemima) when she first came to Warcop; and found them just as kind to her as her own relations, and rather more entertaining.

Warcop   21 May 1936

. . . I feel horribly depressed as I notice the ways of the clan up here – they don't seem quite the cream of the earth as I always wanted them to be & I feel myself the sheerest skim milk of the lot. I *can't* think we were sent into the world just to see who could have the best house & furniture & make it shine the most. Yet I am sadly conscious that I don't come up to standard. My Highland Kate is a pet of a girl, but she's apt to send in cold plates for hot chicken & forget the dusting . . . Aunt Emmie has made Row End a picture & cheered up a bit over damming her beck with a felled tree & raising it two feet so that you can see it from the windows . . . My veins get more & more swollen & knotted – I can*not* sleep for the pain in them & I get stupider every day as the blood flows more slowly to the brain . . . an overdose would be *such* a kindness . . . This place is more sparklingly lovely than ever, but I can't walk much. Still, I *did* get to the bridge once & often get to church.

25 May 1936

. . . So nice to get your cheery letter . . . You can't think how it feels to be useless & unwanted & unfit to do things, when all one's long life one felt enormously occupied, wanted by lots of people & able to rush off & distract any dumps that came along in next to no time . . . There are probably plenty of people worse off who bear it much better, within a few hundred yards. Par exemple, the maiden lady in old Alice Hall's cottage, with two illegitimate children, who has fits; & old Gregson, whose gout is so fierce he has to be dressed & undressed & sit in the little kitchen swearing all day!

Highland Kate is very sweet & nice to me but so nearly dotty I never know what she will do next. I dread having anyone to a meal, she does it so badly. Never mind, man does not live by bread alone – *nor* by the size of his house, though Warcop may think so. I find Mabel kind, but *very* funny –

'Do you not know me? I have married Tim.
What glory is *not* all mine belongs to him' –

kind of thing!

'*Bloomsburia in tres partes divisa est*', they used to say of the district round the British Museum: meaning Fitzrovia, Bedfordia and Ormundia. Fitzrovia, the westernmost of these and the nearest to my home in Regent's Park, had been an artistic quarter even before Chelsea, and in Charlotte Street, its main thoroughfare, there was a house where Constable had lived. The lower part of the street was full of foreign restaurants – that is French, Italian and German – for there were very few Indian or Chinese restaurants in the West End of London at that time, and no Greek. The studios were mainly in the upper part of the street, where it had become Fitzroy Street. Sickert, Duncan Grant, Vanessa Bell and Rex Whistler all had theirs on the east side; but Nina Hamnett, with whom I made friends, lived in a tiny top-floor room crammed with books, next to the Fitzroy Tavern. Stulik still ran the Eiffel Tower restaurant which faced up the street, as he had done in the heyday of Ronald Firbank, Augustus John, Aldous Huxley, Evan Morgan and Nancy Cunard: but nobody went there any more. The first 'room of one's own' that I secured was a ground-floor room in a house where Thackeray had once lived, in Maple Street, taken against Violet's wishes. In 1937 I would have a top-floor studio with a bathroom at 16 Fitzroy Street; and in 1939 a top-floor flat at 107 Charlotte Street. None of these buildings exists any more; and a few yards from the site of Thackeray House in Maple Street rises the Post Office Tower.

Warcop   2 October 1936

. . . Autumn has scarcely shown herself yet, but on this still afternoon the country seemed to hold its breath before the first frost touched the valley. The sunshine filtered through grey clouds as I clicked the Deepgill gate & Roman Fell showed a bronzed freckling where the bracken stood out against the turf, but in the gill there was only a golden stalk here & there & a crisping of the fern & the thorn trees crimsoned over with berries. The beck had such a lovely line of light before it fell over the waterfall & the 'pool beneath it never still' . . . Your father used to say 'I'd like to go to church in Deepgill & to be buried in Deepgill' . . . I don't find Warcop easy to live in or to pray in, but up in Deepgill I can only *think* in Psalms, & worship as I try to take in every light & shade & curve & colour. When I was a child I remember crying in the night because I couldn't still be seeing Abbotsham cliffs; & now I try to fancy the gill in the moonlight & all the rabbits giving a ball!

                                          17 October 1936

. . . The trees here are like flames round the house & make the little room full of golden reflections. I *never* saw beeches so brilliant, but I long for the leaves to fall & let more air in. Tim's trees seem to have stifled me all the summer . . .

Lily could not face a winter at Warcop and Chris, though he loathed the idea of staying in an hotel, still preferred it to being left at Warcop without her. Perversely, for the climate of the Thames valley had never suited her – and she would soon be complaining about her eyesight again – she elected to stay at Moulsford Manor, near Goring. A Golden Wedding anniversary was to be celebrated in December, and this hotel's accessibility to the Woodgers at Epsom, to the Grahams at Cuddesdon, to myself in London and to Oxford friends – such as Ursula Tyrwhitt – must have influenced her decision.

Another near neighbour was King Edward VIII at Fort Belvedere, whose reign was suddenly being speeded to its end. Lily knew exactly how she would act in Mrs Simpson's place. '*Oh* to be Mrs S. & say "I'll die for you or live for you, but ruin you I will not!"' The evening after the Buckles' Golden Wedding luncheon on 13 December I listened with my grandmother to Archbishop Lang's speech on the 'vulgar wireless': this filled Lily with indignation. Two days later she wrote to me: '*You* were *my* chief pleasure. I did so like the things you said & did. I get so edgy now & when people say common things about the King I want to send them out of the room!' As the year was ending, still at Moulsford Manor, '*so* snug' with a private sitting-room, she wrote: 'Did you see that King Edward went miles in the snow to read the Christmas lesson in church in Vienna? The more I think about it the more I feel it was the *Archbishop* who should have resigned – a year ago – when he found he had no influence.'

On their way home the Buckles spent a week at a London hotel. Granny visited Granmumkie. I do not know if they had met since my parents' wedding in 1914: their conversation must have been disastrous, and they never saw each other again. 'I went to see Mrs Sandford. We are such poles asunder even in our ideas of what to say & what to omit that it does not seem very useful to meet.' Chris and Lily also saw Pat and Violet Kinnaird and no doubt had a despairing talk about my future.

I had shown my designs to Ninette de Valois, to René Blum of the Ballets Russes de Monte Carlo and to the playwright Clifford Bax without any tangible results; and I had failed an audition for an acting scholarship before Michel Saint-Denis at the Old Vic. Theatrical ambitions somewhat damped, I enrolled at the Regent Street Polytechnic to learn textile design. Lily wrote from Warcop encouragingly. 'I always did so envy Morris who could think of a lovely pattern at dinner & draw it on his napkin & beautify all the nicest houses in England with it. There is such beauty in a pattern. Did you know there are ten patterns of stars in snow crystals (there may be a hundred, but I have seen a scientist's photos of ten) – all perfect six-point stars, but quite different. The finest has each point like a spray of moss.' There was an accompanying sketch.

My altruistic Granny was very bad with servants. Highland Kate had fled to her native glen and Lily was managing with a 'temporary daily':

Sunday, 28 February 1937

... We are deep in the purest snow I ever saw. Looking down the white-clothed garden to the village & Tim's trees is lovely as a dream – but we have *no* el. fires *or* light *or* tel – everything cut off – & if valiant Dorothy had not pushed through from Sandford to light fires & cook etc we shd have been in a plight ...

24 March 1937

... We have had a tragedy here. Three little boys under six were playing by the beck – very full now from the snow water off the fells – and the little one – only $2\frac{1}{2}$, fell in backwards. 'He never called out, he just went floating off with his eyes open, so I came back for Daddy to pull him out,' said the little brother. Warcop was so good. Jim & Mr Murray [the clergyman] went in over their waists to search & then men & police dragged & searched all down the river. Next morning early they all came back past my window, & a few hours later the big best room was clear & the big family bed all draped & spotless & there in the centre lay the most divine little figure – the cheeks still rosy, the little mouth set in that marvellous wise smile.

Midnight, 14 April 1937

. . . Many true thanks for nice letter. I *do* hope you'll get a lot out of the Poly. course – a lovely design is so divine, & there are such millions of bad ones . . . Read Kipling's *Something of Myself* – all his early life in India writing for the *Pioneer* gives one a good idea of the hard work before he learnt to write the stories that appear to be so effortless. I *would* have liked to write something decent, but I always just missed it.

I had recently formed the ambition to buy back Eden Gate and was full of unpractical ideas for its glorification. It was therefore depressing to learn that it had been sold to strangers, Frank and Georgie Chancellor. But Lily liked them, and so did I when I got to know them later: they became fast friends with my mother, who regularly went to stay with them.

8 May 1937

. . . All the old wing of Eden Gate is to be pulled down & probably the Bow. I don't mind. I think I shall find the old Eden Gate eternal in the heavens with all the generations passing in & out just as they do in one's thoughts. I fear I am past writing a book about it. I grow more & more stupid & *amazed* at life. Why it is so curiously tied & bound & spoilt by people, who, with so little trouble, could make Warcop as pleasant as it is lovely. *And Don't.*

Lily was worried by the idea of the Coronation. 'How *can* the Royalties & poor old Bishops stand so long & what an awful expense! In the circumstances I do think a private coronation would have been far better.' Pat Kinnaird would be on duty as an usher in the Abbey in his Archer's uniform. Violet and I were to watch the procession from a stand built over the porch of Barclay's Bank at 1 Pall Mall East.

Warcop   8 May 1937

I feel terrified lest the Coronation goes beyond human endurance [wrote Lily]. How will Christian get ten girls to their seats after travelling [from Scotland] all night like sardines? How will your top hat endure it if it rains? How will the King & Queen & all their retinue survive it all? We are all gay with flags & crowns & paper wreaths & we all go to Church. Aunt E. lunches with us & there is a vast comic procession of which Mrs Wild does not approve & therefore Mabel is undertaking fancy dresses for all. Mrs Wild gives every child a mug & I have bought six dozen large wooden soldiers made in England, one for each child's plate at tea.

Lily also made a big laurel wreath to go round the War Memorial. I was thrilled by the appearance of King George VI and Queen Elizabeth who, returning from the Abbey, looked like painted, glittering idols in their illuminated golden coach.

In the summer I went to stay with friends at Vence in the south of France, saw the Mediterranean and spent my twenty-first birthday at St Tropez, which was then little more than a fishing village with one-and-a-half hotels. I continued studying textile design at the Polytechnic in the autumn, but my designs were too unusual; I was told they were unsaleable and given the advice to 'go and look in the windows of Debenham and Freebody's' and copy the kind of thing I saw there. Thirty years later I believe I should have done very well with my sketches. I was introduced to an American woman who was setting up as an interior decorator in Paris. She thought my original designs would go down well there and that we might be able to help each other. I was longing to live in Paris anyway, and in January 1938 I set off with high hopes.

'How does the fall of the franc affect you?' asked Lily. I had gone to Barclay's Bank in the rue 24 Septembre and drawn out all the money I had in it, making several pounds' profit. 'Are you being a good man?' she asked. 'Nothing else matters.' No, in her sense I wasn't. On 13 March 1938 Hitler annexed Austria. On the 15th Lily wrote to me in Paris: 'Fifty years ago since your father came into the world at Eden Gate. Granhardie & I have been thinking about him all day . . . *Why* can't the world be more like Warcop – all budding spring & songs of birds – but Warcop isn't *all* that – it's also got little dumb Reggie at the gate & his half-crazy mother, who seems likely to have to be put away in an asylum & Janet says, "Such a mercy if she is," but how would Janet like to be "put away" – & *she* gets very excited & queer nowadays!' On 16 March she wrote, 'If I were you I should come straight home & enlist.'

My stay with the American lady at Neuilly had led to nothing. Visiting English friends gave me dinner in the best restaurants, and I took them on to every kind of night club. Next morning we would reassemble in the Ritz bar: champagne cocktails, then lunch. Edalji Dinshaw, a Parsee friend from Oxford days, arrived; and Prince Felix Youssoupov tried to sell him the famous pear-shaped pearl, La Peregrina. He even offered me a percentage – about £3,000 – if I persuaded Edalji to buy it. I learned some French. In March I caught an appropriate disease, spent a week in the American Hospital, moved to an hotel and ended up in a *maison meublée* in the rue La Bruyère, Montmartre. A Danish friend who ran a smart hat-shop told me that in spring the great dressmakers bought sketches from free-lance designers to give them ideas for their summer collections. I studied *Vogue*, went to bed for a fortnight – living mostly on hot chocolate and Camembert cheese – and made a hundred sketches. Then I put on my best dark-blue suit and steeled myself to knock on the doors of Chanel, Lanvin, Schiaparelli, Maggy Rouff, Molyneux, Robert Piguet, Marcel Rochas. It was hopeless. I had not realized that what the *couturiers* wanted was not a jacket simulating an open book or a skirt *appliqué* with silhouettes of Sacré-Coeur or the Eiffel Tower but a subtle new way to cut a pocket or to turn a hem. After a fortnight I sold one design to a kind Jewess called Rosevienne, whose firm was only in the second grade. (She was later murdered by Hitler.) When poverty and sickness obliged me to return to London – which I did reluctantly as I had fallen in love – I went the rounds of dull English dress-shops in Knightsbridge and Berkeley Square with my portfolio, telling gullible ladies that 'this was what the Paris fashions would be like that summer'; and in a week I made nearly fifty pounds.

Lily had a new occupation to distract her from her afflicted body. 'I crochet squares day & night of everyone's old skeins & balls of wool. Eighteen squares sewn together make a fine blanket & it goes to permanently disabled invalids. The funny thing is it's so really exciting – you have to make shots as to how long a bit of wool will last round the square & what shade can go with what. My last one was like an old Persian rug. The present one is kingfisher wings – all greeny blues & greys & I do it half the night.' Tommy Hall, the postman who had looked after Garry's dog Jock, died. 'In his last hours he was unconscious, but perpetually trying to sort and deliver letters.' Christian was running 'a lovely camp & her pale-faced slum girls are adoring every moment'. My handwriting was 'much better'. The morphia Lily took for her angina depressed her so much she left it off, but nausea continued and the doctor said it was 'heart sickness' and that it was supposed to be a final sympton, 'but nothing seems to finish me, so I just go blanket-ing along & sometimes can walk to the post'. 'Don't fall in love with a lady of the ballet,' Lily advised. But it was a man of the ballet, a high-cheekboned Yugoslav, who followed me back from Paris, and Violet would not have him in the house as it was 'so bad for the servants'. I left St Andrew's Place in a huff. With the 'warm weather & haycutting' Lily was 'a hundred times better' and had a picnic tea in Deepgill. Although my way of life seemed hopeless to Lily, and although I did not write to her often enough, when we met I was nice to her and she forgave everything. My summer visit to Warcop went well. 'I can't thank you enough for all your loving kindness to me . . . your father could not have been nicer.' In mid-September Lily returned to the subject of my joining up. 'I should write, "In the *event* of war being declared I wish to apply, etc." I think & think of you & of 1914.' But Chamberlain brought us craven hopes of peace from Munich.

The futile years since Oxford had humbled my pride. I was ready to take almost any job. I went to Alexandra Palace in search of work in television. I went to Elstree Studios to see the art director Laurance Irving. Dolly proposed that I should publish with my illustrations our family fairy tale, handed down from the days of Lady Charlotte Greville, which had a sung refrain: 'Come with me, my sweet, leave all. Call to mind the wailing wood!' I was interviewed by publishers – Peter Davies (one of the originals of *Peter Pan*) and Michael Sadleir of Constable's – but they wanted premiums before they would take me on. I applied for work at Selfridges and at Bumpus. I planned to open a junk shop and began to pickle Victorian hall chairs and paint them white. Lily suggested teaching in a preparatory school.

1939! At least I wrote a scrappy diary to record those last feckless months of peace. Rose was so unhappy about me that on 3 January at the end of my Christmas stay at Overstrand she said she had nothing to live for. The next day I saw Pat at the bank in Pall Mall and suffered 'a severe scolding over 1938 expenditure, idleness etc.' Lily had come south again. My diary recorded: 'Cold water poured on shop idea. Lunch at Mostyn Hotel w. Granny, Doris Eden, Christian & Ursula. G. unsuccessful, thank God, at Peter Jones. [Whom could she have been urging to give me a job there?] Defend and expatiate on my shop.' '5 January . . .

Drink w. Violet, who lectures me.' On 10 January Lily sent me a cutting from *The Times*. Mr Turner of Marlborough was going out to be Principal of Makerere College in Uganda. 'Go with him!' wrote Lily. But I was too 'busy'. Friends to stay at my studio; friends dropping in for drinks; lunches in Soho; plays, movies, ballets; suppers at the Café Royal; a late-night dive called Coffee Ann; wanderings in search of adventure; consequent visits to the doctor; hangovers; collecting junk from the Caledonian Market; week-ends with friends. A new crony at this time was Michael Block, a Jew of Russian descent whose family ran a dressmaker's shop round the corner in the Tottenham Court Road. He had an exceptional facility in obtaining free theatre tickets (and still has); and we spent many evenings together in fits of hysterical laughter. I could not get over his familiarity with the works of Dickens: it was so unexpected. He was also my guide to the underworld. Meanwhile, the Yugoslav dancer had been succeeded by a charming Australian, with whom I made outrageous scenes of jealousy.

Just as Granny had tried to give me ideas for textile designs, inspired by the wonders of nature seen through a microscope, so her reports on Warcop characters were supplied almost as raw material for a book. How strange, how sad that my book about Warcop and herself would only be written (with her posthumous help) forty years later!

Warcop   2 February 1939

. . . You remember the two old Gregsons? *Good* Gregson, who used to keep the shop, & old *Bad* Gregson who lives at the end of our garden – & (you may not know) *Worst* Miss Gregson, who owns Shoregill & kept house for her brother at the shop. Well, *Good* Gregson has just died after being too paralysed to speak plainly or get about for *thirteen years*. *Worst* Miss Gregson neglected him outrageously & for some years has let no one inside the kitchen where he sat – a helpless mass of dirt & neglect.

Now, *Good* Gregson had both inherited & made & saved a great deal of money, & though *Worst* Miss Gregson owned Shoregill & many other delectable spots she coveted this money very badly. Therefore when *Good* Gregson had made his Will – & a very just Will – leaving farms to his nephews & only a cottage to his rich sister – , she, *Worst* Miss Gregson, always put off witnessing his signature on some excuse! So he died – intestate after all. 'Ha Ha,' said *Worst* Miss Gregson, '*now* his property is divided into only *two* shares – mine & my old *Bad* Brother's & those boys get nothing!' '*Not so,*' says the law. 'It is clear what were the wishes of the testator, though only signed by one witness. The will stands – the nephews get their farms, *but* everything left to *Bad* Gregson will go to his creditors for he is *an undischarged Bankrupt*!' Isn't that a yarn? . . .

But in 1939 I was quite out of sympathy with Lily's idea of what would make a book. In February I had an idea for a fantastic novel about Oxford in the future, and I wrote it while staying with Olivia Cooke at her latest rented Cotswold house near Stow-on-the-Wold. In March I copied it out. In April it was typed.

Warcop   4 March 1939

. . . I wonder every day how you & the novel get on, but the last two days I have been thinking continually about you in connection with Lord David Cecil's *The Young Melbourne*. It's pure delight to read anything so well written, & to me it throws a vivid fresh light on that generation. Also it forcibly struck me that in some ways young Melbourne was very like you: he didn't work much at Eton & not at all at Cambridge, but he read & thought & by twenty-three seems to have begun to work a bit, & made a fine man in the end. We all 'hear different drummers'. *My* drum tells me never to waste a day & to *do* as much as possible. Hardie's is quite different, though his

drum sounds for work too, but it has to be work he likes
& out of doors. You may pull off some fine design or idea
yet . . .

No-one thought I was likely to live last Sunday, but
now I am downstairs again for half the day . . .

A letter has survived that Lily wrote to her eldest daughter six
days after Hitler occupied Czechoslovakia.

Warcop   21 March 1939

Darling Doddie

It's a *week* since you had Dick & his book & not a line
have you sent me! & no one else tells me a thing about
him. He did write last week but told me almost nothing.
Is (the book *any* good? A 'fantasy' dated end of this cen-
   (it
tury doesn't sound to me likely to attract readers. Curious,
Dick's love of 'fantasy' from babyhood. When he was two
he w^d rather trail about in a gaudy silk shawl & a feather in
his hair than play any game . . .

What *do* you think of this crisis? I believe it will be war,
but Hardie doesn't. (He didn't in 1914 either.) I do hope
we hurry up Nat. Service. We always seem to *talk* such a
lot . . .

By mid-March Chris thought war 'inevitable', but Lily
hoped Hitler might 'burst asunder'.

Warcop   8 May 1939

. . . *Such* a pleasure to get your letter . . . I thought the
Archb^p of York – who is worth fifty of Cantuar – hit the
nail exactly, in his address yest^y at the military service at
York Minster. He spoke of 'The Service' being so called
because men served King & Country & not their private
ends, & how when all men love one another & so fulfil the
law, no armies or navies need exist, but *until* then the weak
must be protected & the wicked kept down – & that if the
navies were withdrawn from the seas no ship would be
safe from pirates, as in olden days . . .

What is really badly wanted are books for children like Beatrix Potter's. I know of none now . . . Just lately a goose at the farm hatched out fifteen eggs in a haystack. Her gander stayed *all day* on guard & went with her to get her food day after day. Now they are hatched, she leads them in a long string behind her across the Park to the beck every day & *he* struts at their side. One day a hen came along & took a bit of food from a gosling. In one majestic stride the gander was there & held her by the tail on the ground for some moments – the hen won't try that again. His majestic expression is splendid, & he is so *essential*, for the goose is too silly to ever look behind her & could lose every gosling & never know! . . .

Very occasionally I emerged from my *demi-monde* to go to a dance, and I attended a cousin's wedding at the Abbey. The reception after the latter was at Syon House, and the theatrical splendour of Robert Adam's suite of rooms struck me as more amazing than anything I could devise for the stage. (I would 'collaborate' with Adam thirty years later in the redecoration of Harewood House.)

On 10 May my novel was returned by Duckworth. On 22 May, on top of a bus, I had the idea of editing a ballet magazine. The *Dancing Times* was already in existence – and I had even contributed to it – but most of its pages were devoted to ballroom dancing. My magazine *Ballet* would be all about ballet, music and design. Four days later I talked to the Shenval Press about printing it, then visited Cyril Beaumont at his *boutique fantasque* in the Charing Cross Road to ask for his collaboration.

Warcop   Whit Tuesday [30 May] 1939

. . . I do feel I have lost you this year – & Warcop & Deepgill have been so lovely lately & so heavenly warm this last week. Never have I seen gorse so thick with gold that you cannot see stems or prickles . . . or lilac blossom hiding the leaves . . .

Granhardie fails a bit, but is a wonder for $76\frac{1}{2}$, though terribly depressed at being unable to walk so long or garden so much. People think it is so nice for old couples to be alone together, but when one of them is very deaf & silent & the other wants conversation & to see people it's really quite a discipline. Hardie told me the other day that he might exist without me, but couldn't live: yet if you overheard our conversation in the garden you would know the 'life' was not too easy. 'Chris, these young aquilegias would be lovely near the chairs. Do let me move them out of the back bed.' 'Certainly not, bound to spoil them.' 'Chris, I've watered your young plants.' 'Far better leave 'em alone!' & so on. He doesn't mean it a bit, but how dull it gets!

From my Diary: 'Thursday, 1 June. Telephone madly. Estimate from Shenval Press very satisfactory. Michael & I visit pawnshop. Beaumont. Bank . . . Call for Ma at hairdresser's. Phone Pat about guarantee. See Baron about photos 5–6.30. Taxi to Ronald Crichton's. Drink. Go to *Otello* at C.G. together. Talk to Humphrey Searle, John Bryson. Lyons. Write letters till two.'

On 9 June I was introduced by Ronald Crichton, who had been at Oxford with me, to someone who would become and remain one of my closest friends. Erich Alport was a refugee from Nazi Germany. His father had been a banker and industrialist in Hamburg, but Erich chose to go to Oxford and to become English. By anticipating events he was able to take his mother and a tenth of his fortune out of Germany. He had a house in Mecklenburgh Square. We had all the same interests. Erich's pedantic manner put some people off: not me. I think he liked my vitality and chatter, saw me playing Saint-Loup to his Marcel. (That year I had begun reading Proust.) I was to have in the course of my life five close friends who were Jewish. Of the two whose emigration had been due to Hitler, Erich was the first. Others, like Michael, were the sons of fugitives from earlier persecutions. From my diary: 'Friday, 9 June . . . Dine Ronald Crichton Sussex Place. Eric [*sic*] Alport. Drive through City, Wapping etc. in open car. Drink at Prospect of Whitby. Toynbee Hall – *Le Malade Imaginaire*, sets by Lotte Reiniger. Drive about City & wharfs, beautiful by lamplight. They come in for drink . . .' I moved to a larger flat a few blocks down the street. The diary stopped abruptly on 18 June.

Lily thought there was something improper about ballet and had no idea there could be any art in it: but in July Pat Kinnaird wrote to my grandfather after the first number of *Ballet* had appeared that it had not been a bad idea and that I might reasonably expect to make about £100 a month out of it. Early in August my fantasy *John Innocent at Oxford* was accepted by Chatto and Windus. On 23 August the Nazi-Soviet Pact was signed. On 1 September Hitler's armies invaded Poland. On 3 September Great Britain declared war on Germany. That morning we had our first air raid alert in London. Churchill later described how he and Mrs Churchill, who were then living opposite Westminster Cathedral, 'went up to the flat top of the house to see what was going on . . . Around us on every side, in the clear cool September light, rose the roofs and spires of London. Above them were already slowly rising thirty or forty cylindrical balloons . . .' In Charlotte Street, I too went up on my roof, hoping for a good view of Armageddon. On 5 September Lily wrote: 'I do ache for you – the sooner the wrench is over the better . . .' As I had left the Corps at school without getting the certificate which would enable me to become an officer in case of war I had to appear before a Joint Recruiting Board of the two older Universities to seek a recommendation. During September Poland was overrun by both the German and Russian armies. On 10 October I travelled to Oxford for my interview, was recommended for a commission and walked round to a reception unit of the Oxford and Buckinghamshire Light Infantry to enlist. I should be a

private soldier until summoned to an Officer Cadet Training
Unit.

Warcop   13 October 1939

Dearest Dick

No words to say how thankful I am that you are
accepted. My belief is, you will like it a lot better than you
expect: your life must have been horrid lately & I *know*
your men will love you when you join your regiment &
you will cheer the mess. Granhardie nearly cried with joy
when he read your letter . . .

All my love

G.

PART III

SECOND WORLD WAR

CHAPTER 9

Soldiering in England, 1939–43

Everything to do with the army had always repelled me, and suddenly I was in it. How deep my pacifism had been I am not sure – it returned in later years. Did I join up out of herd-instinct, from an inherited sense of duty, because I knew I should be conscripted sooner or later anyway, or for fear of offending my mother and grandparents? It certainly never occurred to me not to.

My war was divided into two acts: training in England and fighting in Italy, with a voyage round Africa and a land journey from Egypt to Tripoli as an intermission. The period of preparation was odious to me; the 'active service' was more tolerable because of a closer feeling of comradeship and the adventure of being in Italy for the first time. I used to think that 'training' was more 'realistic' than active service, because it was deliberately devised to be as unpleasant as possible, whereas in times of real danger people tried to make themselves comfortable and see the funny side.

Various obstacles had to be overcome before I could find a niche in the army, and once I had found it my chances of surviving the war as an infantry officer were not great. Yet I managed to be recommended for a commission, got through a month or two as a private soldier, caught jaundice and prolonged my sick leave until it was time for me to become an officer cadet, scraped into the Scots Guards, lived down the animosity which greeted me in that regiment, escaped sexual scandals without court martial, was accepted by our 2nd Battalion which had spent years in the Western

Desert, weathered the Italian campaign from start to finish, was discharged without dishonour and lived to tell the tale.

It had been Field-Marshal Sir Evelyn Wood, VC who had settled my father's choice of regiment by recommending the Northamptons, based on a county with which Garry had no connection. At some time in the first months of the war I had to fill in a form stating my choice of three regiments in which I should prefer to be commissioned, and the order of my choice. I wrote (1) Scots Guards – because my uncle Pat Kinnaird, who had served and been wounded in that regiment during the first war, left Barclay's Bank to become its Regimental Adjutant in 1939, and I was much struck by his pretty hat, with its red, white and blue diceboard ribbon and gold embroidered peak, on the hall table at St Andrew's Place; (2) Northamptonshire Regiment – because of my father and (3) Grenadier Guards – because of my grandfather Sandford. I was only 3/64 Scottish, but I daresay my double descent on the wrong side of the blanket entitled me to wear the Royal Stewart tartan.

Contemplating the Warcop woods 'exquisite in livery of gold and brown', Lily thought that 'the *only* decent thing in this war is that there is no hatred of the Germans per se, only of Hitler & Nazis. That German airman last week was so brave I felt as sorry for him as if he were English.'

My service as a private soldier was done in the Royal Warwickshire Regiment. On 15 November 1939 I travelled to Warwick and took a taxi to Budbrooke Barracks, which stood isolated in a modest Shakespearean countryside a mile or two west of the town, beyond the racecourse. At first it was as horrible as starting school all over again: and even at school I had never been woken in the dark by a bugle. The food was disgusting and it rained all the time, yet I found there was something relaxing in having no responsibility except to obey orders. In the evenings I often walked across the fields, thinking that Shakespeare might once have followed the same path, to dine at the Woolpack Inn in

Warwick. In St Mary's Church, in the Beauchamp Chapel, I admired the superb bronze monument of my ancestor Richard Beauchamp, Earl of Warwick, whom King Henry V made guardian to his young son, and who died at the siege of Rouen; and in another part of the church wondered at the chosen epitaph of my bachelor cousin, Sir Fulke Greville, who boasted of being 'Servant to Queen Elizabeth, Councillor to King James and Friend to Sir Philip Sidney'. My grandmother Sandford, who had a very vague grasp of the realities of the latest war, wrote in one of her rare letters: 'How lovely for you to be at Warwick. I expect you are at the castle. I remember teaching Daisy Warwick to bicycle in the courtyard there. What fun we had!'

Lily Buckle was condemned to the isolation, inactivity and boredom of Warcop. In one sense, however, she was not inactive. All the villagers who were not in the armed services soon began to earn high wages in factories or in rent from evacuated townspeople, so that servants became almost unobtainable, and at the age of seventy-five Lily had to learn to cook. Chris's dominant ideas were to help England by spending as little money as possible and by living strictly on rations – which did not make life or cooking any easier. Lily slept very badly, was often in pain, and, being cut off from all her family except Chris, she was without intellectual companionship; so she lived for the postbag. I knew how writing distracted her and I begged her to record her memories of her youth. She therefore began to compose her autobiography, on which part of this book is based, during the first winter of the war.

My stay at Warwick in the days of the 'phoney war', while the French and Germans sat behind their Maginot and Siegfried lines, intensified my love of England and made me feel more than ever a part of it. My thoughts about history had always been mixed up with my feeling for landscape. The sight of hounds tearing up a Cotswold hill, for instance, would make me think of Queen Elizabeth's state progresses across our green and pleasant land or of King Charles II's zig-zag flight after the battle of Worcester. These romantic musings had been since childhood an inspiration to me, and they were a recompense for hardship in time of war. I began to embody my thoughts in a novel; but when I showed the first pages to Erich Alport during a weekend at Polperro in Cornwall – where I recall artistic refugees telling us in awed whispers 'Kokoschka is here!' – this dear, strict, German-born Anglophile Jew scolded me for their sentimentality, and I abandoned the project. I fared better, though, with the genealogical and heraldic researches which I embarked on at that time, and which were undertaken with the same passionate purpose to entrench myself more deeply in England's history. Having decided to order an armorial bookplate, and thinking that since my mother was a co-heiress some Sandford and Greville quarterings should probably be included on the Buckle shield, I began a correspondence with Bluemantle Pursuivant at the College of Arms.

Warcop
8.15 a.m., 24 November 1939

Dearest Dick

You must feel quite used to life in barracks now, I long to know how all goes, but am sure you have no time for letters. I am watching a heavenly sunrise from my bed. The world is such a lovely place & we have turned it into a shambles, with the wireless telling us four times a day in a horrible self-satisfied voice just how the murders & wholesale drownings at sea are going on.

But the bare lilac bush by my window is all hung with melting hoar frost & its diamond sparkles outshine the crown jewels. There isn't a sound in the village except a rook saying a Collect as he flies slowly across.

Europe has turned away from religion & all peace & happiness is left behind. That is how it strikes

Y.D.G.

Above: Violet Kinnaird, the author and Rose Buckle at Le Boeuf sur le Toit (then in the Avenue Pierre I de Serbie), Paris, 27 March, 1938.

Left: Dick Buckle in Hyde Park, 30 March, 1939. Photograph by Cyril Arapoff.

Above: Lily Buckle, Oxford, December 1937. Photograph by Cyril Arapoff. This was taken in the hall of Ursula Tyrwhitt's house, 225, Iffley Road, at the author's request. His grandfather was horrified by the result.

Left hand page, top left: Chris Buckle, 1920. *Top right:* Garry Buckle, autumn 1917. Photograph by H. Walker Barnett Studio. *Below:* Dick Buckle in Rome, March 1945.

Lauretta Hope-Nicholson, London, 1942. Drawing by Augustus John. Author's collection. One of several drawings of Lauretta made by John during the Second World War shortly after the author first met her.

Lily wrote the first part of her memoirs about her youth in Devonshire at a tearing pace and, in spite of illness, household work and crocheting blankets for the Finns, finished it by Christmas Eve, when she had a collapse.

Warcop   26 December 1939

Both arms began to tingle violently, just as I was enjoying a huge batch of letters . . . The pain is more in my head now . . . It's very queer to feel irresponsible – a tiny little old woman keeps running after me & then falling flat in front of me . . . I do think my Book of Remembrance isn't bad. I have got to when I was fifteen & don't think I *can* go beyond another year. Too horrid to describe how violently one fell in love with Douglas Terry when Hardie has been so good to me for fifty-five years! But it's *amazing* to me that when I fix my attention on those long past years the awful mistakes in them stand out like searchlights. I had no idea before how wrong-headed & misguided I was & how I wasted my chances at school by being engrossed in worshipping a pretty mistress, who simply flirted with one girl after another . . .

I was slow to thank Granny for the first batch of reminiscences, but made up for this in time.

Warcop   18 January 1940

Dearest Dick

I do apologise for cross p. card, but I got *so* tired of waiting for a line. *Now* you overwhelm me with kind praise & careful correction of MS. But I only wrote it for you & don't think it could be published. I never stopped to correct or paragraph half of it, wishing to get it done before I got too ill & doubtful if I could.

Warcop   19 January 1940

. . . Here are your corrections returned with *deep* gratitude. Where shall I send Vol II next week? . . . I always want you to read every page directly it's done. No one else ever took such trouble over correcting me except Sir Evelyn Wood. *He* took *real* trouble & read & reread all I sent (but those were galley proofs) & wrote to say, 'How glad I am you kissed Will Hammond!' & 'How I do enjoy Mrs Hutcher, have read her again for fifth time!' But I like praise from you still better, especially in these lean years when I often feel the hopeless idiot that Emmie & Janet & Mabel appear to think me – *& each other!*

. . . It is snowing thick & fast & Hardie is up at Burtergill. He shot four duck this week.

My grandfather had helped the postman by delivering in his car Christmas parcels to outlying hamlets. Most pipes were frozen and the Warcop farmers had 'no water'. As Lily wrote, 'Twenty cows to be watered from one tap inside the farm is no joke – & all the turnips are frozen too.'

Warcop   28 January 1940

. . . I took a week trying to skip my seventeenth year in order not to hurt Hardie's feelings, but I *could* not get on, try as I would, without it. So I thought I would write it all down just to get it off my mind & then burn it & go ahead. But when I had spent most of yesterday over it I decided to let Hardie read it & see what he thought. So down he sat, questioned some commas, but objected to nothing & thought it 'quite all right' – so there it is, & I went ahead quite comfortably with the next year & thought Hardie nicer than ever!

You won't guess what made the blots on this letter – lumps of snow dripping off Purra's fur as he dashed to me to be dried! The birds & beasts feel this weather badly, & my pet old woman opposite the P. Office just died of the cold & nothing else . . .

Although there were Officer Cadet Training Units all over the country, many candidates for commissions in the Brigade of Guards were sent to the one established at Sandhurst, as if they were real Gentlemen Cadets for the regular army, as my father had been: so it came about that I followed him there. Our war-time course, however, was only four months. It was much harder work than being a private and I was bored stiff by wiring, digging, weapon-training and learning about the insides of cars. I was put on a motor-bike to go round and round the oval riding school, ringed by a three-bar fence. 'Faster, faster!' the instructors shouted, then, 'Slow down!' but it was too late. I shot at fifty miles an hour through the fence, destroying it completely, turned a somersault, smashed the bike to bits, landed on my head and was quite unhurt. Drill I was good at. I must have given Granny an exaggerated idea of the pleasures of training, just as I had pretended to enjoy my first days at Marlborough ten years before.

Warcop   17 April 1940

Dearest Dick

We are *deeply* glad & thankful that you like soldiering & are happy at Sandhurst. Your father *hated* peacetime soldiering . . . but when he got a taste of real work & leadership in West Africa he began to love it, & as you know, in the war, could not bear to be away from his men. You will be much the same . . . Archie Buckle's death in the *Times* . . . I sat in the car for a bit at Deepgill gate last evening – fells very clear. The high road *stiff* with lorries full of troops bound for Leith, & we imagine, Norway. Granhardie aches to be there, but, poor love, his memory and hearing get worse . . . John [Graham] returns to King's [Cambridge] tomorrow; his Dean thinks him a marvel – & Tita thinks he will be killed next year. It does not matter *who* is killed – only that each & all should have luck with his honour & trust in God. This world is only prep school.

Warcop   23 April 1940

. . . I have put in some really hard work [on the Memoirs] & got finished up to Aug. 1914 & it has gone to be typed . . . I have been distressed to find how intensely Aunt Emmie dislikes my writing & has let everyone know it . . . But it's very difficult sometimes to know what to leave out – one may leave all the vitality out & spoil the whole thing. And then it seems very conceited to put down nice things people said of one – but yet how they encouraged one to go on! & of course one didn't hear the nasty things. Well, it has intensely interested me all this winter & I should never have done it but for you, & Christian says it will be 'invaluable' . . .

Lily wrote on 20 May that she 'had not liked Winston Churchill until last night, but liked his speech on the BBC *enormously* & every sentence rang true. He may be the right man for the right moment.' Lily had no doubt that we should win the war, though she wished we were 'a better lot & had a finer Government', wondered whether the enemy would 'get across', blamed the Archbishop of Canterbury for being rude to God and liked the King best. She herself 'would far rather be killed than moulder', and she struck me as being too lavish in her readiness to lay down the lives of her grandsons. Suddenly she could keep out of the war no longer. Impelled by a sense of urgency, she decided to visit me at Sandhurst. Camberley had happy associations for her and she needed a change. Her outing coincided with the evacuation of the British Army from France, and she took on the job of looking after its welfare. It was very hot weather. Lily's description of ten days spent at the Cambridge Hotel, Camberley, on the main London-to-Exeter road, was later added to her Book of Remembrance.

On the way down I slept at the Station Hotel, Bedford, to break the journey, hoping to see Mary Graham, who was at school there, but this I found too far out for me to manage. Next morning, waiting for the London train, I noticed officers talking and people looking excited; and I travelled with a charming elderly lady who had heard the news on the BBC. *The evacuation from Dunkirk had begun.*

When I got to the hotel at Camberley it was pure joy to see Dick in his cadet's uniform and so like his father; but the gravity of the war shadowed everything. It was a stranger feeling to walk under the lovely Sandhurst trees again by the lake and to be going to have tea with Garry's son. But the whole atmosphere was changed. Garry's set were all jolly boys fresh from their public schools or crammers. These cadets were mostly grown men, many with wives and families; and the New Buildings only gave bedrooms the size of cubicles. There was a huge room where guests could have tea, but the day I went there in all that crowd of young men I don't think anyone laughed... the quiet was extraordinary. Dick was charming – and as all leave was stopped owing to the crisis he was glad to have me close by, and to come in for a meal when he was free.

Lorries of drenched, worn-out men lying as if half dead, began to pour past the hotel – the men from Dunkirk. I bought £5 of cigarettes and asked all sorts of strange officers in vain to give me a pass for the camp. Suddenly an elderly man who had overheard me and found out who I was said he could give me one for myself and a young officer's wife to go with me, but that no one else and no other car could have the entry. I dashed off to Mr White's garage next door, and Mr White said he would like to drive me himself – he had two sons fighting and badly wanted to see these men. So I spent another fiver on fruit from a good shop close by and off we went – about $1\frac{1}{2}$ miles along the pine woods. When we turned up a side road it had a felled tree flung across and mounted police who said we couldn't pass. However, I sent a pencil note with my pass to the Commandant and presently an orderly came back and said we could come to the C.O.'s tent. After that we stood by the car and I called out 'Chocolates, Cigarettes', and the poor men soon crowded round until I could hardly breathe. They looked half dead – and when I saw a group of ragged officers looking wistful and found they had lost everything too, and had not a cigarette or money to send wires to their people, there was plenty to do, even for me.

The Military Police told me that when the first draft had been brought into this camp a man had been there who took all the men's wires and letters to their people – some hundreds – for which the men gave him the money. Shortly afterwards all these telegrams and letters were found torn up in a field, and the man had made off with the money. What a welcome home to England! It made me wild.

I soon found the men would like me to send more wires, so I went back in the car to do this, and also get more cigarettes and fruit. It was roastingly hot and the big pears and oranges gave pleasure beyond words. I asked what else they needed and found no one had a handkerchief or shaving brush or soap. So next morning, very early, I cleared out Woolworth's for these with great content. I forget what else they wanted, but I think I spent about £60 in two days, and oh! I did enjoy it. The hotel was seething with officers, some unable to put boots on their poor bleeding, skinless feet. One night the bar began to fill and a queue stretched across the road. I thought the barmaid would faint with exhaustion and begged the manager to let me draw the beer, but he said he could not do it. Just as I was thinking of sleep, long past midnight, my bedroom door opened and a voice said, 'I'm the barmaid, and I'm going to kiss you goodnight!'

Next day the men looked a hundred per cent better – shaved and brisk and enjoying the band, vowing they would go back and finish off the Germans next week.

Lily would have liked to stay on, throwing her money about, indefinitely; but her savings were soon exhausted, there was an air-raid warning, she thought Chris would worry about her, and she set off for Warcop, calling on Christian, who was running mobile canteens at Birmingham, on the way. The defeat of the French and British armies had given her a natural feeling of impending catastrophe, and she had one of her presentiments.

Christian's Boiling hot Office,
Birmingham   4.45 p.m., Friday [June 1940]

Dear dearest Dick,

   I had a feeling about that heavenly walk by the lake – it
was too good to be repeated in this world!

She meant that I was sure to be killed. Four years later, when
it turned out that I had survived the war, I did feel I had
disappointed her sense of dramatic fitness.

   But something had happened to me during Lily's stay at
Camberley – and not to me only, to most of my fellow-
countrymen. Up to the night of 4 June, when the evacuation
of the British Army from France was completed, I had no
doubt whatever that the Germans would invade and occupy
our island. But that evening, after the BBC news, Churchill
spoke. In later years, after reading much about and by
Churchill, I came to think that he was not a man I could have
liked – and he and Roosevelt certainly caused untold misery
by handing over half of Europe to Stalin at Yalta – but he was
a hero to me in June 1940. I was sitting with friends in the
oak-panelled mess, hung with very bad water-colours of
hunting scenes, on the first floor of the New Building at
Sandhurst; and when Churchill spoke of fighting on the
beaches I realized in a flash – and I think my friends realized
too – that the war might yet be won. Winston Churchill
worked a miracle that evening, and nothing he did later can
diminish the wonder of it. I never knew until I watched a
television programme in 1980 that the French had thought
we betrayed them by sailing away from Dunkirk.

   It would have taken more than Churchill to make me
interested in soldiering. I was prepared to die for my country
if that was necessary, but to expect me to concentrate on
the mechanism of the Bren gun was asking too much. I
thought only of pleasure and getting to London for week-
ends. All leave, however, was stopped. Our course was

shortened by one month, as more officers were needed urgently.

Warcop   18 June 1940

. . . How *did* you all feel at the RMC yest^y when you knew France had given in? I said to myself, 'Anyhow Dick won't go to France.' G. Hardie is *very* upset – won't help Gen. Perreau [with the Local Defence Volunteers, later renamed by Churchill 'The Home Guard'] lest he is a nuisance, won't give up his gun, won't take any steps about taking in people. Of course I am burning to be off or else busy here . . . Think all schools sh^d break up & families be together. Perhaps RMC will break up? One doesn't know *one* thing except that England must see Germany defeated . . . The French said yest^y they had stopped fighting & now it seems they went on. We asked them to be one nation with us & that they could never be – as well ask Aunt E. & me to be one person . . .

Warcop   20 June 1940

. . . It often strikes me how silly it is that papers, BBC & public speakers are allowed to vilify the enemy – it only embitters & never cures & we all have to make terms in the end . . . I pacify these evil days by walking about the lanes with a very invalid baby who will only be quiet in a moving pram, & whose mother is worn out . . . Jemima [Wild] makes Mrs Chancellor [whose husband Frank had been taken prisoner] her care & sleeps at Eden Gate, which Jim thinks unnecessary – but Jim is working hard over LDV General Perreau in full war paint is driven about by Peggy [Rollo, Jim Wild's niece] and has Merry [Wynne, Aunt Emmie's youngest son] as Staff Officer. He came to see Hardie yest^y to ask him to help also. Hardie, having decided he is too senile to be of any real use, had been haymaking & would not trouble even to pull down his shirt-sleeves to receive him – & in reply to his polite enquiries stated that he was too deaf, too slow & too old . . .

Lily thought she would 'rather like to go to & fro with – say twelve – children, to settle them in Canada, as I like the sea & love children'. The idea of her as a trans-atlantic courier struck me as exceptionally fantastic.

Warcop   27 June 1940

Dearest Dick

I ought to be glad you join your regiment next week, but in one way I am sorry, as I shan't be able to picture your daily life any more . . . I cannot *conceive* how the French will endure life now or how Pétain can bear up for a day . . . 9.30 a.m. Just got a note from Mr White of the [Camberley] garage who drove me free seven times to the B.E.F. camp & to whom I sent a silver ashtray in acknowledgement. 'I shall value your gift as one of my most treasured possessions. What little I did was fully repaid by the pleasure of meeting such a divine person as yourself.'!!

I was now an Ensign in the Third Regiment of Foot Guards; and in July 1940 I reported to the Training Battalion at Pirbright Camp, a few miles east of Sandhurst in pine-clad Surrey. This was hell. For several weeks – during which I had my twenty-fourth birthday – the young officers were on a drill course with newly-promoted corporals, to be chased around the square. There were four drill parades a day, the first before breakfast; and the rest of the time was filled up with weapon-training, attending Company Orders and Commanding Officer's Orders. Our sleeping quarters and the mess, to which we returned for meals, were half-a-mile from the square, so we were bicycling up and down, to and from parades, from seven till six.

My first appearance on the square was marked by a

ludicrous incident. The regulation shirt material worn in the Brigade was a dark brown (not khaki) woollen taffeta. Because I could not contemplate wearing this next to the skin I had ordered some silk shirts in the nearest colour Hilditch & Key could provide – which was rather greener – with facings on the collar, cuffs and chest of the correct material. I did not know that in hot weather drill was done in 'shirt-sleeve order', without jackets, with sleeves rolled up and the Sam Browne belt and brace worn directly over the shirt. My squad had hardly scuttled a hundred yards when there resounded a bellow from the Drill Adjutant. 'Halt that squad, Drill Sarn't.' 'Sir! Squad . . . Halt!' Little Freddie Hesketh came pacing from the other end of the square. 'What is this patchwork garment you are wearing, Mr Buckle?' 'I can't wear wool next to the skin, sir.' 'Leave the parade ground at once and come back properly dressed.' 'Sir.' Stamp, salute. 'Left, right, left, right, left, right,' called the Drill Sergeant. So I bicycled half-a-mile, bowed with disgrace, put on someone else's shirt *over* the offending one, and returned. Freddie spoke to me afterwards in a friendly way, saying he quite understood, but that I must get some plain silk shirts made in no matter what shade of brown or green to replace the patchwork ones; and this I did. (Years later, in Italy, we became friends, and I was drinking with him one evening in a Tuscan valley when he opened a letter from England and exclaimed, 'My God, I'm a peer!')

The depressing thing about Pirbright was that there seemed to be no end to it. There was nothing to look forward to and no one to talk to. Senior officers stared at the new Ensigns as if they were slugs, and even with the young officers I found little in common. When appealed to for a week-end's leave, the Adjutant, tall, pale, lugubrious Archie Pearson, looked as if I had just thrown up on his desk. 'Have you mastered the Field Training Manual?' he asked. 'Do you know all your weapons inside out? It isn't an easy thing to be an officer in the Regiment, you know.' I escaped from the dreariness of life into the novels of Ronald Firbank, which I read and re-read. I collected material for a book about him; Evan Tredegar, Nina Hamnett, Duncan Grant and others produced personal reminiscences which were useful to subsequent biographers. Apart from this, I corresponded fanatically about my quarterings with Bluemantle Pursuivant at the College of Arms.

Unacceptable officers were usually sent on courses to get them out of the way. (In the last resort they were posted to a service battalion abroad.) I was banished to a Physical Training course at the Police College, Hendon. This made a change. At the concert on our last night there I sang for the first time, dressed as a little girl with long hair, an obscene song called 'My Little Pussy', subsequent performances of which would boost the morale of the Central Mediterranean Force and expedite an Allied victory.

In September I was sent to the so-called Holding Battalion at the Tower of London, and life was transformed. It was a small cosy mess and nearly everyone – except the Adjutant – was charming to me. The Blitz had just begun, and from the top of William the Conqueror's White Tower the burning city along the moonlit Thames was a splendid, tragic sight. I found it comforting, despite the bombs, to be surrounded by battlements, ravens and Beefeaters, to read the lesson in the church of St Peter-ad-Vincula and to look out on Tower Green, where my ancestress, the Blessed Margaret Plantagenet, had been beheaded. I mounted King's Guard for the first time; and my mother came down from Norfolk to have luncheon at St James's Palace. Our cousin Maud Cator had established a Red Cross hospital in her park at Woodbastwick Hall, and Rose worked there steadfastly for four years.

On the night of 29 January 1941 a big fire blitz took London by surprise: there was a strong wind blowing which fanned the flames. I was Picket Officer at the Tower, and I found myself handling a fire-hose, which was quite a difficult undertaking. I discovered that it was easiest to control the powerful serpent by holding it between my legs. I should have known that fire-bombs were put out with sand. The next day was the first in centuries that the Ceremony of the Keys was not performed. Another night, I recall Tower Hill running with wine from a bombed warehouse.

If one were not Picket Officer and not on King's Guard, which took the Ensigns about once in ten days, one could spend the evening in London. Disguised as a civilian, I ranged the blacked-out streets in search of adventure. A favourite drinking club was 'Le Boeuf sur le Toit' in Orange Street, named after Cocteau's famous Paris *boîte de nuit*, and mainly homosexual. Here, however, I met a girl who was to be one of my best friends. Lauretta Hope-Nicholson and I took to each other instantaneously. She was pretty, but it was her warmth of character that attracted me, and we were both passionate about pictures. I don't know what she liked in me, but I do know that there is no privation she would not have undergone for me and no exertion she would not have made on my behalf, up to the present day – except to answer a letter. It is rare to have a friend in whose eyes you can do no wrong – or almost none. Lauretta was as loyal to me as my mother, and far less critical.

I had to be back before the gates of the Tower were locked at midnight. I could have returned, after my West End debaucheries, by tube to Mark Lane (where Sir Cuthbert Buckle's mansion had been); but the underground stations, where people slept in serried bunks, depressed me – even if they inspired Henry Moore; and when I could not get a taxi I walked. It was not exceptional for a bomb to land just in front of one, then, as one walked on, for another to land just behind. I had a fatalistic attitude to high explosive; and, anyway, I was usually drunk.

When I was posted to our 1st Battalion, in billets at Chislehurst in Kent, I had a hostile reception, as I had on my first arrival at Pirbright. The Commanding Officer was a bleak man who would persecute me, when occasion presented itself, throughout the war. I was sent on more courses, and on my return from one I found that two nudes by Bernard Meninsky, which I had hung in my attic bedroom, had been tarred and feathered. Come to think of it – which I didn't at the time – it was quite brave to hang male nudes in one's billet at all. Finding myself on a course near Dorking I realized that I ought to visit my great-uncle Caryl Craven, who had recently been operated on for prostate and was ill. I called on him one winter evening. He received me, sitting in an armchair by the fire in his Louis XVI bedroom, a rug over his knees. I thought that, seeing me in uniform, he might approve of me at last: but even when I had made allowances for his weak condition I had to admit to myself that his manner was cold. I did not know that Lily had written to him only a day or two before to remind him to remember me in his will. It was the supreme instance of my Granny putting her foot in it. Nunkie loathed Lily and all that she stood for; and her well-meant effort would be the thing most calculated to infuriate him. He must have thought I had come to follow up her letter. No wonder he was cold. Nunkie died a few weeks later, leaving Boxlands and its contents to Helen Northumberland, the one of his nieces who could best afford to maintain it and keep his collection together. Within months the house was commandeered – later to be sold – and its contents were dispersed.

In a disapproving atmosphere, such as that of B Company at the 1st Battalion, I tended to curl up in silence, and, when snubbed, could hardly summon the spirit to answer back. But as I was by nature cheerful and sometimes even amusing in an unexpected way, my fellow officers, when they gave themselves the chance to get to know me, found to their surprise that they liked me very well. I was just beginning to make friends with Anthony Lyell (later killed, after winning the VC in North Africa), Anthony Balfour and Bill Lawson (both of whom later served with me in Italy) when I was posted to the Guards Depot at Caterham, to instruct recruits. One of the recruits whom I used to watch drilling unhappily on the square, though in the Grenadier company, was George Lascelles, destined to become a great friend after the war. At Caterham an escape from tedium was provided by a dear old boy in the Welsh Guards, Harry Rice, who played me records of opera in his hut after dinner. But during those years of training in England I was seldom out of trouble. On the eve of my departure for the 4th Battalion in the West Country, I planned a party in the garden of my billet for the non-commissioned officers and trained soldiers of my company, with whom I had made friends; and a barrel of beer was ordered. The Commandant, Lord Romney, getting wind of this, forbade it at the last moment – but too late. For when I returned to my billet after dinner the party was in full swing and the Guardsmen could not be induced to go away. More trouble.

Our 4th Battalion, motorized infantry, were part of the Guards Armoured Division, sprawled over Wiltshire, Dorset and Somerset, waiting till the time came to invade Europe. In the summer of 1942 we were in tents in the park of Marston Bigot, near Frome. Here training was more arduous, but life was often enjoyable because I found a few light-hearted companions and made a friend, Maurice Cardiff, with whom I discussed life and poetry – particularly A. E. Housman's – and went on excursions to Bath. One of our regular arguments, I recall, was about whether it was possible to perform an entirely disinterested action: Maurice maintained that it was not, but I said it *was* possible – something of Lily had rubbed off on me. To be in the West Country was in itself a pleasure – to see Alfred's Tower on its hill near Stourhead five miles to the south; to bicycle to Farley Hungerford and study the heraldry in the chapel; to spend week-ends at Glastonbury and talk to the old Rector, who furiously believed that Jesus had come there as a boy ('And did those feet in ancient time . . .?') and in the other

Glastonbury legends – and who, whenever the sceptical Bishop removed the notice-board beside King Arthur's grave, put it back. In the autumn of 1942 the Battalion moved to Porlock near the Devon border, marching part of the way; and I, as usual trying to turn everything into an adventure, reconnoitred an interesting route for my company, which took them round the lower slopes of Glastonbury Tor, loaded with a rich apple harvest, to sleep near the site of Sedgemoor Battle, at Middlezoy, whose aged vicar had what he claimed to be an authentic contemporary portrait of Shakespeare over the chimneypiece of his study; and so through the Quantocks, where Wordsworth and Coleridge had written their 'Lyrical Ballads', to enjoy the hospitality of Mrs Luttrell at Dunster Castle. After a week or two of shooting at each other among the stags of Exmoor, we returned eastward to a camp of Nissen huts at Longbridge Deverill, near Longleat and Warminster.

This was a time when the bloodthirsty authorities got tough, invented fiendish battle-courses and allowed a certain percentage of casualties (i.e. deaths) on training schemes. Two Scots Guardsmen were drowned on successive days in a river-crossing experiment on the Avon near Bradford. It was a wet, cold winter. Colonel Archie Douglas, one-legged and no longer young, was avid for suffering. He pinned an order on the notice-board: 'For the week beginning December the (?)th the Battalion will turn night into day.' The officers looked at each other in consternation. The Guardsmen growled. Was the man mad? We rose to a hearty breakfast at 1830 hours, i.e. 6.30 p.m., drilled, trained, marched, were lectured, and attended Company Orders in the dark; then, as day dawned, we officers changed into blues for a three-course dinner, followed by port, and a piper played round the table. Throughout that winter three-day sleepless manoeuvres took place over Salisbury Plain – there was no escape: if you tried to snatch forty winks in front of a truck a general would loom out of the hedge and demand to know if Imber had fallen and how you intended to evacuate your prisoners. At midnight on the rain-lashed uplands how snug seemed the winding valleys of Avon, Wylye and Nadder below! Yet the West Country with its buildings and its history was a compensation for discomfort. One daybreak, after I had managed to sleep on a hill-top without any cover against heavy rain but a greatcoat over my head, I stood up to see, rising from an ocean of white mist and gilded by a horizontal shaft of sunlight, Glastonbury Tor. Then, to come upon Constable's very view of Weymouth Bay, with coursing clouds (remembered from the National Gallery), was exciting – no less than were the fresh-caught lobsters of Osmington Mills, eaten for supper in a field near Crichel. Back from one of these outings, I could hardly be surprised to find no single Guardsman had turned out to hear a string quartet I had lured (in my role of Entertainments Officer) from Salisbury.

For years our 2nd Battalion had been to-ing and fro-ing in the Western Desert. In March 1943 our 1st Battalion landed with the 1st Division, as part of the First Army, at Algiers. The demand for reinforcements to them both was increasing. My time had come to be posted abroad. Leaving behind the 4th Battalion (who would later take part in the invasion of France and Germany) and Maurice Cardiff (who, because he spoke modern Greek, would be seconded to some curious task-force and 'liberate' Greek islands single-handed), I was driven down the Wylye Valley, gobbling with my eyes what I could hardly doubt to be my 'last glimpse of England', and boarded the London train at Salisbury station.

I had to wait several weeks at Chelsea Barracks, which was quite agreeable – for I saw much of Lauretta – except for more Regimental attempts at intimidation. My last dinner in England was eaten in the long dining-room of the mess overlooking, through railings, the Pimlico Road. My draft got into their buses, bound for Euston Station. It was a fine Sunday evening in April.

CHAPTER 10

Into Action, 1943

Seated in the train to Glasgow, where we were to embark on SS *Orion*, I found myself for the first time alone with the only other officer – and commander – of my draft. Major Patrick Steuart-Fothringham, known as Feathers because of his long untidy moustache, was a taciturn, solitary Scotsman, with a pale bony face, sandy hair and a very faint voice. I thought I remembered hearing something about him. 'Aren't you keen on flowers?' I asked. 'Creatures,' he corrected me. After this the conversation languished, for Feathers had no small talk at all. I wondered if the authorities at Birdcage Walk were having a quiet giggle over their incongruous pairing of this melancholy, eccentric landowner, who was probably only happy on the windswept hills of his northern estate, with the exuberant, hedonistic Buckle. What had we in common – except perhaps a dislike of army life and the fact that we were both odd men out? Yet we got on very well together. Feathers was later to choose me to keep him company in a long difficult mountain battle, and would even recommend me for some award. (Years later I read that there had been a law-suit in the early nineteenth century between a Buckle, who had married a Scotswoman, and an ancestor of Feathers over the ownership of the Grantully and Murthly estates which he and his brother inherited.)

Ours was the last draft to Egypt which sailed round the Cape, for while we were on our way the drawn-out desert campaign and the shorter North African one ended on 10

May with the meeting of the Eighth and First Armies and the defeat of German and Italian forces on the continent. The voyage from Glasgow to Suez took two months. This included a week hiding from U-boats in Freetown harbour, where I was miserable not to be allowed ashore, and three days at Durban, where we were greeted by a stout lady in flowered chiffon, the widow of a former mayor, who stood on the dockside to sing popular ballads through a celluloid megaphone. Thrown together with Feathers, I observed the simplifications of his life. Some theory about the harmful effects of hygiene prevented him from ever cleaning his teeth. He had a silver christening mug, black with neglect, which he used for his shaving water; and this was the only vessel from which, in private or in public, he could be persuaded to drink. He ate and drank very little and his only gastronomic interest was in the correct preparation of porridge. Sometimes at meals, which were served by waiters, as if on a peace-time cruise, Feathers, seated motionless and staring at his plate, would switch off completely like an Indian *guru*, deaf to conversation and heedless of the bewilderment of strangers. Whether he really practised some kind of *yoga* or was merely disgusted with the guzzling, boozing and gabble of ordinary mortals I never liked to ask. Feathers despised physical training, which we were daily called upon to perform: he regarded it as designed solely to beautify the body, and therefore narcissistic, a waste of time. The inference was that all the strength a man needed to stalk deer, endure privations and pursue the enemy must come from within. (Feathers was, in fact, extremely delicate, and died of tuberculosis shortly after the war.) He was amused by the number of books I read and commented, 'When you've found the perfect book you won't need to read any other.' I remembered that Mme du Deffand had thought Racine the least imperfect of writers, but *Athalie* his only *perfect* play. Feathers's one book was no classic, no Bible, no encyclopaedia: it was a short story called

The Specialist about a man who made outdoor lavatories.

Since summer 1941 Lily had begun corresponding with Dolly Sandford, of whom she had seen little since my father's death. My feckless ways were a constant topic. 'Dick writes, "Dolly has *paid all my bills!*" . . . I do love you for being so good to him, but oh! who reproved me for paying them when he was twenty-one? And will he become careful after this?' Dolly was pressed into service: 'Will you *very* kindly . . . draw me a kitten, a puppy & a negro doll on a bit of old cardboard, say 12 inches to 14 – the doll full face & laughing, & the animals in two pieces, a back & a front, with flat feet for standing on . . . I do the dolls by the dozen for Poplar Hospital & the London [Hospital] & the children love them. Also you may have some old black or brown velvet . . . I think of you very often as I have your picture of a cornfield opposite my chair . . .' In 1942 she had written, 'I fear Dick will never learn to care for money & it looks as if he would never have much. *If only* he would come back to religion . . . I don't know what Rose thinks . . .' After my mother and I had stayed at Warcop Lily wrote, 'I saw that Dick could do as he liked with his mother & I thought it better than the old quarrels. She never tried to make him go about with her when he wanted to remain with his books, & he has found how good she is over packing for him etc. . . . Of course one longs to see him more unselfish, but . . . he likes to do a thing *very* well if he does it at all & he keeps himself beautifully neat, & he is charming with children. His wit is uncommon . . .'

My Jewish friend Erich Alport had joined the army as a private – he would later become an Education Officer – and was stationed at Warcop. Lily and he got on like a house on fire, but Chris did not take to Erich at all. To Dolly Granny wrote, 'Dick's great friend Mr Alport is in & out every day . . . & *so* uncomplaining of the heavy work & rough life . . . but poor Chris retires to the el. stove in the dining-room . . .

Mr Alport touched me very deeply last night by telling me he was trying to be a Christian . . .' (My mother told me after the war of her amusement at hearing how, on a particularly wild night, when Erich had a cold, Lily persuaded him to stay at the Old Cottage instead of returning, as he should have done, to camp. My grandfather was *horrified*, not being accustomed to harbour deserters.) Dolly, to whom economizing was a pleasure, had begun to make envelopes out of old sales catalogues, with a rectangle of white paper pasted on one side for the address: some of these she sent to Lily.

Warcop   18 May 1943

Dear Dolly

What a brick you are! I don't know if I always begin by saying that, but I always think it . . . I heard from Dick from the dock & imagined he was joining his regiment which has lost so many officers the last three months in Tunisia, but Rose is sure he went to Cairo round by the Cape . . . When I was eighteen & at Eden Gate we talked of Cairo every day. My brother Chamley was there & he had invented & inaugurated the Camel Corps . . . Cairo is very gay & expensive I think now. Dick won't live cheaply there & he will want to go about & see all he can . . . Peter Graham is a pilot in one of the crack Channel Squadrons now, & *terribly* happy . . . I do rather shake for him . . .

I thought I had finished with courses, but on arrival in Egypt at the depot at Fanara, near the Canal, I was at once put on a 'hardening' course. This was followed by a machine-gun course, which entailed two weeks – at the height of torrid July – of assembling, firing, dismantling and lugging over the sand-hills a heavy weapon which, as an infantryman, I could hardly conceivably be called upon to use. I twice hitch-hiked into Cairo, but the museum was closed and the old quarter with the mosques was out of bounds. I had a few adventures, however, and narrowly avoided rape by an obese Pasha in a carriage bound for a house-boat on the Nile. One day I found the reproduction of a drawing of Lauretta by Augustus John in the *Tatler*, and on an impulse telegraphed, asking her to marry me. She thought I was trying to be funny and did not reply.

Walking in the desert with Feathers, I remarked that a landscape without trees was not very interesting, and was startled by his vehement exclamation, 'This is the most fascinating landscape in the world!' 'Why?' I asked. 'Don't you see that just by looking at the ground you can tell everything that has been going on here for days past? You can read it like a book. See here. There's a man brings a camel through this wadi every day, and he has a dog with a limp. And here some ibis settled this morning. And if you follow that track you'll find a rat.'

Feathers had gone ahead when the time came for our draft of two hundred Scots Guardsmen and Coldstreamers to join 201 Guards Brigade at Tripoli, twelve hundred miles away, so I was in charge. The caravan of trucks set off early in August, and it was a worthwhile experience to steer endlessly westward over the dazzling sand, the royal-blue Mediterranean with its turquoise shallows lying on one's right hand, and to go through towns whose names had long been familiar from the nine o'clock news – Mersa Matruh, Tobruk, Sollum, Derna and Benghazi. I passed the grave of John Bowes-Lyon, a friend with whom I used to drink, in the early days of the war, at the 'Boeuf' in Orange Street.

I had trained for three years and travelled ten thousand miles in order to join a service battalion and, presumably, invade Europe with it: but when I arrived at the 2nd Battalion, which was encamped in a eucalyptus grove in the hills above Tripoli, I was far from welcome. Malcolm Erskine, who had disliked me when he commanded the 1st Battalion at Chislehurst, was now Brigadier of our brigade;

and Jack Milburne, who had commanded a company in the 1st Battalion, now had Support Company in the 2nd: they had doubtless prepared the other officers for the worst. Men who had shared the almost mystical experience of a desert campaign made a joke of Regimental Headquarters and resented new people from England. It seemed to them intolerable that they should have been sent this freak, Buckle, who had probably only got into the Regiment because he was the Regimental Adjutant's nephew, who was keen on ballet and art, and undoubtedly a bugger. Besides, the Battalion was up to strength. When I marched in to report my arrival with the draft Colonel Guy Taylor was barely civil. 'Why have you come here? We don't want you.' 'I hoped to be able to join the Battalion and go to Europe with them.' 'Well, there's only one faint chance of a vacancy for you. David Fyfe-Jamieson, who's in charge of the Pioneer Platoon, is away sick. If he doesn't recover in time to go wherever we are going you can come instead. But you must go on a mines course. The Sappers run a school down near the beach.' He was hoping to kill me off.

I worked hard, however, and passed the mines course. During my stay in the Royal Engineers' camp, which was one of many between the city and the sea, I used to walk along the Mediterranean shore at night, and it was strange to see nothing but naked men as far as the eye could reach. Back in the eucalyptus grove, I set about instructing my pioneer Platoon, whose duties would be to lay mines, clear enemy mine-fields, blow up houses or bridges and bury the dead. They rather enjoyed their new toys. One afternoon, too hot to be bothered, I left them playing and went to sleep in my bivouac – only to be woken shortly after by a shattering explosion. The mischievous and handsome Sergeant Morrison had stuck two German Teller mines together with gelignite and let them off in the middle of the camp. I was told that a chunk of metal had ripped open the Adjutant's tent, while another had whizzed within inches of the

Commanding Officer's ear. I realized that my final disgrace had come and that I should probably be court-martialled. I entered the mess tent before dinner nervously. To my surprise the senior officers were looking unusually happy behind their moustaches. An unfriendly major smiled at me for the first time. I could not understand it. Then Colonel Guy said, 'Well, Dicky, that was a fine bang. If you can make as much din as that we can't possibly do without you in the Battalion!

So I was allowed to keep the Pioneer Platoon, part of Support Company, which was commanded by pleasure-loving Jack Milburne; and for many months to come Jack and I would get drunk together and laugh like mad.

Although we knew General Montgomery had conquered Sicily by 19 August, it was only after we had embarked on our L.C.I.s (Landing Craft Infantry) and L.S.T.s (Landing Ships Tanks) that we were given maps and told we were going to land in Italy south of Salerno; but it was later said – as if to account for the Germans being on the beach expecting us – that every Arab waiter in the messes of Tripoli had known the Allied plan. We spent six days lying in harbour before sailing, then we were four days at sea. I read *Anna Karenina* and re-read *The Tempest, Far from the Madding Crowd* and *A Passage to India* on the way across.

For the last month Churchill had been in Canada, where the Quebec conference had taken place; then, after addressing Congress, he had spent a few nights with Roosevelt at Hyde Park on the Hudson. He was there when we crossed the Mediterranean. Years later Juliet Duff told me that she once asked Churchill, 'What was your most anxious moment in the war?' and he replied, 'The Salerno landings.' He was so far away; and he kept remembering Gallipoli.

On 3 September the representatives of King Victor Emmanuel and Marshal Badoglio signed an armistice 'in an olive grove near Syracuse', though this was kept secret for a few days because of the Italian Prime Minister's fear of

German reprisals. On the same day Montgomery's Eighth Army crossed the Straits of Messina and landed unopposed at Reggio, Calabria.

On 8 September we sighted land: this was the north coast of Sicily. The capitulation of Italy was announced on the wireless, and there was rejoicing on board. We were under the mistaken impression that our landing would be unopposed, whereas quite a lot of us would be dead by the next evening. On the morning of the 9th a Thanksgiving Service was held, and we sighted Capri about noon. Heat mist prevented me from making out a clear outline of the coast, but I could discern white patches of buildings which I identified on the map as Salerno, Vietri, Amalfi and Positano. I was enraptured to be seeing Italy for the first time.

The Gulf of Salerno is separated from the Bay of Naples by the mountainous Sorrento peninsula. Italian friends later told me that they had watched the spectacle of our landing operations from their balcony at Positano, as if from an opera box. We were part of the American Fifth Army. The British 46th Division, the 56th (which included 201 Guards Brigade) and an American corps were to land on the beaches from Salerno to Agropoli. Even from the low view-point of our vessel the harbour was an amazing sight. I counted a hundred and twenty craft: there were many more – L.C.I.s, L.S.T.s, corvettes, cruisers, battleships. Beyond the beach and plain rose a semi-circle of blue mountains – like Westmorland, I thought. Our brigade was the reserve brigade of the division, our battalion the reserve battalion of the brigade; so we were 'out of the blood bath'. Our rifle companies landed from their two L.C.I.s ahead of us, and we in Support Company, with the carriers and anti-tank guns and 'first flight' transport, hit the beach and began to disembark at 5 p.m. I set foot in Italy.

The fireworks of the naval guns firing tracer over our heads at night were spectacular: but the impetus of our first two days' advance was lost, and our depleted troops were held up along the line of the railway which ran through Battipaglia. We 'dug in', took up defensive positions and waited for Montgomery to arrive from the south to relieve the German pressure. It was touch-and-go whether we should be driven back into the sea. I had little to do except blow up a big stone bridge to prevent our lines from being infiltrated by German tanks, and to lay mines, so I made myself comfortable in the vaulted basement of a farm, started cooking enthusiastically for my platoon – supplementing our lavish rations with local onions, tomatoes and apples – and even went sight-seeing. I found a little, unused notebook in a disabled German tank – near which, I recall, lay the body of a tall fair German whom I found attractive – and began a diary which was continued for over a year.

One of the friends who brightened for me the early part of the Italian campaign was Frank Waldron. He was tall and inclined to fat, with a wing of yellow hair, a relic from his days in the RAF, over his left eye. He had a broad, pale, sleepy cat face, with a nose which showed signs of becoming a beacon like Bardolph's in later life. Most of the officers who had served in the desert had developed individualities of dress which would have caused a scandal at home: but Frank was the most un-regimental officer who ever lived. The 'desert rats' who had spent the winter of 1942 out of the line, training in Syria, had all bought huge sheepskin 'Hebron coats' which would be produced as the cold weather came on: Frank's was the most voluminous, with the orangest hide outside and the shaggiest wool within. As the winter progressed, this big soft man seemed to turn up the collar higher and to clutch the garment more desperately around him with the gesture of a defenceless débutante in an evening cloak. Whether he was really reduced to a sponge of self-pity by the exertions of army life, by deprivation of girls and liquor, or whether, like Falstaff, he had merely perfected a self-pity act to raise a laugh, his gloomy prognostications, as he sat slumped on some stone, usually had the effect of cheering me up. 'D'you realize, Dicky, we're a doomed generation? It's all very well laughing, you superficial degenerate. D'you know what our expectation of life is? Eighty-five to one. Honestly, we can't possibly expect to live more than a month at the very most. My God, why did I ever leave the air force! Half the battalion are dead, and the other half are in a state of mutiny. Can you *wonder*, with officers like us?'

On 12 September Mussolini, who had been imprisoned since 26 July, was rescued by German paratroopers from an hotel in the Abruzzi and flown to a conference with Hitler. The next night I wrote:

I go to G Company and am led right forward to a charming house (Gunner Observation Post guarded by us) in a romantic orchard just by the railway, where we lay forty Hawkins mines across a track under the noses of some enemy tanks. Return at 1 a.m. and am just going to bed when Colonel Guy telephones for me and one section. The Coldstream to our right are being attacked. Take Sgt Morrison's section up under heavy shell and Spandau fire to Battalion Attack Headquarters at Morella farm, narrowly missing being blown up by Hawkins laid across the road by Coldstream and left unguarded – but as I am walking in front of the truck I see and remove them. As we come up road twenty-five yards from Battalion Headquarters a shell – from our own guns we think [but we were often thinking that, possibly wrongly] – lands on it, making the tower wobble. I visualize them all dead. Find Colonel Guy with Tom B. and Frank rather shaken up. Sit about with them till dawn, listening to the battle and enemy tanks on our right. No job for us. Result of battle: the Coldstream repelled the attack, which was intended as a divisional one, with a spearhead of fifty tanks, with infantry hanging on to them. Troop-carrying vehicles following up never unloaded. Two German prisoners said our guns prevented the attack developing. Coldstream put out [rendered useless] three armoured vehicles. Only two killed, I believe. I return at 7 a.m. with the section and make breakfast for the others, who had a good night's rest and are still asleep.

On 16 September Churchill cabled to General Alexander 'Cramponnez partout' (Hold on tight), but the worst was over. Kesselring had already begun to withdraw his divisions northwards.

I did not particularly enjoy leading my pioneers up a road under fire from the enemy, but what is called 'courage' comes so much more easily to an officer, who must play a part and set an example, than to the men he commands, who have less to lose; and since I was a bit of an actor I survived various ordeals without being convicted of cowardice. My facile bravado would diminish as the months went by. I disliked burying the dead who had lain for days exposed to the autumn sun. One friend was still recognizable, though dark in colour, jammy in texture and alive with maggots: and I thought of the day he had arrived at Pirbright. On 21 September I had a close shave.

> Our field is dive bombed. I am standing watching A.A. Oerlikon tracer when I hear a patter all round me on the ground. Everyone else has dived for cover. The truck in front is pouring water. A man on the ground screaming 'Help!' I am putting a field-dressing on his wounded leg when I look round and see the Sergeant-Major's servant lying on his back, shirt open, blood pumping from a hole in his heart. Know he is dead, so continue dressing leg. Then see Pipe-Major Raeburn curled up with the top of his skull blown off and brains pouring out. Put dressing on his head in case, as he seems alive. [In fact I put his brains back into his head, replaced the top of his skull and tied it on with a bandage under his chin: but he died later.] Send man across river for doctor. Ian F. wounded in side and leg, Sgt C. in thigh, others slightly. If I had taken cover I should have got it too, as the Germans were spraying the ditch . . .

That afternoon I went sight-seeing. 'Finally locate *all* graves. Drive south to Paestum. Roads crowded with Americans.

Nobly proportioned Greek temples – Doric – thickly occupied by un-Greek-looking Americans . . . Letters from Mama, Granny . . .'

The letters Lily wrote me during the last months of 1943 have not survived. But the letters I wrote to her, to my mother, to Dolly, to Ursula Tyrwhitt and to Erich Alport were all preserved. My mother gave me those she had kept, and Ursula's niece gave me Ursula's after her death. It fell to my lot to go through not only Granny's and Dolly's papers after their deaths, but also Erich's. What is more, all these dear ones copied out extracts from the letters they received, and when I found these extracts too, I was embarrassed that my careless reports should exist in several editions. The explosion made by my blowing up the bridge near Battipaglia had repercussions in England, for Lily wrote to Erich about it in December.

On 25 September I awoke with fever and a pain behind my eyes. I had malaria. For four days I was very ill in a field-hospital, unable to swallow, sleep or lie still. Then I was given a day-long saline and glucose injection, which restored me like magic, and I began reading Balzac. I was first flown to Catania in Sicily, where my hospital was in a brand-new barracks, then transferred to a Red Cross convalescent home at Taormina, where I dwelt in bliss, gazing at the alternative views of Etna to the south and the Calabrian mountains on the mainland, exploring the Greek theatre, making friends with a Colonel Hill from Shropshire who was a keen archaeologist, reading, writing short stories and drinking white vermouth with soda water and lemon peel. After three years of being so highly organized in England, it was strange to learn that I was expected to find my own way back to join the battalion, wherever they were. There was nothing to stop me disappearing into the heart of Sicily and becoming a bandit. Although I was driven into Catania in General Oliver Leese's car, I spent three days there trying to get a lift to Messina. At Messina I attached myself to a convoy of

American gunners bound for Naples. I thought of Ulysses as we crossed the Straits; and the sailor who checked us off the ferry had a ring on every finger, which was unusual in those days. For four days I drove with the Americans up the west of Italy, sleeping in the back of a command car, thanks to the hospitality of the Battery Commander, 'a lanky Texan'. I became barman and jester to the Yanks, some of whom had probably never met an Englishman before, and we revelled in mutual amazement. I enjoyed their exotic food ('Up in the dark. Breakfast of bacon, powdered egg omelette, hot raisins, apple sauce, apple butter, coffee'), the landscape ('Pass Scylla and see Charybdis. Lovely view from the hills back towards Sicily, Messina, Aeolian islands, Stromboli smoking'), playing a card-game called 'Hearts' in the car at night, and the leisure to read Vigny's *Servitudes et grandeurs militaires* at Gallico Marino. I noticed 'the women round Nicastro wearing traditional scarlet petticoat, with overskirt tucked back and fixed in a bustle behind, usually a black shawl on top and some with the old head-dress with a flap hanging down at the back'; we camped at Belvedere, where I invented 'a punch called Belvedere Beauty' and we talked about 'food, monsters, catholicism'; we turned inland at Sapri 'into a different type of scenery: even more fantastic mountains, but wooded – fir, oak, ash, chestnut – with red and white villages in valleys'; we passed through Lagonegro to sleep at Salaconsilino, where the Americans compared the heavy rain to 'a cow pissing on a flat rock'; wound through passes below ruined towers to emerge on Eboli, with 'a view of our battleground, the Salerno plain and the Sorrento peninsula – much sharper now in the colder weather – and Capri shining clear'. Peasants had already begun to plough the shell-pitted fields by the Battipaglia cross-roads. 'Lunch at Pontecagnano. My last meal with the Americans, who have been very good to me . . . They seemed to like being intruded upon.'

There was no way of knowing how far north the battalion

had penetrated. I slept a night at Salerno, then on 30 October drove through the pass at Cava, spent an hour and a half examining Pompeii, saw for the first time the Golfo de Napoli and Vesuvius smoking, then, a month behind the first 'liberating' troops, entered Naples. I was directed to the immense Albergo dei Poveri, built by the first Bourbon king in 1750.

> Find transit camp in the poor house, vast, dark and indescribable – like hell. Passages so big that cars are driven round them. Take half-an-hour to find the office; clock in. No bedding or blankets available and no eating utensils, so put necessities in small pack, leave luggage and stagger forth in the dusk to seek the Town Major for permission to sleep at Transit Hotel. Walk miles, sweating and desperate, misdirected three times, find office shut, in dark, but a clerk gives me a chit and I continue to Albergo Patria in Via Sanfelice.

Suddenly things looked up. I found shelter, drink, food and an old friend:

> Am given candle-lit bedroom; and rejoice to find much wine and whisky in lamp-lit bar. Drink two large whiskies, one Strega and a bottle of Italian 'champagne' (250 lire). Talk to two Americans. A Royal Welsh Fusilier major hints that I can get a lift to the battalion from C.M.P.s [Corps of Military Police]. Dine alone. Then meet Tony Mattei [whom I had known in London through Evan Tredegar], who is in A.M.G.O.T. [Allied Military Government of Occupied Territory]. Sit and gossip with him and others, drinking red wine. To bed a little drunk and read Stendhal.

CHAPTER 11

Around Naples, 1943–4

Unlike Sir Philip Sidney, unlike Milton, unlike Coke of Norfolk, unlike my ancestor Burlington or many another *milordo inglese* who made the Grand Tour with his tutors in search of classical art and landscape, unlike Horace Walpole and Thomas Gray, unlike Robert Adam, unlike Beckford, Goethe, Byron, Shelley and Turner, all of whom had crossed the Alps to descend into the land where lemons grow, I had started my *Italienische Reise* at the southern end of Italy. Rome, Florence and Venice would be for me the centres of future happy explorations, but it was on Naples that my dreams were focused throughout the winter of 1943 and until the following summer. Although I would have to play a small part in the tedious business of pushing the Germans northwards, Naples, the ancient capital of pleasure, was always a glamorous and consoling thought at the back of my mind during the early months of the Italian campaign; so that those autumn days, the wild winter and the incredible spring which I saw break through the sacred rocks of Italy, were seen then, and are seen still, through a mellow Virgilian glaze. Having read how the courtiers of the Restoration cast up their eyes and prepared their yawns behind baroque fingers when the King began for the hundredth time a description of his flight after the battle of Worcester and his escape to France, I try to remind myself that the minute details of daily life – food, friendship, sight-seeing, love-making and battle – cannot be so fascinating to others as they are to me, and to confine my narrative within acceptable bounds. Yet it must be stated that the five months I spent with the 2nd Battalion before they returned to England, leaving General Alexander and myself behind, held a special character of gaiety and adventure which set them apart from subsequent campaigning further north.

On this first visit to Naples, although I went dutifully every day to the transit camp to beg a lift to my battalion, who were by this time beyond the Volturno, I was held up for five days, which I spent mostly in the company of Tony Mattei. Tony was a British-born Maltese, descended from a noble Roman family; and his knowledge of Italian had earned him his job of facilitating Anglo-Italian relations. He started me off on my first words of Italian, fed me in the darkest black-market restaurants, took me to the most ornate churches and showed me the most breath-taking views, so that I came to regard him as the magician who held the keys of the enchanted city on its curving bay. In fact Tony introduced me to Naples as Sir William Hamilton had introduced so many Grand Tourists from England a hundred and fifty years before. He was an amusing as well as an instructive companion, and if he ran out of factual information or true stories would imperturbably invent.

I had a link with Naples. My great-great-great-great-grandmother Elizabeth Berkeley, Lady Craven, later Margravine of Anspach, had spent her last years and died there. I knew this, but did not know that I could see her monument – as I did in 1965 – in the Protestant cemetery near the station. A great-great-grand-daughter of King Charles II and Louise de Kéroalle, she was one of the most flamboyant characters to scandalize London society and tour the courts of Europe during the late eighteenth and early nineteenth centuries. Her travels took her as far as St Petersburg and Constantinople. Whether at her instigation or not, her lover, the Margrave of Anspach, Brandenburg and Bayreuth, sold his principality to his uncle King Frederick (the Great) of Prussia in 1790. His wife died in the following year. After the death of Lord Craven six months later, Elizabeth married the Margrave in Lisbon and brought him in triumph to London.* Although she was now a Serene Highness, Queen Charlotte would not receive her at court; so she had to content herself with the privilege of driving in her coach 'within the ride of Hyde Park, where royalty only enters' and with a constant succession of parties and theatricals at Brandenburgh House, near the river at Hammersmith. She had been a friend of young William Beckford, whom she called 'Arab', at the time when his good looks, talents and high spirits – as well as his wealth – dazzled the *beau monde*; and she remained one after his disgrace and ostracism in 1784. They both loved literature, music and the theatre; and when William entrusted to her the manuscript of his *Vathek*, she wrote: '*Etrange arabe . . . je suis endormie et j'ai fait le rêve de la vie de Vathek – quel rêve – Bon Dieu, d'un bout à l'autre ce n'est que Beckfordism* – but seriously, 'tis fine, horribly fine . . .' She thus coined the word I would later apply in my mind to my own love of the fantastic and to the exhibitions I should design in the middle years of the twentieth century. Widowed for the second time, Elizabeth moved to Naples, where she gardened furiously at her villa at Posilippo and, from her palace in Via Chiatamone, scared the wits out of the more staid English Grand Tourists. I am sure I should have got on with her very well.

Just as in the course of battle we hardly gave time to mourn the deaths of comrades, being more interested in the next meal, so in my Neapolitan excursions I was callous of the appalling privations suffered by the teeming poor of that city, which Tony and his Allied Military Government could do little to alleviate. We licentious soldiery looked to the starving Neapolitans to provide us with black-market food, music and sex: while they battened leech-like on us shabby

---

*Lady Craven's character is said to have inspired Schiller's heroine in the play *Kabale und Liebe*.

Inglesi and richer, smarter Americani, hanging on for dear life.

Naples was basking in the remains of summer. My diary provides a few snapshots in the November sun.

> Take a horse-drawn *corricolo* from the transit camp, to which I am to report daily at 12, back to the Albergo Patria, driven by a young man called Gennaro, while his friend Salvatore sits with me inside and teaches me parts of the body in Italian. He says Germans do not believe in God. Meet Tony and we walk to lunch at a Restaurant Falstaff, very dark and full of Americans with tarts . . . Violins . . . white and red wine, macaroni, veal, potatoes, peas, two helpings of parmesan cheese, bread, two apples, salad of celery and potatoes . . . Great gossip . . . Vesuvius spouting flame . . .
>
> Two thirds of Naples has to evacuate itself this morning from 10 to 2 as the electric light is being turned on for the first time and time-bombs are feared . . . Read in Botanical Gardens . . . Drive with Tony to Posilippo to see 'the most beautiful view in the world'. During dinner with Hugh Cudlipp and Cyril James, who run all the British newspapers out here, an air-raid warning . . . all the waiters disappear to the cellar, leaving the bar locked . . .
>
> Wander through back streets, where palaces with courtyards and great armorial gateways are hidden among slums . . . Into Gesu Nuovo . . . acres of coloured marble, painted dome, golden altar, a sunbeam lighting up a figure of the Virgin above it. Watch a fat white priest in smoked glasses taking confessions . . . G. & I go up the hill in a taxi, a long drive to 92 General Hospital. Find D. (leg), Frank (foot and jaundice), S. (unconscious, with bad wound in guts). Walk round wards asking for Scots Guards. Find big Richardson (shrapnel on face); Creighton (rupture); McGovern (abscess on eye); Clark, ex-drummer at Pirbright (armpit); ex-Sgt Stewart (all over); Fulton (foot), etc. Hitch down hill in dusk. Find Mendelssohn's Violin Concerto (BBC) beautifully playing on wireless at hotel . . . Read *Psychopathia Sexualis* in bed . . .

A beautiful Bourbon Neptune fountain in Piazza G. Bovio. Lose my temper and strike out at a boy who climbs on to the carriage, demanding food . . . Lunch at Falstaff, this time to electric light, but to the same tunes on mandoline and violin – 'La Donna é mobile', 'Toreador', 'La Cucaracha', 'Santa Lucia', 'The Merry Widow Waltz' . . . . the proprietor very obsequious, saying 'for us everything is possible' . . . After dinner get rather carried away talking about Proust . . .

At last I got a lift to our Brigade Headquarters, crossed the Volturno and found Colonel Guy, Feathers and two others playing cards in Hebron coats 'at the bottom of a hill'. 'The cold compared to Naples is astonishing'. I was still in summer uniform. 'My Pioneers are disbanded. I am to have a special Patrol Group – as far as I can see, to do all the dirty jobs the companies don't like.'

I had arrived just in time for the first battle of Monte Camino. Colonel Guy Taylor was going back to England, and Feathers, though still only a major, would be in command. I drove with him and the company commanders to reconnoitre the area in which we should concentrate before attacking the mountain. For the first time I saw its three peaks, 727, 963 – to be known because of a ruin near the summit as Monastery Hill – and 615, which would be the last we had to overcome before we went down the other side to cross the Garigliano.

November 6

Fine, cold morning . . . Find Jack Milburne (my Support Company commander) at Teano, a circular walled village; the pipe band playing down below in a ravine. Autumn colours. We stack the jeep with luggage and drive on to the battalion in the chestnut woods.

In the dark the Coldstream can be seen attacking [the hamlet of] Calabritto. In this they suffered bad casualties from mines. The Grenadiers on the right are climbing up Bare Arse Slope to 727. We set off in single file, Right

Flank, F Company, Battalion HQ, G Company, down-hill, being in reserve and guarding the Coldstream's left flank, to face down the valley. Tedious, sleepy march down bad track, ending for us at a cottage, which becomes Battalion HQ Companies dig in around and to the front of us. The cottage has four rooms leading one out of the other like a Cotswold house, and is cleaner and neater than most Italian hovels. Several eager families in a shelter in the garden produce light from wicks floating in olive oil. Nothing doing for us tonight while the Coldstream die on the mines and the Grenadiers clamber up the rocks by moonlight. Jack and I sleep on top of a straw-mattressed double bed in the furthest room. Many religious pictures on the wall and the peasants' clothes heaped in baskets all around.

My next day's excursion and its consequences illustrate as well as anything in Tolstoy's *War and Peace* the confusion of battle, in which subsequent historians have to rack their brains to find a pattern. Inadequate information or briefing, orders misinterpreted (in this case by me), a fault in map-reading or the lack of a map, darkness or bad weather, all these can affect the judgement, causing wrong decisions or delays.

November 7

The Coldstream have taken Calabritto. I am ordered to take a patrol to find if the lower slopes of M. Camino beyond the Cocuruzzo [stream] are occupied. Take Sgt Woodside, Hirst, Brickell. Pass Coldstream HQ and am warned against mines. We pick our way forward down the gorge to the river, find elaborate wired mine-fields with obvious trip-wires and notices, and go through them; then, on far slopes, wire entanglements and prepared positions – abandoned. Pick a chrysanthemum and return just in time – one o'clock – with the information, hot and tired. After lunch I have to walk another three or four miles to tell David Forbes, Coldstream Commanding Officer, about patrol. [He died of wounds that night.] Loot odd painting from a bombed church. On return, hear the battalion are to go up the hill after the Grenadiers. I am to go straight off with a large patrol to contact the Grenadiers, find a concentration area for the battalion, place guides for them and recce a route for the attack on 615 tomorrow. Take both Sgt Dixon and Sgt Woodside, etc. As we leave the cottage minus greatcoats the rain begins in earnest. The climbing consists of leaping from crag to crag, slipping, tumbling, grasping, tugging. On the way up we meet a stretcher carried by eight men, who say what hell the hilltop is, and that they have been hours getting down. Rain, cold, thunder and lightning. We are sniped from the left and cross over to cling to the precipice on the right of Bare Arse Slope. Arriving at the top [727], greeted by a blazing stonk on Grenadier positions, rocks splintered and flying all around us – crashing noise. I send Sgt Dixon and Black back to warn John [Weir] that the climb this way would be impossible for a battalion in the dark. (I had not been told that it was anyway up the muletrack to the right of Bare Arse Slope that the battalion was planning to go.) I continue and find the Grenadiers – first seeing a hysterical man howling with his arms above his head. Find Hugh Cholmeley commanding in a trench on the off side (precipice) from the rain and shells. Some of the Grenadiers have been without food since they came up – or water – and no medical aid or means of evacuation. It is now dusk. Go with the Grenadier Patrol Officer round the hill to look at the approach to 615. I go on alone, but before I can examine ground thoroughly a mist comes down and, afraid of being lost, I return . . . After waiting about till 9 in the rain, misery and shells for the battalion, I think they may have taken my advice and decided not to come. The Grenadiers are out of wireless touch. Rather than sit still and freeze without cover in sodden clothes behind a rock, decide to take patrol back to meet battalion or if they have not started rejoin them. On the way down I ponder (mistakenly no doubt) on the futility of the operation, and think that the mountain could as well be by-passed and its defendants ignored and starved out. Meet Sgt Forsythe and signallers going up to lay line. Arriving at bottom I find the Grenadier main HQ, where the Adjutant tells me the Battalion [Scots Guards] are going up the mule-track. News to me! I dash with patrol left to Saraceni, where by luck I meet G Company waiting at a crossroads. Tell first John, then Alastair, then the Commanding Officer, my story. They have just been told by a Berkshire patrol that the mule-track leads nowhere. Remembering the precipice, and not having been told to look out for the track, I am apt to confirm this. We walk back to main Grenadier HQ and after awful difficulty the CO gets through to the Brigadier on the wireless. He says, 'If mule-track impassable, go up Bare Arse like the Grenadiers.' Being told the top cannot be reached this way before dawn, he says, 'Await further orders.' [But the Berkshires and I were both wrong in thinking the mule-track was a *cul de sac*; and as the battalion had to go up the mule-track it would have been better if they had gone up then.] F Company, who were helping the Coldstream that afternoon, operating independently, were never stopped going up, and under Bones R. clambered up to their disaster. With the soles of my desert boots seven-eighths off, soaked and exhausted, I drag back to the cottage, and after trying to dry myself, get into bed between two other snoring officers.

November 8

I stay in bed all day. Rain. Hirst goes back to the chestnut woods to fetch socks, cigarettes and *La Chartreuse de Parme*. Talk to Bobby B. about our mutual relations.

The weather changed again: the 9th was fine. With our Intelligence Officer, I looked up at the formidable mountain and we recited poetry to each other. I obliged with Yeats's 'Long-legged Fly'. 'That civilization may not sink, its great battle lost . . .' A peasant gave us apples. Battalion headquarters were now in 'an attractive group of buildings near San Clemente'. I wrote my diary, sitting in the sun; and talked in French to some 'charming Mauritian pioneers, being used as porters' about 'their island, the King and Queen'. This had unexpected results. They laid at my feet a sack of potatoes, wine and a walking stick. From the god-like euphoria induced by their devotion I had a rude awakening.

Interrupted in the middle of an excellent stew cooked by the Mauritians by the arrival of the Commanding Officer [Feathers]. Right Flank and G Company are to go up the mule-track tonight. I am to go with the Commanding Officer as Staff Officer. Adjutant to stay at the bottom. Rather annoyed. We assemble at the R.A.P. [Regimental Aid Post, where the doctor was] at Mieli at the foot of the mountain after dark. A drunk man arrives, having had more than one rum ration, crying, 'Shoot me, sir, shoot me!' and vomiting. Men are to carry one blanket, wear greatcoat. Start uphill. Right Flank, G Company, Battalion Headquarters in single file, up and up very slowly, stopping and falling asleep on our feet every twenty paces. Very hot walking with impedimenta: very cold as soon as one stops. As soon as we arrive at the top, i.e. the ridge between the Grenadiers and the lower slopes of Monastery Hill, facing 819, Right Flank start rounding up Spandau nests and sending down prisoners. We establish Battalion Headquarters just below the ridge in a trench with rocks above; a smaller trench for Gunner major, another for Signallers. G Company to the left forward, Right Flank higher up and more in contact with the enemy.

For five days I lived in a foxhole with Feathers, exposed to the enemy and the elements; and we were quite happy. Although, in our eyrie two thousand feet above sea level, the fleshpots of Naples seemed far away, we were not out of contact with the human race, for our Signallers in the next trench maintained wireless communication with the Adjutant and Brigade Headquarters; and the Divisional Commander, General McCreery, even came up to visit us. One night I found a stranger in the Signallers' trench, who turned out to be a hygiene expert from the War Office who had flown out to see that we were taking our anti-malaria pills. 'Poor soul!' I wrote. 'He has left a dinner-party at the General's to visit us up the mountain. We discuss ants and Italy. He gives me Oxo cubes and chestnuts and takes a note to Mama.' (The generous and rather sentimental letter he was kind enough to write to my mother on his return to England was of course copied and passed on to Lily and to Pat Kinnaird.) A mule-train came up the mountain with our rations every night, but the Italian porters showed a tendency to mutiny because of the Germans' accurate shelling. I found that the effect of blast from a near shell was to make me scream obscene abuse. Together with the Oxford and Buckinghamshire Light Infantry we attacked and were counter-attacked, but the well-placed and well-fortified Spandau posts on Monastery Hill prevented us from capturing that three-thousand-foot peak. I wrote a mock newspaper *Camino Griff* ['Griff' was the current slang for 'news'] and five manuscript copies were circulated among the companies. Its slogan was 'The Lowest Circulation at the Highest Altitude'. When on the evening of the 13th we were warned to evacuate the mountain next day and to 'dissipate our dump', a party of Queens' were very angry at having to carry down the boxes of ammunition they had just carried up:

November 14

Rain. Mist. A few shells . . . The tracks have all become rivers. We thank God we are going down tonight. I wander round companies for the last time and gossip in rain. Iain Moncreiffe, who came up the hill two days ago, has been run over by a huge boulder which hurtled downhill into a wadi; but he is still fairly alive. Evacuation starts with Ox and Bucks at 5.30. I go downhill early with Iain and my boys to contact REs who are laying mines across the track after everyone has passed. We lie in wet grass, talking heraldry. See everyone through. Slither down path in dark, guarding rear. Luckily the Germans hold off their guns – very civil. A Fusilier blows his leg off on the mines through coming down the wrong way. We get to the bottom about 10 and check out through the Brigade Intelligence Officer beyond Mieli. Go on lorry, icy cold, *via* traffic blocks to our Battalion area in a muddy valley east of Roccamonfina. Find everyone about 2; eat cold stew, take off sodden clothes, scrounge blankets, sleep in front of Commanding Officer's car, the new padre in the back. I was last off the mountain . . .

Was it really less than three weeks since I had been feasting with Tony Mattei in Naples? The first – unsuccessful – Battle of Monte Camino was over.

Our ten days out of the line, between the two battles of Monte Camino, resting, tidying up and making a pretence of training, survive radiant in my memory: there were the joys of friendship, landscape, food and drink. Would this happy interlude have been forgotten if I had not kept a diary? We were to retire to a village on the Neapolitan plain, surrounded by mountains from which there were breath-taking views; in the company of Iain Moncreiffe, with whom I found I had more and more in common, and of Anthony Balfour, my old friend from Chislehurst days, who had come from North Africa to join the Battalion while I was away sick, I could gossip and get drunk. Even the slow move back to our rest area through 'golden woods and wet, muddy valleys' was enjoyable.

> Anthony [who, being Second-in-Command of a company, had not been up the hill] comes to fetch me to lunch with Right Flank, i.e. Bobby Bulkeley, Anthony, Iain and David Moncreiffe (in bed) [who] are in a feudal hovel . . . Sardines, pickles, jam, figs, cheese. Very hungry. Talk about Beckford, schools, Wykehamists. Bobby shows snaps, including one of Mr Churchill arriving by plane in Teheran with no one to meet him. Piles of chestnuts in

every corner and under the family's bed. David M. [Iain's young cousin, whom I had first met when he came up Mount Camino to replace a wounded officer, and whom Iain was to succeed in 1957 as eleventh baronet] in bed in the smallest room in the world, with a huge fire, reading Shakespeare. Walk back with A. and I. through an afternoon like autumn in England, feeling holiday-moodish. I make a punch of red wine, rum, whisky, vermouth, oranges, apples, lime-juice and sugar, for eight.

Even a two-hour talk next day by the new Divisional Commander, General Templer, in a disused church of St Sebastian, during which he offered 'no compliments or promises, but plenty of good ideas for training and fighting – right but depressing', and which I listened to with 'frozen feet', did not lower my spirits. Half-an-hour's drive next day brought us to Zuni, below the Rocchetta hills, where the battalion had fought in my absence. 'My platoon are billeted in a row of pink cottages. We officers live in an upper room which gives one way on the nearby hills, the other on a monastery garden full of golden oranges and red persimmons.' Battalion Headquarters, where I used to dine most evenings, was in a large house which, with its outbuildings, surrounded three sides of a courtyard. 'Fantastic Italian-Victorian interior, with many hideous paintings, trompe l'oeil ceilings, plaster statues.' Frank Waldron arrived from hospital, 'wearing his enormous Hebron coat'.

We were settled for a while in this attractive village, whose surrounding landscape made me feel I was Byron, Keats and Shelley rolled into one, and my three special friends were all present. There were a few regimental duties to perform, but for the most part we could 'fleet the time carelessly as they did in the golden world'. I have already described Frank, who had just recovered from jaundice. The tall, fair and elegant Anthony Balfour, whose mother was a Lascelles, must have

been the most sybaritic officer in the Brigade of Guards –
which is saying a lot. He was well up in the London
theatrical world, knew Hermione Gingold and Hermione
Baddeley, and had a 'camp' sense of humour. He referred to
the lower classes as 'slaves' and was apt to run them down in
his jeep if they got in the way. Iain Moncreiffe, a skeleton in a
false moustache, was so delicate that he could only have got
into the regiment by bribery or family pull. He was always
lost in dreams of ancestral splendour: but though his
historical, heraldic and genealogical lore seemed to merge
with mythology, it was also related to a realistic political
sense and a rigorous code of conduct. He was a very kind man
– which perhaps Anthony was not. Neither Anthony, who
had been a peace-time soldier and now took over command
of Right Flank, nor Iain, who commanded one of Anthony's
platoons, was cut out for war-time soldiering – but perhaps
that can be said of some of the best soldiers. Iain was often in a
state of Pictish rage at being passed over for a captaincy.
Frank had no patience with Iain's snobbery and regimental
ideas; and Iain was not much interested in Frank, who
descended from few Scottish kings. Anthony, Iain, Frank
and I derided the 'keen-ness' of new arrivals from England,
and complained incessantly of the young Adjutant's efficiency. Yet John Weir, later killed at Anzio, would go
down to history as 'probably the best Company Commander
in the Brigade'.

When we had a church parade in the courtyard I watched
'bewildered Italians hang over balconies to observe our
northern ritual'. A 'grimacing little deaf-and-dumb dwarf'
with a 'gift for pantomime' attached himself to Battalion
Headquarters. 'He has a motor-car ballet and a drinking
ballet,' I wrote. 'Anthony is terrified.' Frank also swore he
had seen 'a legless creature drag itself across the courtyard and
drink a puddle'. When Frank and I dined in Right Flank
with Anthony and Iain we found them in 'a Cecil Beaton
room with crimson, olive green and gold wallpaper, with

curly satin-covered sofas, old photographs in fretwork frames shaped like trophies, and a pianola' which made very odd noises one night until we discovered we were playing *Aïda* backwards. I read aloud short stories I had written in Egypt and Sicily. Iain had discovered a Guardsman who wrote poetry, and he recited some of it.

Next day Feathers took the officers on to some high ground to practise a military form of conceptual art, known as a TEWT, tactical exercise without troops.

> A wonderful day. Drive up to Rocchetta among the hills, passing David Loder's grave. (I had spent a weekend with him at Glastonbury.) See a fantastic Jacques Callot funeral procession leaving the village to go up the mountain road to a chapel: three very small children, a peasant in rags holding a cross, the priest in a surplice, the plain wooden coffin borne on shoulders, two women in shawls, a few men with their hands in their pockets, and last, a boy carrying a pick and shovel. No pomp except the salutes of twenty Scots Guards officers . . . We cross a little cultivated valley to higher hills (where, while I was away, Anthony did well). The most splendid view I have ever seen. Foreground of autumn woods; the village of Rocchetta on its hill; the cultivated plain; the sea and Ischia one way; the other way endless mountains, blue and grey, some snow-capped, with purple cloud shadows travelling across; Croce, Camino, Cassino rising from the flat green plain; and the gap between them which is the road to Rome. There are one or two solitary figures going about their errands in the hills.

I left a company party for which I had made a punch in dixies – 'ten gallons of wine, two gallons of vermouth, two gallons of rum, one gallon orange juice, sugar', at which there was a 'brains trust' with 'questions about Ireland's neutrality, the House of Lords and miners' wages (fierce discussion)' to talk as soberly as possible to two men who had run away just before we climbed Mount Camino, and whom I had to defend at a Court Martial on the following day. This was held in the former Royal Palace of Caserta, 'the last flourish of Bourbon pride'; and I walked up the 'stupendous staircase' and round the state apartments. There was a cloud of discontent hanging over the battalion, the 'five-year men', who considered themselves due to be sent home on leave, infecting newer arrivals with their grievances. Nevertheless we were ordered into action again, for Monte Camino had to be taken, and we left Zuni on 2 December.

> Talk to McCuaig, the poet. Give him Keats, Tennyson and a notebook. Leave in convoy . . . Eastern hills beautiful under snow. Pass through a battery of twenty-five-pounders near Roccamonfina, making a deafening noise. A vast barrage is going down on the mountain. De-bus and eat stew in the dark near Conca. The battalion moves in single file along a muddy rocky track to San Clemente – about four miles, very slow going. Sleep in a field beneath a fig-tree with the padre, who snores. Cold but no rain. Half a million shells on Monte Camino in the night.

I made up a song to be sung to the tune of *Tipperary* and sang it to my platoon at the foot of the mountain:

> It's a long climb up Mount Camino,
> It's a long way to go,
> And we'll all need a drop of *vino*
> For the mule-track's very slow.
> Good-bye Calabritto, Farewell Bare Arse Slope!
> It's a long, long climb up Mount Camino,
> But the last time, we hope.

The way up was indeed slow. 'I have to lead the battalion up the mountain . . . G Company grumble and swear about their Everest packs. Whenever the swearing rises to a roar I halt the battalion for a rest. Eventually halt for ten minutes every ten minutes.' I read later that General von Senger, commanding 15th Panzer Grenadier Division, who were defending the mountain, proposed to withdraw to a new line west of the Garigliano; that Kesselring reported this to Hitler, who forbade him to allow a retreat; and that the Führer's interference was 'brushed aside'. If the general could have heard us grumbling as we climbed he might have decided to hold on a little longer. We pushed on next day over ridges which had been strongly held three weeks before, to see new cultivated fields cradled between peaks and to look down at last on the Garigliano valley, 'the Promised Land for which we have all been fighting', with the famous Abbey of Cassino beyond and, to the south-west, a calm sea.

The second battle of Monte Camino was over, but it still remained to keep in touch with the retreating enemy. On the night of 9 December I was ordered to take a patrol to report whether some bridges over the Garigliano leading to Route 6 (Via Casilina) had been blown. I was thus for an hour or two the forrardest man in our division.

> Anthony says he can give me no men . . . most of Right Flank, including Signallers, drunk . . . I get Cpl Musgrave and one Morrow, however. Heavy rain, of course, sets in. Iain points out roads to me between intervals of being sick, which he is every night apparently. [Years later Iain discovered he had an allergy to onions and garlic.] Set off at 9.30 into the unknown – no information about the enemy or Americans on our right, so scared stiff. Walk along road except for once when we think we hear movement and make a long and muddy detour. Shelled accurately by our own guns throughout . . . See five dead donkeys. Find two bridges intact, the third – a big one – blown.

It was Anthony's birthday on 11 December, so on the 10th when I went to dinner with him in his hovel I took him a glass lemon found among the debris in mine. The Germans always smashed everything in the peasants' houses, china, glass, furniture, before retreating. 'We drink punch by the fire, with Italian eyes glaring at us from the surrounding gloom.' History would reveal that the British and German casualties during the second battle of Monte Camino were almost equal – 941 and 974. The name of this obscure mountain would join those of Namur, Dettingen, Egypt, Waterloo, Alma, Tel-el-Kebir, Modder River and God knows what other victories among the Battle Honours of the Scots Guards; and today anyone watching Guard Mounting at Buckingham Palace, if he were able to get close enough – which is improbable – could read 'Monte Camino' embroidered in gold on the Colour borne by the Ensign of the Guard.

I got into Naples to buy Christmas fare for the company and felt 'outlandish in my muddy boots, with my tall stick'. We celebrated in a flat land near the mouth of the Garigliano. It was the best time of the year for views. My diary recorded 'A blue cloudless day, with the whole bay from Ischia to Gaeta clearly visible'; 'a triumphal march of pale golden clouds'; 'the mountains behind Gaeta clear but delicate as if painted on a pearl'. Returning from dinner with F Company in a jeep without lights, I was overturned with the jeep on top of me, face downward in a stream. I crawled out with no bones broken, but got 'three stitches in the back of my head, the poet McCuaig holding a torch'. I wrote buoyantly to Ursula Tyrwhitt on the penultimate day of 1943:

> Snow-top't mountains, white villages and ruined castles. It is like dancing in a ballet conceived by Shelley, décor by Turner, music by Debussy. So far I am still dancing. I wish you could come round for a gossip between the acts. Smoke hangs above Vesuvius like an unanswered prayer . . . The other day an officer in the Cheshires looked at me recognizingly and asked if I came from London. I said Yes; and he said 'Thought I recognized the accent.'

We were to move back for our rest at last. I went ahead, looking for billets, and early one morning, crouched over a hole dug in a garden, watched the sun rise behind Vesuvius, 'the smoke bright pink'. Anthony returned from a brief staff job wearing what he called his 'new brooch' – it was the Military Cross. He, Frank and I went off on leave together. Instead of stopping at Sorrento, which was organized as a leave 'resort', we pushed on to out-of-bounds Positano on the south side of the peninsula, off which lay I Galli, the three rocky islands which belonged to Massine. In the 'vertical village' of Positano I made my first 'Italian' friend, Countess Nora Gaetani d'Arragona, who was in fact born Pattison, of the Anglo-Italian ship-building firm (her great-great-grandfather had built the Naples-Pompeii railway), with a German mother. Frank photographed Nora's two-year-old daughter, Raimonda, who would become a dear friend of mine a quarter of a century later. On the way back to Aversa, we heard *La Traviata* and *Il Barbiere* at the San Carlo in Naples, which had been opened up for the troops; and as I yielded the best place in the box to Anthony he said, 'Pass the tiara.' He and I visited Herculaneum which I found 'not so nice as Pompeii' because 'the squalid slum houses which overlook it, with their washing hanging out, ruin the illusion'. We admired the House of the Cervi, however, and Anthony said they must have been 'stinking rich' and given 'marvellous parties'.

We heard that our immediate attack across the Garigliano was to coincide with a landing south of Rome. Our 1st Battalion was coming from North Africa to take part in the latter, and when Anthony was ordered back to a depot before joining them as a company commander I was so depressed I 'started drinking rum and orange before tea'. I never saw him again. Years later I found out that he was my third cousin once removed on my mother's side, and my fifth cousin once removed on my father's side.

[Aversa]   [19 January 1944]

Dearest Granny,

I get your letters regularly – the last written on 3

January . . . We are really very lucky to have Italy as a battleground and not Russia or Burma. Do write a little larger on your airgraphs as they are so hard to read when reproduced in quarter scale . . . Stone pines are very pretty, like romantic umbrellas. In the next war we must have telephones to ring our relations up on every night.

[Cellole, on the Appian Way,
   below Minturno]   [22 January 1944]

Dearest Mama

Your Christmas gaieties [at the hospital at Woodbast-wick Hall] sound exhausting. I had a charming letter from Diana Cator saying how wonderful you had been for the last four years and how everything was due to you for the smooth running of the hospital and the men's good behaviour . . . Letters are very quick nowadays. I should like the Joseph Severn book [by Lady Birkenhead] as I hope soon to be seeing Keats's last resting place . . . I have just made myself a fearfully smart hat with the Balaclava helmet you knitted four years ago and my small star stuck in it. But it rather needs a veil.

Four days later

Sitting in roaring sunshine . . . Tonight I have ordered soup, corn-beef hash with potatoes, onions and green peas, and pancakes with treacle and orange salad: so you see we do not starve . . . I wish you could be sitting in the sun here with me in a yellow linen frock, screwing up your eyes . . .

For six weeks we occupied various positions north of the Garigliano near Minturno, facing, westwards, Scauri and the Gaeta promontory, and, northwards, the Auruncian mountains. I was now Intelligence Officer and in attendance on our new Colonel, but I still went patrolling. One lovely morning when I was out sniffing around the enemy lines, gathering flowers and a new kind of anti-personnel mine, our

Battalion Headquarters was hit by a stray shell. Everyone there was wounded, and the Commanding Officer died a few days later. My patrol had perhaps saved my life. On 24 February I went out again to question peasants about the Germans' habits and positions.

> The old man in S. Vito proves unprofitable, cannot walk, never leaves his garden, has seen nobody. Give him bully beef and cigarettes. He gives me three eggs. So on to another farm where I find an old woman of eighty-four and her deaf and dumb daughter, about forty, living alone in considerable boredom.

Years later my account of this patrol was quoted at greater length in the Regimental History, whose compiler commented:

> Eggs were not the sole commodity Lieutenant Buckle collected; a brother officer alleged that he 'walked over to the German lines in daylight, rummaged about at will, and usually returned with odd curious books, abstruse and pornographic. One day he returned with a bridal dress which he wore for dinner in the evening.'

The 2nd Battalion were to go home at last, and as I had been abroad so little time it was unlikely that I should be allowed to go with them. We withdrew to Sorrento and I recorded 'a blossom fringe round the slopes of Vesuvius'. Our 1st Battalion, back from Anzio, were in billets nearby: they had lost their Commanding Officer, fourteen other officers and 122 Other Ranks killed or died of wounds, nine officers and 303 Other Ranks wounded, and four officers and 213 Other Ranks missing, mostly prisoners. Our battalion headquarters was in a magnificent villa overlooking the bay. Feathers refused to allow me to engage an Italian chef to lend variety to our officers' dinners because he could not make porridge. My personal attempts to enliven (i.e. shock) the mess perhaps went too far, for Iain Moncreiffe told me years later that I came into dinner one evening announcing, 'My dears, I've just slept with a Cardinal's nephew.' On 18 March Vesuvius obliged with an eruption, the biggest since 1899. Next day I was Picket Officer, as I had been on that other fiery night at the Tower of London in 1940.

> After dinner go to a party at the sergeants' mess . . . Dance wildly with Sgt MacDonald . . . walk to a terrace overlooking the sea to watch the eruption . . . Forks, fans, fingers and flowers of flame rising in the air; and a thin scarlet stream running down to the left – towards Naples . . . Turn out the guard and to bed about one.

Three days later, returning with Iain from a trip to Naples, where I was entertained by the first of several Salvatores and Gennaros ('600 lire'), none of whom was a Cardinal's nephew, I thought the city was 'thick with artificial smoke', but it was ash from the volcano; and when the wind changed two days later a grey snow fell on Sorrento, which created a fog so dark that vehicles needed lights at midday, and we needed umbrellas, which we had not got, to avoid pollution.

The 2nd Battalion sailed for England in April; the 1st Battalion relieved Poles in central Italy; and I was posted to the Infantry Reinforcement and Training Depot, known as the IRTD, a kind of Pirbright, which was growing up outside the village of Rotondi 'on a great inland plain on the way to Benevento, surrounded by spectacular mountains'. During the three months I spent there Rome fell and the Second Front was launched in Normandy; my aunt Christian Buckle became a nun at last, my uncle Eric Graham became a bishop and I became a captain. I was also able to watch the advance of spring in the Italian countryside, and to explore more of the province of Naples.

> I have a room with Hugo Charteris and Giles Mundy in one of the better houses of the village. Most officers live in tents in the camp. A central mess in a great sunless house with a courtyard and variegated wallpapers. There are about a hundred officers of all five regiments of the

brigade. Over four hundred Scots Guardsmen . . . I am to be Training Officer to our company . . . Montesarchio, a town with a castle on a hilltop nearby (a Poussin outline) was the Roman Caudium. This is where the Battle of the Caudine Forks took place.

I heard the morning bells of Easter, however, in Naples, with Salvatore

> . . . in a sinister *pensione* on the top floor of a barrack-like house in Vicoletto Berio, one of the narrow lanes with steps which climb the hillside in the poor quarter north of the Via Roma. My bedroom is vast, with dark brown gilt-embossed wallpaper, a triple bed, scarlet blankets. The house is run by a bearded old man and two old women, and presumably kept going by a tart (about thirty-five) with frizzed yellow hair, who bounces in wearing a blue taffeta dressing-gown to look at us, rolls all over us and waves her tits about.

No 1. I.R.T.D. [Rotondi] C.M.F.   13 April 1944

Dearest G

You will notice the change of address . . . This bit of country is very beautiful, a cultivated inland plain planted with poplars; and all around it hills higher than any in the British Isles [as I thought], with castles and monasteries – we climb them daily! The wild flowers are innumerable – anemones, snow-drops, crocus, periwinkles, grape hya cinths, cillas, orchids, Star of Bethlehem, campion, violets, primroses, daisies. You wonder what has given the mountain paths their carefully swept appearance, until you see the women dragging great bundles of brushwood downhill at a run. The charcoal-burners pursue their ancient calling five thousand feet above sea level; and one sees strange beehives of timber being prepared, to be covered in earth, lit and left to smoulder. Tuesday was the *festa* and the local saint, Sta Maria della Stella, was carried in state round the village with a brass band playing selections from opera, virgins lining the streets, all the married women and children singing a different tune, choirboys in cyclamen and gold trying to look holy and asking passers-by for 'caramelle' and cigarettes . . .

The villagers of Rotondi went out to work at four in the morning, 'singing gaily'; my Guardsmen and I put on a show of being busy in the heat of the day; in the evening drink flowed in the officers' mess; after nightfall I went 'late walking', as Falstaff called it, in the woods. I was surprised to find that from the top of the mountain which rose steeply above our camp I could see 'grey-blue Vesuvius, Naples and even ships in the harbour'; while from the same viewpoint in the afternoon light 'the plain and hills towards Benevento were like a tray heaped with opals'. I was at last able to make an excursion to explore the historic promontory dividing the Gulfs of Naples and Gaeta, and drove with Richard Coke through Posilippo and Pozzuoli 'where St Paul stayed a week on his way to Rome', to Lake Avernus, 'the mouth of hell', and to the cave of the Cumaean Sibyl, which was full of Americans. On 16 April, when visibility was better, I returned with Colin Dalrymple to the Cape of Misenum.

> We leave the car and walk up to the summit (only five hundred feet high), by a path thick with iris, vetch, white hyacinth, wolfs-bane, lizards and butterflies. This is the perfect day of the year to look at the famous view: the sea very blue and all the surrounding mountains, islands and lakes clearly visible. One's eyes move from Capri, round the Sorrento Peninsula, the mountains hiding Salerno, Vesuvius, the glittering suburbs [central Naples being hidden], Posilippo, Nisida, the network of lakes, bays and beaches below us, Procida silhouetted against Ischia, the Cuma rock, the Campania, Monte Massico and the hills by Mondragone, the Minturno hills beyond, Gaeta, the Ponza Islands – all indigestibly blue and beautiful . . . We are given some excellent wine by a farmer with four grandchildren.

But I was in considerable discomfort, having caught an inconvenient disease from Salvatore (or Gennaro), which was cured by pills from a friendly army doctor in Naples. After a day or two in bed in my billet, I emerged to find our valley 'lit by the green flames of poplars'. I designed an outdoor theatre for our new Entertainments Officer, Michael Howard of the Coldstream. That April I went on leave with Hugo Charteris and stayed at a villa at Ravello next to that in which the King of Italy was swearing in a new government. May brought 'asparagus and artichokes', 'cuckoos and cowbells', 'hawthorn and asphodel', a baby born in our billet, a change from battle-dress to khaki drill, 'a pink moth outside my mosquito net' and a new mess waiter 'just like Dorothy Hyson'. I saw Trajan's magnificent arch at Benevento and visited the 1st Battalion in 'the very centre of Italy'. The coast road to Positano, where I spent a week-end with Andrew Cavendish, was 'heavy with the scent of Judas trees, overhung by valerian and many-coloured geranium'.

On 5 June Rome fell – and my theatre opened. 'Walking home at night I stopped to listen to a man playing a guitar on a first-floor balcony. Neighbours leaning from their windows. Moonlight.' Next day the village was hung with 'pretty Italian flags'; and there was 'a large and silent audience' for the news of the Second Front in the mess after lunch. On the 8th I got leave to go to Rome. My companion was Peter Tunnard, known as Daisy, with whom I spent much of that summer and the following autumn in a state of giggles. He was so social that it was a joke. From Syria and Lebanon he had carried letters of introduction to Cairo, from Cairo to Naples; and he was armed with more for Rome. I should not complain as it was through Peter I saw the inside of many palaces – which made a change from my solitary exploration of monuments and churches. I was breathless with expectation as we came over the Frascati Hills and down to the Roman *campagna* 'in time to see a salmon-pink sun disappear into the sea'. We did not know whether we should be sniped at from roof-tops or welcomed as heroes, whether we should find the city evacuated or whether there would be food, water and light. We ignored huge signs warning 'ROME OUT OF BOUNDS. TURN BACK NOW,' passed the Colosseum, and were somehow accepted by a polite Italian receptionist at the Albergo Flora in the Via Veneto, although it was taken over by the American secret police – who ignored our intrusion. The only amenity lacking was water, which had to be fetched from taps in the street. Next day, which was fine, I was 'early awake'. While Peter paid calls – and even, I think, went to a smart wedding – I walked round the Forum, found the Piazza di Spagna and the house where Keats died – and made love. On the 10th I visited the graves of Shelley and Keats, then found a Turkish bath in the Via Poli. On the 11th I gazed at St Peter's, saw a collaborator lynched, went to a lunch party at the Grand Hotel and had tea with Princess Colonna. When we drove back to the IRTD, we took the coast road, and I saw where Anthony had died at Anzio.

Before my Neapolitan honeymoon ended I was determined to see Capri, but it had been taken over as a rest camp for Americans (the British were allowed Ischia) and was out of bounds. However I picked up in Sorrento a boy called Tonino, whose brother had a motor-boat; I supplied the petrol and changed into 'a white silk shirt, blue shorts, a white belt and a white tie with blue chrysanthemums'. (It seems odd to have worn a tie with shorts.) Two fellow officers came along. Even my prose style rose to the depraved occasion. 'As we approach the enchanted island across the swaying straits, Capri looks like the discarded diadem of some sea-goddess.' We drank vermouth *frappé* in a garden, 'surrounded by flowering Americans . . . talked about Pontius Pilate, Tiberius and Oscar Wilde . . .' then hurtled up to Anacapri to visit Munthe's Villa of San Michele, where I found among the good doctor's Roman fragments the tombstone of one 'Marcia', which was Tonino's surname.

On 10 July I paid 'what may be the last of many visits to Naples . . . the harbour full of silver balloons. Capri clear as a cake . . .'

CHAPTER 12

◆•◆

The Grand Tour Continues,
1944–5

I joined the 1st Battalion at Greve, south of Florence, on 27 July, a few days before my twenty-eighth birthday, and became Second-in-Command of G Company. We were in 24th Guards Brigade and part of the 6th South African Armoured Division.

Warcop   24 July 1944

Dearest Dick

Many happy returns from the bottom of my heart. I won't send a cheque as I can't run to one equal to your rank & I don't think you can need one, but I'll send you books and handkies if you tell me which & what . . . I felt sure Col. Guy Taylor [killed a month before] would be a great loss & do feel for you. But to give your life for your country is so fine one can't grudge it – & I do think those are most blessed who go while still young. I never could wish Garry back.

Doris, at Epsom, is worked to death billeting bombed people & tearing across the downs in her car, lying in the mud when bombs pass over. 180,000 moved from London area in ten days *is* a record, but what it must cost!! We have a pretty young woman and her baby sent by Doris nearly three weeks ago, & think it best to take them free and let them keep their billeting money. It's a fag to cook for them, but two families can't cook dinner together in one kitchen, & we manage . . .

John [Graham] visited Cairo Cathedral & saw a fine memorial put up by the Egyptians & the first name on it

241

was 'Lieut. Chamley Turner'. I *was* pleased to know it was there. The Grahams can't get into Forbes Court [Broughty Ferry, near Dundee, which was to be my uncle Eric's palace as Bishop of Brechin] yet . . . Peter [Graham] shot down a plane & is doing Deputy Squadron Leader & a lot more flying now. He sounds likely to marry by Christmas. Hitler's smash-up sounds hopeful. I hope you march into Florence & stand on the bridge by the Arno & clasp your heart as Beatrice passes by!

Y.D.G.

We forced the Germans slowly backwards and the Scots Guards were the first troops to enter Florence. After retreating north of the river, the enemy destroyed all the bridges except the Ponte Vecchio, which they blocked by blowing up the houses at either end.

4 August 1944

Shelley's birthday. We leave in buses at dawn, B Company leading. Yesterday the Coldstream pushed forward to San Gersole, two miles beyond Impruneta; and we are given company objectives on low hills in the outskirts of Florence just beyond them. A beautiful red dawn, very still, with no gun-fire; and I feel exalted at the prospect of perhaps seeing Florence before nightfall. The Company Commanders are ahead early for a recce with the Commanding Officer, so I lead the battalion forward in three-tonners, passing through Impruneta, which is thoroughly knocked about. We de-bus at S. Oriolo, near Coldstream Battalion Headquarters . . . The morning continues quiet . . . We file forward on foot through vineyards and lanes . . . and arrive at Andrew Cavendish's company HQ at S. Gersole. He is very pleased with himself having had a scrap with a few Germans left behind in the big getaway last night and captured a gun of sorts. We push on downhill and up again, eating plums and nectarines off trees on the way, to our objective M. Cuccioli, which is not held . . . The Italians welcome us with wine and water . . . About 4 we get word to move . . . Marching up a long lane with high walls overhung by trees and vines, we get into the lush southern suburbs of Florence, thick with splendid villas in gardens behind armorial gates. Through a gap in a broken wall Florence is at last visible, white and serene below, with blue hills rolling all around. The Germans have apparently retired north of the Arno, but Spandau fire can be heard from the far bank . . . We do not go right down into the town . . . Each of our platoons has a good villa and a garden, and we in Company Headquarters are the guests of Commendatore Orlando at his handsome house which looks down on the other three. It is a big, white, modern villa with a terraced garden, a long winding drive and a view of eastern Florence, with Fiesole behind. Orlando is a fat, very hospitable manufacturer of fifty and speaks French . . . Mrs Orlando is a nice-looking dark woman. Their younger daughter (twelve?) is here, but two sons were caught across the river when the Germans stopped the traffic . . . Spandaus still fire, but we are not shelling the town. Towards evening German guns start shelling the eastern suburbs south of the river in front of us . . . Orlando gives us vermouth. Rain sets in about six. I bicycle down to settle some muddle about billets and get soaked . . . Orlando opens three bottles of sparkling red wine from Verona . . . Each company is tonight sending four men in two rubber boats to see if they are opposed in crossing the Arno: all are fired on and return. Anthony S. has today been killed when his car ran over an S mine; and Hugh S. was killed when he showed himself on the river bank . . .

6 August 1944

Tennyson's birthday and mine. Orlando gives me a leather pocket book with his card and a sprig of sweet-smelling herb. The girl gives me a vase of flowers and Mrs Orlando makes me some pancakes with raspberry jam for tea. All this in addition to wine at lunch and supper. We are being relieved by Canadians tonight and going back to the Siena area for a week or two's rest . . .

Warcop   6 August 1944

Dearest Dick

Twenty-eight years ago it was just such a lovely warm Sunday as this & I was holding you in my arms wrapped in a Shetland shawl, just ten minutes old, and Jim Wild came in & put his finger into your tiny fist & wished he had a son like you. Now, Jim has gone beyond the stars & you are fighting in Florence. Mummie is nursing in Norfolk & I am very very old but still going & have just been looking after another baby on the lawn, whose father is also in Italy, Driver Jelley, R.A.S.C. Tomorrow we take in yet another 'bombed out' . . . Poor Alice looks in pretty often, v. sad: she comes down from Helbeck to take flowers to Jim's grave . . . I am better & walked to Row End yesterday, my 1st visit for weeks past. We are having divine still warm days & sit out all the afternoon. Hardie shoots & comes in too done to make fresh tea . . . Tim market gardens. No news at all.

My true love & every best birthday wish.

Y.D.G.

My diary from summer 1944 to spring 1945 suggests that I was growing increasingly impatient with my fellow officers; there are also signs that they were often longing to get rid of me, for during the winter I was twice sent as liaison officer to adjacent troops or to organize the comforts of our officers' holiday villa in Florence. On different dates I would record how 'R is a booming bore', 'D is incredibly drunk and rude', 'C without ever being amusing is never serious. Incessant banter is so middle-class and tiring. B is always trying to be funny.' My closer friends of this period were Coldstreamers: Michael Howard, who later became a pre-eminent military historian and a Fellow of All Souls, Simon Phipps, who later became Bishop of Lincoln, and Andrew Cavendish, who later became Duke of Devonshire.

Another friend was more unexpected. The Battalion had

picked up an Italian boy partisan in the Chianti hills and the Guardsmen had adopted him. As he spoke some English he acted as interpreter, made himself useful and was attired in khaki drill. One morning at Fagnano, near Siena, when I was sticking branches of greenery into curtains of camouflage netting hung round a courtyard of the villa to form the background for a concert-party, the boy appeared asking, 'Can I help you, Captain Buckle?' and proved skilful. I drove him to San Gimignano, that towery hilltop town, and we looked together at the frescoes of Bennozzo Gozzoli, and Ghirlandaio's 'Death of Sta Fina'. Later in August I wrote: 'There is a bathing place in the River Elsa . . . The mill-stream falling from a high rock makes a perfect showerbath . . . When Franco sits in the middle of the shaft of falling water it parts and spreads all round behind him, like the tail of a huge white peacock in glass beads.' I told Franco I was a ballet critic, and he told me he wanted to be a stage designer. Later, when Florence was free of Germans, he left us to return to his home there. I had tea with his family and he showed me his designs. After the war he was taken under the wing of Lucchino Visconti, and became known throughout the world as Franco Zeffirelli, designer, director of opera, plays and films, one of the great men of the theatre of our time.

On 10 September, on leave in Rome, I realized that I had been a year in Italy: I was the only officer in the regiment who had landed at Salerno and had not left the country since. That day Princess Doria showed me the picture gallery in her palace, perhaps the grandest private collection in the world; and Henry of Bavaria, who had been a friend of Iain Moncreiffe's at Oxford, took me to Keats's house. It was with this exiled prince whose father, the legitimist King of England, had been one of the most able German generals in the First World War, that I first saw the Sistine Chapel. The Dorias, by descent the most English, and by conviction the most defiantly anglophile, of Roman aristocrats, had suffered accordingly. The Allies had made the Prince mayor, or

Sindaco, of Rome. He, his wife and daughter proved the kindest of my Roman friends.

11 September 1944

Up the Capitol steps to Michelangelo's splendid Piazza del Campidoglio. There is a small exhibition of sculpture in the Capitoline Museum on the right: 'The Dying Gaul', the Venus and the lovely Spinario, which I never thought I should like so much. Also some charming Vanvitelli views of Rome. I go next door and ask for the Sindaco. Prince Doria shows me the Council Chamber where he was installed in office, and the smaller room where the Giunta meet twice a week. Then his own office, with the sitting-room next door (chintz sofa and armchairs), which has the small balcony commanding a bird's-eye view of the Forum, with the tree-clad Palatine behind, and the Aventine and the blue Alban Hills with White Frascati. He says he often works on the balcony in the evening, and that the view is best with the pink glow of sunset on it. Below us the Mamertine prison where St Peter lay, and to the right the crazy pavement of the old Via Sacra, winding uphill to the site of the Temple of Jove, which stood where we stand now . . .

Although the Allied armoured divisions were advancing from Normandy towards the Rhine and the Russians were approaching Warsaw, in Italy the British Eighth Army and the American Fifth, of which we were a part, had been thinned out to supplement the forces in France, and our progress was slower. Our 1st Battalion, Scots Guards, were held up throughout the winter in the mountains between Florence and Bologna.

My grandfather was eighty-two. My cousin Peter Graham was a prisoner. Doris's eldest boy was serving in Holland, her second in India. My mother's cousin's Red Cross hospital at Woodbastwick Hall in Norfolk, where she had nursed so faithfully throughout the war, had been emptied of servicemen and filled up with old women, which she liked much less: but she never complained. I caught a new kind of jaundice called 'infective hepatitis' and enjoyed a long bacchanalian convalescence at the Palazzo Sermoneta in Rome, staying with Hamish St Clair Erskine. 'You are a most uncomplaining person always,' wrote Lily: but I was becoming a much less courageous one. The pleasures of Rome – which included Michelangelo, the fire-lit library of the Olympian Duchess of Sermoneta, the fountains of Bernini, the Dorias' Caravaggios and their Velasquez portrait of Pope Innocent X, festal dinners, voluptuous nocturnes and tender aubades – made life seem too desirable to lose. My wine merchant had his shop opposite the Trevi fountain and even the manner in which he addressed my bills – '*Al illustrissimo e gentilissimo Signore, Capitano Buckle*' – was baroque. Yet Christmas had to be spent in the Apennines near Castiglione-dei-Pepoli. 'In the snow all the coloured military signs which burgeon particularly at cross-roads look like Christmas cards or decorations – one or two actually *are* Christmas cards! . . . I say *Buon Natale!* to a poor old woman in a black shawl, who seems greatly cheered.' The Marchesa Origo, a distinguished writer, lent us her Villa Medici at Fiesole as a rest house for our officers. Nearly five hundred years before, Lorenzo de' Medici, whom I did not know to be my ancestor, had discussed Plato with his friends there, looking down on Florence. Queen Victoria had stayed there, and Princess Mary and Lord Lascelles had spent part of their honeymoon there, spied on by Ronald Firbank, who was writing *The Flower Beneath the Foot* over the wall. The Coldstream villa, where I often dined, also had a royal connection: L'Ombrellina, south of the river, belonged to Mrs George Keppel, King Edward VII's former mistress. Tony Mattei, who had shown me Naples and later cropped up in Rome, walked smiling through a door, to wave his fairy godfather's wand over Florence: he introduced me to an amusing old Venetian anglophile interior decorator called Count Medin, with whom I spent much time that winter.

Sheds containing public lavatories for the troops had been erected at the corner of the Piazza della Signoria opposite the entrance of the Uffizi (through which I never passed). Because of the *apartheid* of our South African friends these were labelled 'black' and 'white'. I always used the black ones. In January I was sent to another snowy mountain outpost as liaison officer to some Americans:

> Drink a bottle of rye whisky with one Lieutenant Geiger, who is tall, husky and married to a gangster's daughter. In peace-time his job is driver and bodyguard to the man who runs the 21 Club in New York. While I draw a caricature he plays the mouth organ to me . . . The Americans think me crazy. My cough is terrible . . . Work on a short story . . .

My mother had gone to stay with, and look after, Lily and Chris.

Warcop   7 February 1945

Dearest Dick

Splendid to get your mail yesterday & to see your mother's happy face over here. You do write so cheerfully too, & the war seems as if it might end next week & all five grandsons be left intact! Why can't one rejoice with all one's heart & soul? I feel too weighed down by the awful misery in Germany to think of anything else . . . *You* sound chilly but serene with your books & Americans. Well, your mother is taking the *most* marvellous care of us – never shows boredom & sings as she goes about the little house. Yesterday she even set to in the cold & helped Hardie & an old man to shovel in two cartloads of coal, & looked as smart as ever after it. I can't get over her good looks! As a girl she was definitely plain with merely good hair & legs. Now, at fifty, she is quite strikingly attractive & *miles* better looking than Doris & Tita as well as appearing to be at least ten years younger than they are . . . She finds some fresh improvement she can make every day & keeps Hardie so cheery & content he hardly knows himself!

. . . Rose brought me a fine clump of budding aconites which will be a golden glory when I get down this morning . . . I have been correcting the last MS part of my 'Book of Remembrance' . . . Your new book is sure to be clever, but I hope it may be something more after all you have seen in the last five years. Personally I prefer true stories now to any fantasy . . .

I had been anxious to leave something behind me if I were killed and I laboriously copied out the feeble and fantastic stories I had written in Egypt, Sicily and Italy. Andrew Cavendish took them home to be typed. Luckily none was published. The only good thing about this book might have been its title. For some surrealist reason I was determined to call it 'The Trousers of the Saints': to justify which I had written (in Taormina) a poem to serve as epigraph.

> Heaven was full of double beds,
> New books by Proust and lilac trees.
> Iced *crème de menthe* was served in jugs
> By narrow-hipped Norwegians,
> Who spent whole mornings combing out
> Their yellow or green-golden hair.
> Whispers were heard among the woods,
> Where Negroes lurked; no one at all
> Could fail to find his cup of tea.
> But Polydore threw grapes at God,
> Made water on the Holy Hill,
> And stole the trousers of the saints.

Warcop   15 March 1945

Dearest Dick

. . . I don't often bore you with letters, but I think of you day & night. In fact, every time I wake I begin to pray for you, John, Peter & Andy. You will have heard of John [Graham] baling out his plane just a month ago when it caught fire near Venice after dropping its bombs . . .

THE BRIGADE OF GUARDS

Presents

AS
IMPROPERLY
DRESSED

A REVUE

TEATRO NUOVO
SPOLETO

SATURDAY MARCH 10TH AT SEVEN O' CLOCK

You mother is good as an angel to us both. She went with me to Kendal to be X-rayed yesterday & looked after me like a courier & kind nurse in one. An exhausting show, but the drive was wonderful – though the solemn great fells show no touch of spring yet. Kendal market was golden with wild daffodils from the lake sides . . .

Does time really exist? After Kendal today I fell into a deep sleep & when I woke I was standing on the steps of Eden Gate & my mother came up them in her dear old garden hat, rather hot from gardening, & I said, 'Mother, you have been working too hard. She looked at me so

MUSICAL DIRECTOR	.	.	.	.	Major H. J. L. Green	(C. G.)
BUSINESS MANAGER	.	.	.	.	Lt. D. E. C. Price	(S. G.)
STAGE MANAGER	.	.	.	.	Sgt. Cormack	(S. G.)
WARDROBE	.	.	.	.	Lt. the Lord Herschell	(C. G.)
ASSISTANT PRODUCER	.	.	.	.	Lt. M. E. Howard	(C. G.)
THEATRE MANAGER	.	.	.	.	Sgt. Pollock	(S. G.)

The Revue written and produced by
Captain C.R.S. BUCKLE, Scots Guards.

●

PRESS COMMENTS

« *This sort of thing would not have been tolerated in peacetime* »
HOUSEHOLD BRIGADE MAGAZINE

« *A revolting mixture of smut and sentiment* »
JAMES AGATE IN « THE SUNDAY TIMES »

« *... the bottom ...* »
PRAVDA

●

Please adjust your dress before leaving.

Front and back pages of the programme of *As Improperly Dressed,*
a revue staged by the author at Spoleto in March, 1945.

kindly, with little beads of perspiration on her face, & said,
'Oh *no*, dear, but I fear you had a hard morning in Kendal!'
It was as vivid as real life & I thought, 'Oh how *silly* I have
been not to live at Eden Gate lately, there's no other place
to touch it!' Exactly what your father used to feel.

We were withdrawn from the line – I never saw Bologna –
and the two Guards Brigades serving in Italy met at Spoleto

for rest and re-organization. I produced a revue in the Teatro Nuovo (which would be the core of Menotti's Spoleto Festival in post-war years): *As Improperly Dressed** had three riotous performances. When the battalion went north again to face some hard battles south of the Po on the Adriatic coast, I was sent to Florence as housekeeper at the Villa Medici. My fighting days were done.

There was a race between the Allies and the partisan army of Marshal Tito for the taking of Trieste. To the disgust of the Yugoslavs, General Freyberg of the Second New Zealand Division (who had buried Rupert Brooke in 1915) received the surrender of the city on 2 May. On 6 May, by which time I had returned as Second-in-Command of Right Flank, we crossed the Isonzo, motored along the cliff road and entered Trieste. With the coming together of Germany's Western and Eastern enemies trouble was anticipated. The grey-clad partisans, with their red stars, had machine-guns at every street corner. Our Battalion Headquarters and the officers' mess were installed in the big Albergo Savoia Excelsior on the waterfront, and each company had an allotted task in case of emergency. Meanwhile, intent on pleasure and privacy, I took a room in a *pensione* half a mile from the Savoia. On the night of 8 May I was scared out of my bed there by the sound of shooting. I rushed to the window. Partisans were firing their rifles in the air. The war in Europe was over.

In war or peace, my Grand Tour, which I had started at the wrong end of Italy, had to be completed. In Florence Henry of Bavaria had taken me to tea with Berenson: in Venice I visited Contessa Morosini, whose famous beauty in years past had won the Kaiser's love. In Venice, as in Rome, a few masterpieces were brought from their shelters and exhibited

---

* The expression 'As Improperly Dressed' is a technical one which must seem strange to anyone outside the Brigade of Guards. If a guardsman is walking about camp or barracks without a cap and passes an officer, he holds his arms rigidly to his sides, jerks his head to the right or left, and after three paces, faces front and swings his arms out smartly again. This is called 'saluting as improperly dressed'.

for my sake and for that of a handful of Guardsmen I brought to see them: I particularly recall Cima's 'Baptism', Carpaccio's 'Courtesans' and Tiepolo's 'Santa Tecla relieving the Town of Este from the Plague'. In the Grand Hôtel des Bains de Mer on the Lido I was shown the room where Diaghilev died. In Trieste Ferruccio Tagliavini sang *Werther* for me. In Padua I saw the Giotto chapel; in the castle of Mantua, Mantegna's painted room; in Vicenza the Palladian houses. In Verona I thought of Romeo and Juliet. On leave with Michael Howard on Lake Maggiore, near to where the fleeing Mussolini was captured, I was shown the hanging gardens of Isola Bella by Countess Borromeo. In Milan Cathedral, the aged Archbishop, supported by two angels, preached to me against '*la bomba atomica*'.

PART IV

LAST YEARS OF
LILY AND CHRIS

CHAPTER 13

Winter at Warcop, 1945–52

The Old Cottage, Warcop. Drawing by Robin Tanner.

The besetting sin of the old is that they expect letters: in this
Lily was the most grievous sinner of all. Today the telephone
has almost abolished correspondence except from strangers
in need of information: but I belong to an intermediate
generation whose frequent recourse to the irresistible
instrument has not yet destroyed the appetite for written
news of distant friends, and I can sympathize with Lily's sense

of neglect. She regarded the telephone as an expensive and unsatisfactory branch of semaphore, only for use in emergencies. If you rang her up, she said, 'Yes?' in an untypical, brusque, parade-ground manner which made you feel you were wasting her time. (In those days telephones were always installed in the least accessible corner of the house.) Since in England in the 1940s few people motored two hundred miles just for a week-end, Lily felt as cut off from the descendants in whom she took such an interest as if they were in Australia. She longed for letters and was upset when the Warcop post brought none. I feel just the same in Wiltshire, in 1980.

Lily had reason to be pleased with her daughters and their children when they came to stay – although Tita struck her as rather too possessive of her brood: and she would soon be a great-grandmother. In 1945 she very much liked Elizabeth Graham although she thought her too much 'a Norton Buckle' in looks. Peter Graham married his Sylvia, and John was due back from Germany: both brothers were to go up to King's College, Cambridge. Andy Graham was home on leave from Burma. Jane Woodger was training to be a physiotherapist. As for Jane's elder brother Mike, Lily wrote, 'I really *never* met so delightfully learned and modest a young man – no, not even Douglas Terry! Very good-looking, too – and so interested in every kind of thing from guns to Hover flies and edible fungi.' On the other hand, 'Dick has been in England three weeks, but all we know is that he *intends* to come up and see us.' When I did visit her I struck her as 'fit and well and kind and charming, but desperately keen on starting to run his magazine *Ballet* again . . . To me it's ten to one he loses a fortune.' She associated ballet with immorality and wrote to me: '*You* went off the rails, I fear, at Oxford, if not before, & it's not easy to get back. I dread you never having a wife & the Buckles ending in you & not a *really* happy you either.' How much did she know? Had one of the aunts been talking? Lily was distressed, in 1946, that

Andy Woodger was not married in a church; yet she enjoyed his wife's letters, thought she had 'good taste in books' and hoped 'all might be well yet'. Peter's son, born in March, was to be called 'Michael James', which for some unknown reason she considered 'silly names'. When Christian came on leave from her convent, '*How* she cooked and washed and cleaned!': but she was 'for ever praying – in the empty church – anywhere – '; and Lily thought this excessive. 'God isn't an Eastern potentate'. Doris, who didn't pray at all, was another 'pure angel' to her parents when she came to stay. Both Mike and Jane Woodger got engaged. Mary Graham too. Mary's youngest brother Martin had won a scholarship to Glenalmond, and Stephen was going to Sandhurst, hoping to join the Black Watch. John Graham left Cambridge for Ely Theological College in August. Judith was back from the Argentine, but had broken her leg. This was an excuse for Lily to make, in October 1946, another excursion to the Cambridge Hotel at Camberley, which had been her headquarters after the evacuation from Dunkirk, and which was near Judith's nursing home. It was Lily's last trip away from Warcop. Judith's eldest son Edward came over from school at Charterhouse 'enormously grown & improved since Christmas, & the governess brought Adrian, aged six, whom I had never met before. *Quite* the handsomest, jolliest, cleverest small boy I *ever* met!'

Warcop   14 December 1946

Dearest Dick

No letter from you among the bed-full I have had – & also Hardie – for our diamond wedding & my eighty-first birthday . . . Everyone sent me a bulb (or more) by my request as a cheap & really nice gift, & our tiny room is full of bowls of shooting spears of green & also some lovely cut anemones wh. I deeply enjoy. Weather has been desperate. I think it is a month since I even got to post. I am so thin I have to sit on my hands in my bath! But we carry on – & I *am* glad to have saved Hardie £16 by not having Nurse for a month. He gets fussed over money in his old age – without any reason. I have had *none* for ages . . . I have given the Graham and Woodger families all I had to save death duties. Now I carry on with Hardie [paying me] rent for the cottage, out of which £24 goes to Cousie [a Buckle cousin] & £24 to Stephen [who was at Sandhurst] . . . Judith's second son [Timothy] sounds a marvel – top in every exam . . . Dick, don't forget you are the head of the family & *must* keep an eye on us all.

I had been demobilized in March 1946, and a few days earlier moved into a house I had bought, 6 Alexander Square, near the Brompton Oratory. It was a conventional Regency house with trees in front and a garden behind; but the 'square' had only one and a half sides, the traffic rushed by and when, during the very first night I slept there, I heard the underground railway rumbling beneath me, I decided to move as soon as possible. In fact, I was to sell the lease at a two-thousand-pound profit less than two years later. Meanwhile my mother, who had resumed life back at Overstrand with Nanny, her garden and her village duties, arrived with some furniture she had bought for me in country sales, to make me curtains out of mattress ticking and hessian, which were available without coupons. I went by bus or taxi daily to the office of *Ballet* in Frith Street, Soho. The magazine, which continued for seven years, was never a success and as Lily had predicted, lost me and my friends a good deal of money. Costs were higher than before the war, paper was scarce and expensive, advertising was hard to get. Yet, looking back, I realize that my spell as editor of *Ballet*, like my time in the army, was a step towards my becoming a serious writer – which was something Lily had always hoped that I might be, but which I only began to become after her death. It seems that I was destined to evolve in the most roundabout way, and as if by accident.

My Grandmother Sandford, who had left London during

the bombardment, was back in her Paddington flat. Pat and Violet Kinnaird were living in Surrey. Violet occupied herself with the Surrey Red Cross, of which she was eventually to scceed her cousin Helen Northumberland and Lady Onslow, to both of whom she acted deputy, as President. Pat travelled daily to and from Barclay's Bank in Pall Mall East. I had been bidden to lunch with him there one day shortly after my return from Italy. Archie Pearson, who had been Adjutant at Pirbright when I first joined the Regiment and who later succeeded Pat at Regimental Headquarters, was the other guest. I suddenly realized that the object of the occasion was that they should both tell me how well they thought I had done in Italy – after all the trouble I had been in before. I was overwhelmed, knowing that I could have done much better.

Back in Tedworth Square, Dolly Sandford and her last remaining maid, the faithful Parsons, settled down happily together in the crammed and dusty house like two mice in a furniture repository. Dolly had never thrown away anything in her life – not a dress, not a hat, not a newspaper, not a piece of string. The L-shaped drawing-room on the first floor was so full it had to be given up – except for purposes of research. Books were two deep in the bookcases; the grand piano, the sofas, the armchairs, the tables and the floor were stacked with parcels. Any concern for appearances was abandoned. Nevertheless, once a year I would carry eight heavy pots of aspidistra from the mangy back garden up to the drawing-room balcony, and once a year carry them down again. I visited Dolly mostly at tea-time on Sundays. She lived in the double ground-floor room, an upright piano laden with parcels separating her sitting-room at the back – with its springless sofa and armchair – from the dining-room in front. Half of the dining-table, covered in a crimson rep cloth, was free from parcels. The electric bulb hanging low over it had a shade painted with chrysanthemums on a black ground, and cast a cosy pool of light.

Countless packets of China tea were kept in the bottom of a big bookcase, the upper part of which held bound volumes of *Punch*. On the chimneypiece, in brass shell-cases from the First World War, were peacocks' feathers. From a three-sided window seat with red cushions one looked out on the trees of the square. There was something charming about the house and the atmosphere surrounding Dolly in spite of the clutter and the dirt. I once asked her if she did not find it awkward, having to share her only bathroom with Parsons. She was astonished and exclaimed, '*Servants* don't have *baths!*'

The beauty of fells, trees and flowers hardly made up to Lily for the isolation of life at Warcop. All Chris asked was a regular routine: gardening, the *Times*, and almost daily walks with his gun. Lily wanted something more, and although she persevered in trying to make Chris comfortable, as he grew deafer and less communicative, she became more bored and impatient. Tim Chamley at Warcop House never ceased to be 'kind', but his wife Mabel, Lily's sister Emmie at Row End and her cousin Janet Irving were 'odd' – which was the expression Lily used for people with different standards of behaviour from herself. Before old Mrs Wild died Lily had begun to see her once or twice a week, thus ending at last the ancient feud between Warcop Hall and the descendants of farmer Matthew Chamley at Warcop House. Lily's increasing weakness necessitated nurses and at least a daily servant, but her relations with these women were not always happy. A maid gave notice when she heard Peter and Sylvia were coming on a visit, and a new nurse, who arrived immediately after this refused to 'act as parlour-maid' or carry the tea-tray into the garden, so she left too. When Lily's eyes were worse than usual she crocheted blankets 'for Austria'. Listening to Christmas broadcasts, she 'loved the King, as usual'. Then the crocuses would appear among the snowdrops and suddenly 'cheerfulness kept breaking in'. When she had nothing new to read Lily turned to old favourites. 'I have been enjoying Mrs Gaskell's *Wives and Daughters* as if it were a new book.' Trollope's Signora Nerone always made her laugh and his Dr Thorne still reminded her of her father. Palgrave's *Golden Treasury* was a great resource: and in February 1946, she wrote to me: 'Last night I read Keats. His thrush: "Oh, fret not after knowledge, I have none, /And yet the evening listens", and Shelley's "From the contagion of the world's slow stain /He is secure" are to me the finest sentences men wrote.' '*Worst*' old Miss Gregson, who kept the shop at the Eden Gate end of the village, was dying, and Lily was ashamed that she had never prayed for her 'until yesterday'. It was an event when Chris shot a few rabbits and a snipe. Lily re-read the letters I had written her from Marlborough, and wished I wrote as regularly now that I was thirty. Billy Wild had sold all the timber in Cemetery Wood. 'If *only* Tim would cut his awful yews!'

When Lauretta arrived from France in August 1947 we went straight up to Westmorland for a long week-end and stayed at the inn in Appleby. In her sepia brush drawings of Appleby Castle and the Eden Lauretta already showed the influence of Jean Hugo, the French painter, great-grandson of Victor Hugo, whom she had brought to stay with me in Alexander Square six months earlier. I had admired Jean's designs for the ballet before and since the war; he and I became friends at once and collaborated later on a number of projects. Lauretta would shortly marry Jean, but my Granny, knowing nothing of *his* existence, at once saw in *her* a possibility of continuing the line of Norton Buckles. After tea in the garden of the Old Cottage, being left for a moment alone with Lauretta, Lily questioned her about her 'intentions'. She said it was improper for her to stay under the same roof with me at Alexander Square unless we were married. Lauretta laughed and said it was a cook I wanted, not a wife. But Lily persevered.

Warcop   23 August 1947

Dearest Dick,

Is Lauretta really going off to France next month? I fear you will miss her badly if she does. It must be horrid coming back to an empty house every evening. I really have no wish left except that you should be happily settled – & it does seem *too* sad if Garry is to have no descendants after yourself . . .

Always my love
Y.D.G.

I did like Lauretta . . . I hope she got a *Picture Post* I sent her, with a rather good article & illustrations of tropical butterflies.

Immune from seduction by tropical butterflies, Lauretta would soon be the mistress of a romantic house amid vineyards in Languedoc; and I should have to learn to cook. In time the seven Hugo children became as dear to me, almost, as if they were my own.

In my grandfather's diary, no less meticulous than his own grandfather's log-book of voyages to India, but of a less sensational nature, he recorded the mild monotony of Warcop life. Barometer readings, wind and weather, my grandmother's movements (she was always referred to as M – for Muddis), visits from relations, walks with his gun and his latest dog, the changing of razor-blades, and trips every six weeks by car or bus into Appleby for a hair-cut – these were the basic contents. The little dark-blue leather-bound diaries from Smythson's in Bond Street – which were my mother's invariable Christmas present to Chris until she realized his eyesight was deteriorating and began to send larger common cardboard engagement books – were written up in a handwriting so small that I needed a magnifying glass to decipher them after his death.

1 January 1948
Slight rain in night.
28.85. 34° W. Cloudy. Drizzle.
M. down to lunch but did not go out.
Janet. Owen [Wynne] came to say goodbye.
Cutting kindling.

2 January 1948
Rain at night.
28.90. 43 °S.W. Drizzle. Cloudy. Damp. Mild.
shifting wood and kindling.
clearing up front garden.
M. did not go out – down to lunch.
Emmie came in.

3 January 1948
Rain at night.
28.60. 45°. Cloudy. Rain evening.
Across river saw 1 cock 1 hen.
tired & did not go out afternoon.
Janet & Emmie came in for a few moments.
Hesford brought Morphia.
M. did not go out. down to lunch.

Shopping at Gregson's; calling on Tim; writing to the Telephone Manager at Lancaster; getting in Dent to clear a pipe in the kitchen and Hutchinson to stop a leak in the bathroom; taking two of the eggs Windsor Chamley had brought him to Emmie; seeing the first snow on the fells; meeting Christian when she came on leave from her convent; lending the *Field* to Tim; walking to Flitholm with Christian; having a fall; raking weeds out of the path: these were the events of January 1948.

My own engagement diary for the same month is crammed with the names of choreographers and dancers. It was at the end of January that I moved from Alexander Square to Bloomfield Terrace. This was a smaller but much more interesting house in a quiet street near Chelsea Barracks, which I bought from Lauretta's exotic godfather, who was notable for having played Herod in the first English production of Oscar Wilde's *Salomé*, but whom I never met.

In February I began writing about ballet for the *Observer*. I also had a holiday in Malta. Pat Kinnaird died suddenly at Barclay's Bank in March. From then on poor Violet had nothing much to live for except the Red Cross and perhaps me. Lily wrote: 'It seems such a pity that Mrs Sandford, Dolly & Aunt May all have houses in London & yet she [Violet] has to hunt for another & be all alone in it.' (She might have included my unmarried aunt Eva Sandford, who had given up being Lady-in-Waiting to the Duchess of Gloucester, and Cynthia Thomas, who had separated from her husband.) But none of my Sandford aunts or great-aunts would have dreamt of living under the same roof as her sister. I helped Violet to move into a flat. We sometimes went to the ballet together; but she startled me one day by refusing an invitation on the grounds that Thursday was the evening she had to pull her own curtains. John Graham was ordained in May. A frost in June killed all the fruit in the Old Cottage garden. On 21 July Lily wrote to me: 'I am getting to be a horrid creature – people vex me & I can't get over it. Janet said this afternoon, "You *will* enjoy the ————s, and getting E. to tell you all the scandal & then you must tell me!" I longed to throw a cushion at her head.' On 31 July I was introduced to George Harewood, and began planning an opera section in my magazine *Ballet,* which later became *Ballet and Opera* and, later still, two magazines, *Opera* and *Ballet.* In August my mother went to stay at Helbeck Cottage: my grandfather recorded 'Rose came in' and Granny wrote to me 'Your mother has been down to see us three times, looking very fit & smart.' In September I spent three nights at Warcop. In October Mary (Graham) Holtby had a daughter. Chris was eighty-six on 18 October. Both my Grandmother Sandford and Tim Chamley died in November.

After my September visit to Warcop Lily and I never saw each other again. I do not know what I could have said to her to earn the gratitude expressed in the following letter. Gin may have loosened my tongue.

Warcop   15 September 1948

My Dearest Dick.

I am *still* chewing the cud of all the dear comforting things you said to me. You see I had thought long since that you had ceased to care 2d about me – and you wrote *so* seldom & said less & it is common for old people to grow dull & less cared for & I had tried to accept the inevitable. Therefore your flood of affection moved me enormously & I felt quite overcome, though quite unable to grasp it at once. I know Hardie thinks he couldn't live a week without me, but that is mostly a matter of comfort: he can't remember to keep in the fire or order his meals, also in ordinary daily life he hardly speaks to me until tea-time or seems to know I am here. But he roused up for *you* & was really delighted with you – & he thought, as I do, that your face & voice had become so like your father's, & that you were doing more work; & that you *looked* well – like a man who was leading a decent life – not living at night clubs etc. He said several times, after long periods of silence, 'Well, I *am* pleased with Dick. He is turning out *far* better than I expected!'

Heaven bless you, Dick
Y.D.G.

On 14 January 1949 I received a telegram from my grandfather saying that Granny had died in her sleep that morning. My mother came down to London from Norfolk and we travelled up to Warcop on the next day. Judith and Christian were already there. Out of consideration for my feelings Chris had not been exact in his telegram. Lily did not die in her sleep. She had got up to make tea in the early hours, and her night-dress had caught fire from the electric stove in her bedroom. She died of burns and shock. Both my grandfather and the housekeeper behaved with promptitude and efficiency: yet when my grandmother's body was laid on her bed, the two expert women of the village were not immediately sent for, as would have been usual, to do what was necessary. This delay made their task harder when they arrived at dawn: but they spoke with awe of finding the General seated by his wife's body, reading the Bible, as he had clearly settled down to do several hours before. Christian told me this a quarter of a century later.

Lily was buried in the cemetery on the hill near her mother and Agnes. Christian lined the grave and I covered a wooden cross with moss to stand at its head.

Even some of the most devout believers fear death, but I think Lily had been perfectly sincere in insisting that she looked forward to it: her faith in God's mercy was unwavering and her confidence that He would unite her with her father, Chamley, Garry and the Bishop of Gibraltar was absolute. 'This world is only prep school,' she had written to me in 1940. 'There is *nothing* in death.' She had always known exactly what God was like and never hesitated to describe Him. He was a creative genius, an artist-scientist (like Leonardo da Vinci – only she did not say so), who for His own pleasure (like Pygmalion or Dr Coppelius) devised the miraculous machinery of our bodies, and (like a weaver of fifteenth-century tapestries) filled the world with trees, wild flowers and butterflies for our delight. In return we had to 'put our backs into' life, work harder, do better and be suitably grateful to Him in our prayers. On the other hand, God was 'not an Eastern potentate', and would *not* want Christian to spend so many hours in prayer that she had no time to talk to her mother. Lily had always been so sure about the proper ordering of life on earth – almost as if she had a direct telephone line to the Archangel Gabriel – that her children, when young, had said she ought to have been pope. I can indeed see her as a firm, benign, undenominational ruler of the church, presiding over definitive symposia, which would be followed by tea in the garden.

Although the eyes of Netley Hospital's 'Eye-closer' were themselves closed for ever, my grandmother continued to exert her influence from beyond the grave. The warm-hearted woman whom the young officers in South Africa had nicknamed M.O.A. – 'Mother of All' – lived on, to some extent, in all her numerous descendants: but she made a sensational come-back into my life fourteen years after her death. It was not until the 1960s, when I was preparing to write something about her, that I set in order all the letters Lily had written me. Then, the strength of her will – and her determination, disguised by countless jokes and blandishments, that I should fulfil my early promise and do some work of note in the world – hit me like the blast of heat from an open oven door. I had never felt her presence so strongly, even when she was alive.

Lily had always worried over who would look after Chris if she died before him. A few days before her death she answered an advertisement in the local paper; and after her funeral Chris engaged the woman who came in response to this letter, which had been written without his knowledge. He lived on for four years.

When Chris first crossed Regent's Park to visit Mrs Turner in 1880 Lily had just lost her copy of *Julius Caesar* on the way back from school; and as he had used the same edition for his Woolwich exam he brought her his copy next day. Although he exerted himself over fifty years later to watch the production of *Hamlet* I designed at Oxford, I never thought he could have opened a volume of Shakespeare again. In this I was wrong, as I learned from Christian years later. Alone in the Old Cottage, he read through the whole of Shakespeare at least once. He also enjoyed re-reading

Winston Churchill's war histories. At Christmas 1949, Doris Eden's youngest boy, Christopher, stayed with him to paint his portrait: for eight days running he made in his diary the unusual entry 'Two sittings'. Chris grew deafer and blinder and he lost his sense of taste. Still, he regularly did the church flowers, worked in the garden, drove to Appleby to have his hair cut and received the Sacrament. On 25 October 1951, there was a general election and he walked to the school to vote. In the middle of 1952 the writing in the diary became shakier, the entries shorter. Nevertheless my grandfather, who was himself in his ninetieth year, noted on 6 August: 'Dick's birthday. 1916.' A month later he made his last entry.

I was sent for on 28 November. (The magazine *Ballet* had gone into liquidation four days before.) Tita and Christian were already at the Old Cottage. My grandfather was conscious, but incapable of speech and breathing convulsively. His legs had begun to mortify. His bed had been moved down to the dark little dining-room. My aunts and I took turns to be with him, day and night, four hours at a stretch. When off-duty I slept at Eden Gate. It was painful to see the brave old man suffer and be powerless to help. It seemed that he could not die. In the watches of the night I sat wondering how I could hasten his death. After three days I decided that it was my duty to ask the doctor to put an end to his agony. In fact, Chris died the next evening, 1 December 1952.

It was freezing weather and Warcop was white. Dr Hesford had been endlessly kind to my grandfather, whom he admired, so when I went to see him off at the creaky iron gate of the Old Cottage I gave him the silver hip-flask which Chris must have taken out hunting half a century before. As I stood at the gate, shivering without a greatcoat, the doctor told me, as an instance of my grandfather's sense of duty, a story that was new to me. One day during the war, when rationing was in force, the General noticed that his weekly joint of meat was larger than usual and he commented on the fact. My grandmother told him that the butcher, after distributing the village's rations, had found there was some meat left over, and he had allowed her to buy it. The next time the butcher called he found Chris waiting for him, to say, 'No meat this week.'

I never remember a stiller or starrier night. Partly because I was relieved that my grandfather's sufferings and my vigils were over, but also because I was proud of the simplicity and nobility of his life, ended like Granny's in the house where mine had begun, it seemed to me, as I walked back to Eden Gate, that the trees and fells of Warcop, the stars and the full moon all joined together in one hymn of praise. I opened the heavy Warcop House gate, the click of whose latch had announced to my great-grandmother Turner as she lay dying at the Old Cottage a visit from her brother Tom; took the path through the frozen Crooks, which joined the other path from the church and school on which my grandmother had met the postmistress waving a telegram – 'It's all right, Miss Lily, he's coming home to marry you!'; entered the domain of Eden Gate, where my father had been born in similar wintry weather; and passed through the Wilderness, which Lily had first seen 'thick with dewy primroses and wood anemones' in 1884.

When I was sorting my grandfather's papers and putting together his diaries, which I had never opened before, I had the idea of looking to see his entry for the day that Lily died. I should have known better than to expect a mention of the event: for how could he express in words that sudden ending of a lifetime's love? He had written:

Heavy rain at night
29.30. 43° W. cloudy
Christian arrived 5.15. Cash in house 21 shillings.

Acknowledgements

I should like to express my gratitude to the following for their invaluable help:

My aunts Mrs Joseph Woodger, Mrs Eric Graham and Sister Christian C.H.N. gave me their reminiscences. A letter from my grandmother to the first is quoted; the second wrote to me to confirm my grandmother's account of her presentiment of my father's death; the last told me things I did not know about my grandfather's final years. My cousin Miss Woodburn gave me information which led to my tracing the Chamley pedigree a few generations further back; and Miss S. J. Macpherson, Archivist-in-Charge of the Archives Committee at the Record Office, County Hall, Kendal, provided more valuable facts about the Chamleys. Colonel G. E. Braithwaite of Ledbury gave me the benefit of his researches into the history of the Braithwaite family in Westmorland. That my mother's memories were indispensable goes without saying.

Mrs James Blackett-Ord of Helbeck took considerable trouble to help me over the history of various Westmorland families. Miss Rosemary Olivier allowed me to copy passages about the Buckles at Wilton from the diaries of her aunt Edith Olivier. These documents could not be quoted in the present volume but will, I hope, be revealed later. Lord Glenamara gave me his recollection of the unveiling of the Warcop War Memorial. Lady Longford supplied the source of a half-remembered opinion of the Duke of Wellington's. Mr Alexander Schouvaloff, Mr Felix Hope-Nicholson and Mr Daniel Pettiward helped me with vital details of research.

It was my old fellow-campaigner Professor Michael Howard who recommended C. R. M. F. Cruttwell's *A History of the Great War*. I have quoted from this and from David Erskine's *The Scots Guards 1919–1955*.

I am grateful for permission to quote some sentences from the catalogue of *Ursula Tyrwhitt: Oxford Painter and Collector*, an exhibition arranged for the Ashmolean, Oxford; and from *U and Non-U Revisited*, published by Debrett. Other paragraphs are reprinted from *The Adventures of a Critic*.

The parts played by Mr David Dougill, Mrs Anthony Harriss, Mrs Alexander Schouvaloff and Mr Robin Baird-Smith in bringing this book to its present shape are described in the *Apologia*. Miss Gillian Gibbins of Collins went through the text with meticulous care and helped me eradicate the grosser errors. David Dougill also read the proofs.

Mr Robin Tanner generously gave time to draw for me the illustrations of the view from the 'Opera Box' and of the Old Cottage at Warcop. His drawing of the cottage, which he has never seen, was based on two old photographs and two new ones specially taken by Mr Mark Blackett-Ord of Warcop Hall. Mr Tanner's drawing of the view from the 'Opera Box', which he *had* seen, was aided by a photograph by his foster-son Mr Dietrich Hanff. Miss Astrid Zydower was kind enough to fall in with a very complicated idea of mine for a decorative and symbolic title page. My cousin Mr Christopher Stewart Buckle and Mrs Gill, Archivist at the West Sussex County Council, helped me to trace the signature of the Lord Mayor, Sir Cuthbert Buckle, to the Guild-hall, whose Deputy Keeper of Records, Miss Betty Masters, made it available to me; it was then photographed by Mr Godfrey New.

The following old photographs were copied and enlarged by Miss Zydower: Lily Turner in the Wilderness, the river Eden, Eden Gate, Dolly Sandford sketching, Garry Buckle with Dick, Mrs Sandford with Dick, Rose Buckle with Dick and Dick in Rome. She also photographed the watercolour by Dolly Sandford of Rose Buckle at the Old Cottage. Dolly Sandford's watercolours of The Fox, of the lane between Warcop House and the Old Cottage, and of Warcop Bridge were photographed by Malcolm Case of Shaftesbury, who also photographed Amy Stobart's drawing of Lily Buckle and Augustus John's drawing of Lauretta Hope-Nicholson (Mme Jean Hugo), and copied the two photographs of Chris Buckle. The photograph by Photo Studios Ltd of John's drawing of Ursula Tyrwhitt is reproduced by courtesy of the Royal Academy of Arts. The photographs of Derek Hill by Cecil Beaton is reproduced by courtesy of the Cecil Beaton Collection/Sotheby's.

INDEX